Management
Science
Knowledge

MANAGEMENT SCIENCE KNOWLEDGE

Its Creation, Generalization, and Consolidation

ARNOLD REISMAN

QUORUM BOOKS

Westport, Connecticut • London

658
R 37 m

Library of Congress Cataloging-in-Publication Data

Reisman, Arnold.
   Management science knowledge : its creation, generalization, and
consolidation / Arnold Reisman.
      p.   cm.
   Includes index.
   ISBN 0–89930–739–6 (alk. paper)
   1. Management science. I. Title.
T56.R542   1992
658—dc20   91–44705

British Library Cataloguing in Publication Data is available.

Library of Congress Catalog Card Number: 91–44705
ISBN: 0–89930–739–6

First published in 1992

Quorum Books, 88 Post Road West, Westport, CT 06881
An imprint of Greenwood Publishing Group, Inc.

Printed in the United States of America

The paper used in this book complies with the
Permanent Paper Standard issued by the National
Information Standards Organization (Z39.48–1984).

10 9 8 7 6 5 4 3 2 1

To Ellen

Who "stands beside me" and has always been there—
with wisdom, empathy and love.

Contents

Illustrations

TABLES

Acknowledgments

This book represents the cumulative results of a process spanning over three decades. In the early sixties Elwood Buffa challenged me to encapsulate the existing body of equipment replacement analysis knowledge into a single chapter. Many sleepless nights and much anxiety followed. The outcome is replicated as Chapter 16 of this book—a generalized model; a taxonomy of all its special cases; and a classification of the landmark developments in the field.

That first experience in consolidating a knowledge base, while at the same time expanding it, has led to similar activities in other branches of operations research/management science (OR/MS).

Over the decades and perhaps unwittingly, a number of journal editors in chief have made this book possible by publishing articles that were not quite run-of-the-mill. These editors recognized the need for doing research on research and for making the knowledge base of each subdiscipline more user-friendly for novices, mentors, and for practitioners. The more outstanding among them are Robert Thrall (*Management Science*) and George B. Maxey (*Journal of Hydrology*) in the sixties; Marty Starr (*Management Science*) and Sumner Levine (*Socio-Economic Planning Sciences*) in the seventies; George Nemhauser (*Operations Research Letters*) and Dundar Kocaoglu (*IEEE Transactions on Engineering Management*) in the eighties; William Dunn (*Knowledge in Society*) and Ralph Segman (*Journal of Technology Transfer*), and once again Dundar Kocaoglu in the nineties. To each of them I am forever grateful.

Just as I am thankful to the editors of journals for giving me a vote of confidence, so I am thankful to those academic administrators who have exhibited a greater than run-of-the-mill breadth of vision. Outstanding among these is Burton V. Dean, a man who removed many an obstacle from my path and always showed appreciation for my efforts and results. This book could not have taken the form that it has if not for the many former graduate students who, over the years, have been put to the test and proven their ability to do the kind of integrative work, in their respective fields, that Dmitri Ivanovich Mendeleyev did for chemistry in creating the Periodic Table.

I want to thank Mrs. Tedda Nathan for her contributions in creating the manuscript for this book. Her efforts went far beyond typing and formatting the various chapters. She handled many of the administrative aspects involved in creating a book of this kind.

Lastly, the production staff at Quorum books under the direction of Nita Romer did a superb job of copy-editing the manuscript. Although I have published many professional papers and over a dozen books, I have never been forced to pay as much attention to detail in citations and referencing as I was in the process of producing this book. While that created more work for me and my associates, I am indeed thankful to Ms. Romer and staff for their insistence. As a result the final product is much more user-friendly.

Preface

Bertrand Russell has been known to say that a simple problem in arithmetic about *A, B,* and *C* going up a mountain can become an involved problem in psychology if *A* is identified with oneself, *B* with one's most hated rival, and *C* with a schoolmaster who assigned the problem. Conversely, problems due to emotional bias that affect discussions of strategies for doing research can be avoided if the objects of the discussions are not identified directly with anyone's particular approach, strategy, or results, but made a part of a more general framework. Such a framework should delineate the many different strategies for pursuing research and discuss their attributes, both the benefits and the costs. Clearly, the benefits and costs should be viewed from the varying perspectives of the researcher, the institution, or the society at large.

This book is concerned with classifying, discussing, and illustrating the various strategies and tactics for creating new knowledge, and for unifying, consolidating, and/or generalizing on existing knowledge in the management sciences.

Each of the philosophical, strategic, and tactical concepts discussed are amply illustrated. The illustrations reflect the breadth of the management sciences. Much of the text, by design, is sourced from refereed journals serving archival functions in the various subareas of management science.

This book is intended for graduate students about to enter the less structured and ill-defined world of research, and as a guide for their mentors. Project managers in industry and government who forever have to face ill-defined and unstructured problems may derive much benefit from the systematic approaches to problem solving discussed in this book. Lastly, the book is intended for funding agency executives as a means of improving the classification of research proposals. It is hoped that the book will also enable future textbook authors to present their material in a much more unified fashion, allowing the readers/students to see each bit of new material presented in its proper context.

This book may be used as:

1. A text or supplemental reading for courses in research methodology.
2. A text or supplemental reading for courses in engineering design.
3. Supplemental reading in courses on the history and philosophy of science.
4. Suggested reading for anyone embarking on a master's or Ph.D. dissertation in any field of science.
5. Lastly, it is suggested as a source book for anyone, including seasoned researchers, interested in systematically going about finding voids in the literature and hence topics of potential research.

Part I

The Challenge

Chapter 1

Introduction

One offspring of World War II is the field of operations research (OR). In the course of that war, men of various origins and professions were thrust together; they pooled their resources and attacked their tasks on a scientific basis (McCloskey 1987). Since then, the development and the use of science in management has appeared under a number of different labels. However, the idea of using science in management has roots in the writings of Charles Babbage (1832), a British mathematician, and in the work of Frederick W. Taylor (1919), a U.S. engineer. Taylor's contemporaries Henry L. Gantt (Buffa 1973), Frank and Lillian Gilbreth (Frank Gilbreth 1911), and others made many of the landmark contributions to the field. Today various disciplines perform overlapping and often similar functions; among these are management science (MS), industrial engineering (IE), operations research, systems analysis (SA), systems engineering (SE), industrial dynamics, econometrics, cybernetics, and more recently, management information systems (MIS), decision support systems (DSS), artificial intelligence (AI), expert systems (ES), as well as many combinations and permutations of these fields. Like the occupants of the tower of Babel, the various disciplines are developing and speaking their own languages. MIS types do not know the language of OR, and vice versa. Yet, scholars and practitioners are busy developing models: structural models, mathematical models, heuristics, algorithms, and various specialized computer routines.

Students of management are required to learn the jargons of many disciplines. They must converse with economists about marginal analysis, elasticity, and diminishing returns; with financial experts about the cost of capital, and the desirable, if not optimum financing mix; with psychologists about projective techniques, latent needs, and nonrational behavior; with engineers about feasibility analysis, optimum design, and production schedules; with sociologists about acculturation, social norms, and subcultures; with marketing types about brand switching, adequate exposure, and developing media; and with statisticians about standard error, least squares, and correlation.

With the advent of models, serious students of management need a good working knowledge of several branches of mathematics: mathematical programming, optimal control theory, queueing theory, dynamic programming, complexity theory, and the whole list of mathematical concepts that precede those mentioned. In addition, such students need to be able to correlate, memorize, integrate, and go for long stretches with little sleep. Now that modeling of management decision making has become popular, many people build models. Journals publishing these models are getting thicker, more numerous, and ever more mathematically fashion conscious (Reisman 1991a).

This book has grown out of a concern for the overburdened graduate students and for the conscientious faculty members who find literature in their areas coming out at a rate faster than they can read it, much less absorb it. This concern also includes practitioners who must search to find the one model that will fit their particular situations or models that can be altered to fit those situations. Lastly, there is a concern that we are losing sight of the problems facing us while we seek to mold answers. We, the model builders and algorithm developers, have a debt to these people. We owe it to them to sit back and reflect. We have been so preoccupied with methods of solution and with methods of optimization that we have developed many models that are applicable only to a particular problem of a particular problem grouping—a subset of a particular discipline. We have seen the details but lost sight of the whole. This book attempts to develop a foundation, the methodologies and examples to help synthesize the knowledge within our respective areas, and through generalization and systematization, show its interconnections, interrelations, and limitations. By doing this we will make this knowledge more "user-friendly." We will make it easier to learn, to assimilate, and hence to use and to teach.

The science of management needs the kind of integrative thought given the science of chemistry by a Russian named Dmitry Ivanovich Mendeleyev (1889). Before Mendeleyev developed the periodic table, chemists knew of many seemingly unrelated elements just as management scientists today know of many seemingly unrelated models. The periodic table established the systematic interrelationship between chemical elements. This table removed many burdens from the students of chemistry. In a very straightforward fashion, it pointed the way to the discovery of new elements. Mendeleyev developed this chart by reflecting on the work of others; he achieved a new synthesis that demonstrated a pattern and gave meaning to formerly unconnected elements. Many areas of management science are now ripe for this kind of integration (Reisman 1968; Reisman and Buffa 1962; Sloane and Reisman 1968).

This work should require neither a genius nor a Russian. Within our lifetimes, similar work has been done in many areas of endeavor, for example, in digital computer programming. Some of us can remember when someone looking for a computer solution to a problem was faced with a dilemma similar to that of management science practitioners today. The computer user of yesteryear had to search through the program library of IBM in hopes of finding a program to fit the problem. The alternative to finding such a cannned program was writing, from scratch, specific computer instructions in machine language for a specific problem. Today, with the help of generalized user-friendly compilers, users rarely have to develop their own detailed instructions or search the libraries for applicable canned programs. There is little reason why such developments cannot take place in many areas of management theory, marketing strategy, production systems, and finance.

Such work has been done in queueing theory (Kendall 1953); scheduling theory (Salvador 1972; Graham et al. 1979); forecasting (Chambers, Mullick, and Smith 1974); manufacturing and operations management (Reisman and Buffa 1964; Escueta, Fiedler, and Reisman 1986; Reisman 1979); managerial and engineering economics (Reisman and Buffa 1962; Reisman 1968; Reisman and Rao 1973; Reisman, Fuh, and Li 1988); finance (Sloane and Reisman 1968; Reisman 1966; Reisman, Weston, and Buffa 1964; Srinivasan 1972); computer selection (Clark and Reisman 1981; Egyhazy 1976); manpower planning (Reisman, Song, and Ikem 1991; Balinsky and Reisman 1972, 1973; Fildes 1979, 1985); inventory theory (Javad 1980; Reisman 1981; Menipaz 1982); higher education planning (Huckfeldt 1973; Reisman et al. 1973, Reisman and Kiley 1973); transfer of technology (Reisman 1989b; Zhao and Reisman 1992); countertrade (Reisman 1991b, Reisman, Fuh, and Li 1988); management in general (Reisman 1979); and in the strictly engineering area of hydrodynamics (Stokes 1880; Taft and Reisman 1965; Reisman 1965, 1971). Lengthy as this list of examples is, it is not exhaustive.

The need for generalized models is apparent in university teaching, in research, and in practice. After graduation from engineering school, the author's first job involved analyzing a hydrodynamic system, which behaved in a way unlike anything learned in school. Being impatient with library research, which at the outset seemed to promise little usable information, I derived my own equations, starting with Newton's laws of motion, for the behavior of water flowing under unsteady (time dependent) conditions. To my chagrin, I later discovered that the equations, which I thought were a contribution to the state of the art, were in fact special cases of the Navier-Stokes equations (Stokes 1880) of fluid motion developed over a century before. It would have been of great help to me if my undergraduate instructors of fluid mechanics had shown me that what was being taught was a small part of a larger picture. I would have been well served to learn more about the "kernels" of scientific thought in fluid mechanics.

In hydrodynamics, such generalized models have existed for over a century (Stokes 1880). Yet only during the last two decades have some of the leading engineering colleges started to introduce this general model in their undergraduate curricula.

The more highly motivated arguments against the introduction of the general equations invoke the psychology of human learning. It is well recognized that human learning is incremental. It best proceeds from the familiar to the less familiar and then to the unknown. It best proceeds from the particular to the general. This incremental approach has been the philosophical basis of our educational system from kindergarten through the doctoral program. This approach has also accounted for much of the incremental progress in science and in technology. The arguments for it are strong and valid. In the various areas of management science at a given stage of development, much can be gained by proceeding from the general to the particular. After learning some of the basics of the field, the student ought to be shown the overall picture. With some general theory and an understanding of the organized relationships between the various elements a student can gain much insight into the science. Furthermore, a generalized model or a taxonomy of a field of knowledge will allow a researcher or practitioner to quickly determine the properties of models not previously reported in the literature (Reisman 1988a).

The great and fast-developing need for applications of management science will ensure that general models of the Navier-Stokes type, once developed, do not take a century to be introduced where they will do the most good.

In all fairness to my earlier profession of mechanical engineering, I should point out that the reason the more general models were not discussed in courses on fluid mechanics was that the methods for solving any but the simplest cases were either nonexistent or so cumbersome, time consuming, and costly that they were hardly ever used in actual practice. High-speed computers have changed that. Today both engineering practice and management practice rely more and more on mathematical analysis and less on rules of thumb. In both professions, science is making great inroads in areas once the province of art. These inroads may be enhanced through a synthesis of existing knowledge. Perhaps the methodologies pursued in the generalizations to be discussed in this book are not the ultimate methodologies. The concepts discussed here, however, are irrefutable. To be sure, like many irrefutable truths, they are not original. All sciences have progressed, and are progressing, along lines similar to those that now characterize the science of management; the great strides in chemistry, physics, mathematics, and biology, were made by generalizing on and systematizing existing knowledge.

Historically, motivations for model building were

1. Given a real-life problem, how can I most realistically express it in mathematical terms? Having formulated such a model, what mathematical or computational tools are available for obtaining solutions?

2. Given a mathematical method or solution, what model can I develop to solve the problems I am faced with?

3. Given a mathematical method of solution, what models can I develop to publish a paper?

Similarly, the motivations for algorithm developers were

1. How can I solve a specific class of problems more efficiently, for example, in less time or requiring less computer memory?
2. How can I solve a somewhat more complex type of problem?
3. How can I solve a new class of problem?

The motivations for data collectors were

1. What data do I need to validate my model?
2. What can be learned from the data?
   a. What are the patterns therein?
   b. What hypothesis do they support/reject?
   c. What are their predictive or prescriptive uses?
3. What data might be needed in the future by whom, where, when?

None of these motivations is necessarily bad. Although some may be considered more noble than others, none necessarily performs a disservice to the emerging profession; that is, if the profession can now rise to the call of building some models or developing algorithms based on the following premise: Given a field of endeavor, how can I develop a generalized model or algorithm that will embody all previous works and classify them as special cases, that is, as cases with special limitations, approximations, or assumptions, and/or how can I classify or codify and unify the data available (Reisman 1987)? When all the existing literature in a field is thus classified, students in that area will have a much easier time correlating one work with another, and more importantly, they will get an overall picture of the field. This picture will put everything that has been done in its proper perspective; it will show all that needs doing; and it will show the steps to be followed to model situations not previously modeled or quantified (Reisman 1988a, 1989a). Similarly, practitioners will be able to turn to such work and will no longer need to spend so much time in library research or, alternatively, filing away like a pack rat all the various models as they come out. The chapters that follow discuss and describe some ways and the means for achieving the above ends.

NOTE

This chapter is reprinted by permission from Arnold Reisman, "Some Thoughts for Model Builders in the Management and Social Sciences," *Interfaces* 17(5): 114–20, 1987. Copyright 1987, The Institute of Management Science, 290 Westminster Street, Providence, RI 02903.

REFERENCES

Babbage, C. 1832. *On The Economy of Machinery and Manufacturers*. London: Knight.
Balinsky, Warren, and Arnold Reisman. 1972. "Some Manpower Planning Models Based

on Levels of Educational Attainment." *Management Science*, Application Series 18 (12): 691–705.

———. 1973. "A Taxonomy of Manpower—Educational Planning Models." *Socio-Economic Planning Sciences* 7(1): 13–17.

Buffa, Elwood S. 1973. *Modern Production Management.* 4th ed. New York: John Wiley and Sons.

Chambers, John C., Satinder K. Mullick, and Donald D. Smith. 1974. "Forecasting Techniques." In *An Executive's Guide to Forecasting*, 42–70. New York: John Wiley and Sons.

Clark, Jon D., and Arnold Reisman. 1981. "Problem Definition and Formulation: The CHEVS Taxonomy." In *Computer System Selection: An Integrated Approach.* New York: Praeger Publishers.

Egyhazy, Csaba. 1976. "A Taxonomy for Multiple Objective Decision Making," in "A Multi-criteria Decision Model Within A-Methodology for Computer Systems Selection." Ph.D. diss., Department of Operations Research, Case Western Reserve University, Cleveland, Ohio.

Escueta, Emmanuel S., Karen Fiedler, and Arnold Reisman. 1986. "A New Hospital Foodservice Classification System." *Journal of Foodservice Systems* 4(2): 107–16.

Fildes, Robert. 1979. "Quantitative Forecasting—The State of the Art: Extrapolative Models." *Journal of the Operational Research Society* 30(8): 691–710.

———. 1985. "Quantitative Forecasting—The State of the Art Econometric Models." *Journal of the Operational Research Society* 36(7): 549–80.

Gilbreth, Frank B. 1911. *Motion Study.* New York: D. Van Nostrand Company.

Graham, R. L., E. L. Lawler, J. K. Lenstra, and Kan A. H. G. Rinnooy. 1979. "Optimization and Approximation in Deterministic Sequencing and Scheduling: A Survey." *Annals of Discrete Mathematics* 5: 287–326.

Huckfeldt, V. Eugene. 1973. "A Classification Structure for Models," in "A National Planning Model for Higher Education." Ph.D. thesis, Department of Operations Research, Case Western Reserve University, Cleveland, Ohio.

Javad, Shahriar. 1980. "Multi-Echelon Inventory System in Health-Care Delivery Organizations." Ph.D. thesis, Department of Operations Research, Case Western Reserve University, Cleveland, Ohio.

Kendall, D. G. 1953. "Stochastic Processes Occuring in the Theory of Queues and Their Analysis by the Method of Imbedded Markov Chains." *Annals of Mathematics Statistics* 24(1): 338–54.

McCloskey, J. H. 1987. "US Operations Research in World War II." *Operations Research* 35: 142–52, 453–70, 910–25.

Mendelyeev, D. I. 1889. "The Periodic Law of the Chemical Elements (Faraday Lecture)." *Journal of the Chemical Society* 55: 634–56. (Reprinted in *Faraday Lectures*, Chemical Society 1928, *Lectures Delivered Before the Chemical Society.* London: Chemical Society, 1869–1928.)

Menipaz, E. 1982. "A Taxonomy and Shibboleth of Inventory Models." In *Proceedings of the Second International Symposium on Inventories.* Budapest, Hungary.

Reisman, Arnold. 1965. "On a Systematic Approach to the Analysis and Synthesis of Complex Systems Involving Unsteady Flow of Fluids." *Journal of Hydrology* 2(4): 291–308.

———. 1966. "The Cost of Capital: A Reconciliation of Some Existing Theories Through

Generalization." *Mississippi Valley Journal of Business and Economics* 1(2): 67–82.

———. 1968. "Unification of Engineering Economy: The Need and a Suggested Approach." *The Engineering Economist* 14(1): 1–24. (And the American Society of Mechanical Engineers, ASME Paper 68, WA/MGT–9.)

———. 1971. "On the Understanding of Unsteady Flow." In *Heating/Piping/Air Conditioning* (a series discussing the analysis of hydraulic transients and providing a unified approach to hydrodynamics) 43(6): 92–94; 43(7): 72–74; 43(8): 79–84; 43(9): 104–8; 43(10): 101–7; 43(12): 59–64.

———. 1979. "What is Systems Analysis in General?" In *Systems Analysis in Health-Care Delivery*, 3–33. Lexington, Mass.: Lexington Books.

———. 1981. "Classification of Characteristics of Inventory-Control Problems." In *Materials Management for Health Services*, 240–43. Lexington, Mass.: Lexington Books.

———. 1987. "Expansion of Knowledge Via Consolidation of Knowledge," presented at the Second International Symposium on Methodologies for Intellegent Systems, Charlotte, N. C., October 14–18. ISMIS–87 *Proceedings*, 159–72, ONRL–6417, Oak Ridge National Laboratory.

———. 1988a. "Finding Researchable Topics Via A Taxonomy of a Field of Knowledge." *Operations Research Letters* 7(6): 295–301.

———. 1988b. "On Alternative Strategies for Doing Research in the Management and Social Sciences." *IEEE Transactions on Engineering Management* 35(4): 215–21.

———. 1989a. "A Systems Approach to Identifying Knowledge Voids in Problem Solving Disciplines and Professions: A Focus on the Management Sciences." *Knowledge in Society: An International Journal of Knowledge Transfer* 1(4): 67–86.

———. 1989b. "Technology Transfer: A Taxonomic View." *Journal of Technology Transfer* 14(3&4): 31–36.

———. 1991a. "An Epistemologic View of OR/MS with Implications for the Management of Technology." Technical Memorandum #672, Department of Operations Research, Case Western Reserve University, Cleveland, Ohio.

———. 1991b. "Enhancing Nonprofit Resources Through Barter." *Nonprofit Management and Leadership* 1(3): 253–65.

Reisman, Arnold, and Elwood S. Buffa. 1962. "A General Model For Investment Policy." *Management Science* 8(3): 304–10.

———. 1964. "A General Model For Production and Operations Systems." *Management Science* 11(1): 64–79.

Reisman, Arnold, B. V. Dean, V. Kaujalgi, V. J. Aggarwal, P. Lewy, and J. S. Gravenstein. 1973. "A Task Analysis in a Clinical Speciality Providing Data For a New Curriculum for Anesthesia Personnel." In *Socio-Economic Planning Sciences* 7(3): 371–79.

Reisman, Arnold, Duu-cheng Fuh, and Gang Li. 1988. "Achieving an Advantage With Countertrade." *Industrial Marketing Management* 17: 55–63.

Reisman, Arnold, and M. Kiley, eds. 1973. *Health Care Delivery Planning*. New York: Gordon and Breach Science Publishers.

Reisman, Arnold, and A. K. Rao. 1973. "A Generalized Scheme For Classification of Investment Models." In *Discounted Cash Flow Analysis: Stochastic Extensions*,

260–67. Norcross, Ga.: American Institute of Industrial Engineers, Monograph Series.

Reisman, Arnold, Moon Ho Song, and Fidelis Ikem. 1991. "A Taxonomy of Manpower Forecasting and Planning." *Socio-Economic Planning Sciences* 25(3): 221–31.

Reisman, Arnold, J. Fred Weston, and Elwood S. Buffa. 1964. "Toward a Theory of Optimum Financing Mix." Working paper no. 50, Western Management Science Institute, UCLA, Los Angeles, California.

Salvador, Michael S. 1972. "A Taxomonical Summary of Flow Shop Scheduling Problems." In *Systems Analysis in Health-Care Delivery*, Arnold Reisman, 93, 94. Lexington, Mass.: Lexington Books, 1979.

Sloane, William R., and Arnold Reisman. 1968. "Stock Evaluation Theory: Classification, Reconciliation, and General Model." *Journal of Finance and Quantitative Analysis* 3(2): 171–204.

Srinivasan, Sundaravaradhan. 1972. "A Taxonomy of Portfolio Selection Models," in "A Multi-period Behavioral Model For Portfolio Selection Problem." Ph.D. thesis, Technical Memo No. 256, Department of Operations Research, Case Western Reserve University, Cleveland, Ohio.

Stokes, George G. 1880. *Mathematical and Physical Papers*. Vol. 2, 1–7, 36–50. Cambridge, England.

Taft, Martin I., and Arnold Reisman. 1965. "The Conservation Equations: A Systematic Look." *Journal of Hydrology* 3(3/4): 161–79.

Taylor, F. W. 1919. *Principles of Scientific Management*. New York: Harper and Brothers. (Reprinted in 1947 in *Scientific Management*, New York: Harper and Brothers.)

Zhao, Liming, and Arnold Reisman. 1992. "Toward Meta Research on Technology Transfer." *IEEE Transactions on Engineering Management* 39(1):13–21.

Part II

Some of the Ways and the Means

As the title implies, Part II of this book provides a number of "how-tos" to address the challenges of Part I.

Chapter 2 delineates the various strategies for pursuing research in the management sciences. For each of the strategies described, the chapter addresses the potential benefits as well as risks to both the researcher and to the state of knowledge.

Chapter 3 addresses the means for consolidating knowledge while expanding it. Several ways to achieve that objective are delineated and embedded in a suggested taxonomy of taxonomies. Selected works from both the "hard" and the management sciences are summarized to demonstrate the variety of knowledge-consolidating role models and to test the effectiveness of the *taxonomy* of *taxonomies*.

There are many paths leading to knowledge creation. Chapter 4 offers one step-by-step methodology for systematically identifying voids, and hence researchable topics, within a given field of knowledge. The method is based on transforming a descriptive taxonomy into a prescriptive one. Two disparate literature surveys, one for combining probability distributions in rational group decision making and the other for perishable inventory theory are used to demonstrate the efficiency of the procedure.

The more mature a problem-solving discipline or profession, the greater is its dependence on its science base and less on its art form of knowledge. In Chapter 5, the knowledge base for problem-solving disciplines or professions is subdivided into three categories: data, methodology, and problems. The chapter goes on to discuss the significance of the availability of knowledge in each of these categories and in each overlap between them. Lastly, a systematic approach to finding and specifying literature voids in each of the above categories is discussed and illustrated. Such specifications may be viewed as topics with a research potential.

Chapter 6 draws a parallel between mission-oriented research and real-world problem solving. It then provides three alternative strategies for solving non-textbook types of problems. Lastly, it provides an anatomy and a morphology for the problem-solving project life cycle and discusses the mix of mentalities needed as the stages progress from the feasibility study to preliminary design and ultimately to implementation.

In recognition of the fact that creativity is often needed in research as well as in real-world problem solving, yet it is rarely taught, Chapter 7 summarizes a number of techniques to aid in creative thinking.

On Alternative Strategies for Doing Research in the Management and Social Sciences

INTRODUCTION

In Chapter 1, we challenged the management science community to do more research that is unifying in nature and that tends to compress knowledge while significantly expanding it. In Chapter 3 we delineate a number of taxonomic approaches to classifying knowledge and point out the need for yet higher order contributions, namely those that embed that which is known in more generalized theoretical frameworks. Here we delineate a number of alternative strategies for that type of research. To round out the chapter, we also discuss research strategies that do not necessarily contribute to the objective of consolidating knowledge. Lastly, we comment on some of the pitfalls of each research strategy and the relative ease or difficulty in overcoming such pitfalls depending on the strategy chosen.

DISCUSSION

We start toward the above goals by assuming that the symbols X, Y, and Z in Figure 2.1 represent three different models, each addressing some specific aspect of a field of knowledge.

For example, X could stand for the basic economic lot size equation as developed by Harris (1915); Y would be an extension that accounts for planned shortages; and Z an extension accounting for noninstantaneous replenishment, for example, simultaneous production and utilization (Reisman 1981). One objective of a taxonomy is to show in an explicit fashion the domains of problem characteristics which each of these three models is capable of addressing.

We next circumscribe, as in Figure 2.2, each model by imaginary boundaries that represent the model's realm of knowledge and/or of applicability. For the examples cited, the realm of knowledge for X is clearly the economic replenishment of products consumed or sold, where the demand is assumed to be

Figure 2.1
Models

X   Y

Z

Figure 2.2
Models and Domains of Problem Characteristics

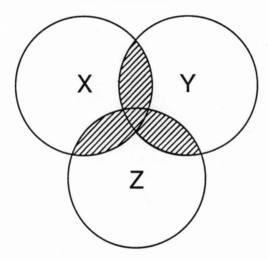

constant and known, the setup/reorder and the holding costs are the only cost considerations, the replenishment is instantaneous (e.g., full batch), and where no shortages or stockouts are planned for, yet no buffer inventory is kept on hand. Its intended applications are clearly in manufacturing, warehousing, retailing, and more recently in the services such as in hospital management of consumables and of disposables. The above remarks also apply to Y and Z except that Y also allows one to establish the economic level of planned stockouts. Clearly the optimum is based on finding the least cost replenishment involving setup/reorder costs, holding costs as well as the costs of shortages.

Model Z, in this case, differs from model X only in that it allows for distributed as opposed to instantaneous replenishment. Such is the case where the item is produced at a rate faster than it is consumed or sold. The resulting Venn-type diagram allows us to, symbolically at least, point out that there are overlaps in the domains of the problem characteristics that are addressable by the respective

Figure 2.3
Models—Domains of Problem Characteristics and Universe of Problem Domains

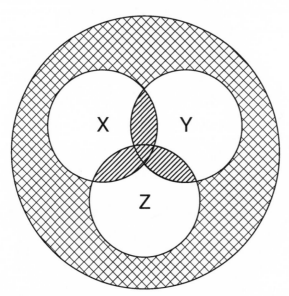

models. The Venn diagram also shows us that there are regions of dissimilarity in these domains.

The above cited examples of three different inventory–control models clearly have a great deal of overlap in terms of the realm of knowledge they represent and also in terms of their universe of applicability. Hence the cross-hatched portions of Figure 2.2 would be much more extensive than shown.

Lastly, within Figure 2.3, we encompass the universe that embeds the problem domains of these three models. Models X, Y, and Z are the early and therefore rudimentary treatments of a vast field now known as inventory-control theory. The potential breadth and depth of this field, its "universe," is shown taxonomically in Table 2.1 (Reisman 1981; Javad 1980). As can be seen from Table 2.1, the domains of models X, Y, and Z are small microcosms in this universe. This allows us to show the extent of this universe, which is not addressed by any of the three models.

If one can embed into the potential universe representation all of the known knowledge in that field, then the space remaining points out the arena of potential research. A good taxonomy of a field of knowledge does all of the above in an unambiguous and easily discernible manner.

One can use the notion of Figures 2.1 through 2.3 in reverse order. By identifying a field of knowledge or the universe of problem domains in that field of knowledge, one can then explore which subset of a problem-characteristics domain should be addressed by a modeler and in what order. The priorities might be set by real-world requirements, by the modeler's skills, or by the relative

Table 2.1

A Taxonomic Scheme for Classification of Inventory-Control Systems

Category				Code
Demand	Deterministic	Static		(d_1)
		Demand		(d_2)
	Stochastic	Stationary		(d_3)
		Nonstationary		(d_4)
Ordering Cycle	Continuous			(o_1)
	Periodic			(o_2)
Lead-time	Zero			(l_1)
	Deterministic			(l_2)
	Stochastic			(l_3)
Stock Replenishment	Instantaneous			(r_1)
	Uniform			(r_2)
Number of Items	Single			(i_1)
	Multi	Dependent		(i_2)
		Independent		(i_3)
Time Period	Single			(p_1)
	Multi	Finite Horizon		(p_2)
		Infinite Horizon		(p_3)
Number of Supply Echelons	Single			(e_1)
	Multi	General		(e_2)
		Arborescence	General	(e_3)
			Parallel	(e_4)
			Series	(e_5)
Item Characterization	Consumable			(c_1)
	Perishable			(c_2)
	Reusable			(c_3)
Treatment of Excess Demand	Backorder			(t_1)
	Lost Sale			(t_2)
Objective of the	Cost Oriented			(o_1)
	Service Oriented			(o_2)
Modeling	Exact			(m_1)
	Approximate			(m_2)
Solution Method	Optimization			(s_1)
	Suboptimization			(s_2)
	Heuristics			(s_3)

From Reisman [1981]

Figure 2.4
Ripple Process

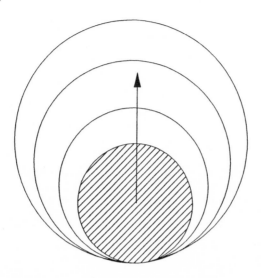

ease of obtaining solutions. Irrespective of the motivations, given a bounding of a problem's characteristics domain, one can then proceed to develop a model or a theory to address the problem domain so identified and bounded. In Chapter 4 we show, in a taxonomic form, the realm (universe) of knowledge for perishable inventory-control theory. Using a fairly exhaustive literature survey (Nahmias 1982), we show what part of that universe has been explored. By elimination we then specify the characteristics of models that have yet to be developed (Reisman 1988).

Taxonomic work is important because it is an end in itself and because it is a means toward a number of different ends. One of these ends provides direction and/or guidance to expansion or generalization of knowledge. The expansion of knowledge, however, can be pursued in several distinctly different ways. We next consider some of these approaches.

THE RIPPLE STRATEGY

The most common way in which management science research is done these days is implied by Figure 2.4. It has been referred to as the incremental approach. The figure, however, suggests another name—the *ripple process*. Typically, this approach takes what is known for *n* dimensions and develops a model, solution or a theory for $n + 1$ dimensions of the same type of problem domain. Using the examples cited earlier, both models Y and Z were incremental improvements over the Harris Economic Ordering Quantity (EOQ) equation or model X.

Figure 2.5
Embedding Process

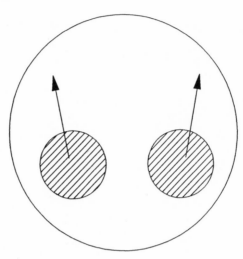

EMBEDDING STRATEGY

The process shown in Figure 2.5 we shall refer to as the *embedding process*. This is a case where several known models or theories are embedded into a more generalized formulation or a more global theory. If we use the incremental approach designation synonymously with the ripple process, then correspondingly we can use "big leap forward" for the embedding process designation. Using the above examples, one could argue that combining models X, Y, and Z into a single equation allowing for shortages and for distributed replenishments as shown in Reisman (1981) represents embedding. However, it is not a big leap forward—a matter of magnitude. Some better examples of the "spirit" of the embedding strategy can be found in discounted cash flow formulations within engineering economy (Reisman 1968, 1971). In these references, the author has combined all aspects of discounted cash flow analysis known up to the time of writing into a single general model (equation). The equation is then shown to be reducible to each of the classical and each of the state-of-the-art models for investment and for equipment replacement decision-aiding analyses. Moreover, a taxonomic scheme for classifying all potential subcases is provided, and its robustness for distinguishing between the different landmark models is demonstrated. Much of this work is encapsulated in Chapter 16 of this book.

The developments were later extended to explicitly consider inflation, variable discount rates, and stochastic considerations in Reisman and Rao (1973).

Lastly, the same approach has been brought to bear in unifying the then emerging field of stock-price valuation modeling in finance (Sloane and Reisman 1968).

Figure 2.6
Bridging Process

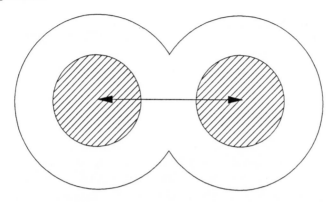

BRIDGING STRATEGY

The third type of process, indicated in Figure 2.6, involves the bridging of known models or of known theories. Examples of this are many. The most recent ones involve merging of discounted cash flow or present value analysis with the theory of scheduling (Lawrence 1987) and of quality control with queueing network theory (Hsu 1987). Although Figure 2.6 represents the bridging of but two disciplines, there is clearly no theoretical limit to the number of disciplines that can potentially be so coalesced. In fact, examples abound of multidisciplinary bridging. Among these is the bridging of stochastic network theory, plant layout algorithms, and simulation, which has yielded a better way of organizing and utilizing flexible manufacturing systems (Wu, Co, and Reisman 1988).

Unfortunately, bridging of disciplines can also be labeled the big-leap-forward approach. Often such bridging results in major expansions of knowledge in the respective fields. The resulting whole is often greater than the sum of the resulting parts.

TRANSFER OF TECHNOLOGIES STRATEGY

Another approach to the generation of knowledge, if not to knowledge consolidation, is what may be labeled as *transfer of technology*, as shown in Figure 2.7. Often by analogy it is possible to use what is known in one discipline to model problem domains falling in some other, perhaps even a disparate, discipline. This does not fall exactly in the bridging category because it does not typically impact the state of knowledge in the ''mother,'' or source, discipline. The distinction is further emphasized by comparing Figures 2.6 and 2.7. Again examples of these forms of contributions abound. One area representing this type of research is the use of inventory theoretic models, and in fact, results in improved cash management practices in a multilevel, geographically distributed

Figure 2.7
Transfer of Technology Process

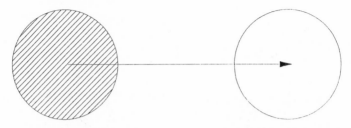

gasoline storage and retailing organization of a major oil company (Anvari 1979). In another example, the recognition of an analogy between traffic flow in the Lincoln Tunnel and a converyor-belt-based, order-picking operation of a magazine and paperback book distributor allowed for a quick, cheap and effective solution to increasing throughput and reducing worker fatigue (Reisman et al. 1982). Applications of queueing theory in the New York Port Authority study (Edie 1961) found the optimum vehicle speed to be thirty-five miles per hour—quite slower than intuition would dictate and what management thought was optimal. In the order-picking operation a slower belt speed reduced the staging "waiting lines" at the bundle-banding operation (toll gate) and the line shutdowns due to "accidents" involving some picker's inability to keep up with the belt at any given time.

CREATIVE APPLICATION STRATEGY

The creative application process as shown in Figure 2.8, is closely related to transfer-of-technology type research. In this mode, one applies directly, not by analogy, a known methodology to a problem not previously so addressed. New applications of the various optimization methods fall into this category. Thus the early applications of linear programming in agriculture (Heady and Love 1954; Boles 1955) fall into this category as do the applications of integer programming to airline crew selection (Spitzer 1961), to radio frequency selection (Mathur et al. 1985), and so forth.

STRUCTURING STRATEGY

Sometimes it is possible to identify a universe of problems that is virgin, or unexplored by management science or social science type modelers. These are often publishing bonanzas. Figure 2.9 symbolizes this strategy. The field of finance was in such a state in the late fifties (Solomon 1959). Much to my surprise, the oldest form of doing business known to man—barter, or countertrading as it is now known and used in over 30 percent of world trade (United Nations 1986)—is still pretty much in that state, albeit some work is on the way (Reisman, Fuh, and Li 1988; Reisman, Aggarwal, and Fuh 1989).

Figure 2.8
Creative Application

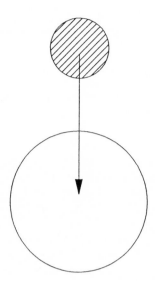

Figure 2.9
Structuring Process

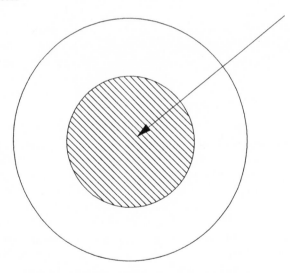

Research in such settings will be labeled the *structuring process* in recognition of the fact that the process requires observation and documentation of the organizational phenomena, for example, the flow and the processing of resources such as materials, energy, money, people information; decision disciplines; and so forth. Lastly, the process requires the structuring or abstracting of observations in the form of models. Clearly the models can take on mathematical, statistical, or conceptual (e.g., graphical and/or computer-aided) formats. Much of the quantitative social science structuring research is statistical in nature. That is, empirical data are subjugated by one or several pattern seeking methodologies such as cluster, discriminant, or factor analysis or by the relationship-seeking regression techniques.

Glaser and Strauss (1967) call this approach to discovery of knowledge *grounded theory*. They stress the need for discovery of theory from data which are systematically obtained and analyzed. Their message is essentially that good theory evolves from well-conceived data acquisitions, from several comparison groups, and from the rigorous analysis of such data. Moreover, they attempt to direct sociological research away from its preoccupation with validating theories that were "generated by logical deduction from *a-priori* assumptions."

By footnote, they point out that Merton (1949)

never reached the notion of the discovery of grounded theory in discussing the theoretic functions of research. The closest he came was with "serendipity"; that is, an unanticipated, anomalous, and strategic finding gives rise to a new hypothesis. This concept does not catch the idea of purposefully discovering theory through social research. It puts the discovery of a single hypothesis on a surprise basis. Merton was preoccupied with how verifications through research feed back into and modify theory. Thus, he was concerned with grounded modifying of theory, not grounded generating of theory. (Glaser and Strauss 1967, p. 2)

By this note they indicate the existence of a bridge between the above *structuring* strategy and the *empirical* validation strategy to be discussed next.

EMPIRICAL VALIDATION STRATEGY

It must be recognized, however, that there are instances when the general preceeds the particular, for example, known general theories or general models must await, as did the Navier-Stokes equations in physics (Stokes 1880), the empirical validation and/or implementation. When such is the case, it is often required that the general be made specific in order to be externally validated. Creating the empirical or the phenomenological basis or foundation for the theory is clearly a necessary process whether it preceeds or follows the theoretic developments. Whereas the embedding and bridging processes tend to explode knowledge, this process, as implied by Figure 2.10, is more imploding in nature.

RESEARCH STRATEGY CHARACTERISTICS

In the spectrum of research strategies, empirical research is the most labor intensive process. This is so irrespective of whether it is directed at theory validation as discussed in connection with the implosion process of Figure 2.10,

Figure 2.10
Empirical Validation

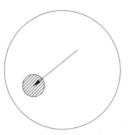

or whether it is an attempt to find patterns, clusters, and therefore meaning to a collection of data. It takes much effort to design and pretest the proper data collection instrument. It takes extensive effort to collect, mechanize, and analyze the data. Although this kind of research is very important in providing an empirical or real-world underpinning to a theory or in reducing theory to practice, it is still within the spectrum of strategies, the process that is most prone to inconclusive results and all that this implies. On the other hand, in the spectrum of strategies discussed earlier, this type of research requires the least creativity and the least need for a breadth of vision.

Generalization/unification research of the big-leap-forward variety is the least labor intensive. This approach typically does not require much, if any, computerization, nor does it particularly get involved with the development and testing for effectiveness or for efficiency of any algorithms. Often it requires no data collection, and validation is easily obtainable inasmuch as published works serve as the basis and the stepping stones for the generalization. Therefore, the generalized framework should reduce to all of these known and published models or theories, as special cases, by a process of simplification. Although it may appear that this is circuitous type reasoning, in fact it isn't.

This strategy is the most prone to result in significant contributions within the shortest time span and the least effort, but it requires the most creativity and breadth of vision. The embedding process may, however, result in much criticism, especially from those who are most comfortable with analysis as opposed to synthesis or design. "So what?" type reactions will be common.

The other strategies discussed earlier in the chapter fall in between the above two extremes. Bridging disciplines may require validation that the resulting theory is meaningful and/or useful. The levels of creativity required in this process are not as great as they are in the big-leap-forward approach, yet they are greater than required for the more mechanistic ways of empirical or of incremental approaches.

The incremental process, or the ripple process, is probably one of the more difficult ways of getting a breakthrough of any significance, inasmuch as it typically requires an extension of a well-developed body of theory where the "cream" has already been "skimmed off." Almost inevitably, this approach requires the highest level of technical competence, albeit in a rather specific arena. However, it offers one of the most well defined starting points for a researcher. It is the most comfortable thing to do for those who have no experience, talent, or disposition to move about in uncharted waters without a compass. It is probably the safest strategy for succeeding by the high IQ type who is most comfortable in textbook or academic environments. The ripple effect, or incremental approach, is most prevalent in highly explored, highly developed domains of knowledge—not necessarily domains of practice. It is best suited for those with great skills for analysis, but who lack the additional creativity needed to do synthesis or design. Whereas the empirical and the structuring strategies, done at their best, take the researcher into the real-world organizations, the incremental type research is doable in isolation, or as Kaplan (1986) put it "in our offices or in laboratory settings." The incremental process is best understood by reviewers and editors of scientific journals and by university search, promotion and/or tenure committees.

The bridging of disciplines approach requires technical versatility as well as competence. That is, the researcher must be equally comfortable with technical matters in each of the disciplines he or she is bridging and must be knowledgeable and convinced that the bridging is indeed necessary or desired.

The transfer-of-technology process requires a bit of vision, a recognition of the analogous relationships that describe the domains in both the mother or source discipline and the receiving discipline. The latter being the discipline or area being structured, modeled, and so forth by such efforts. Although the strategies delineated in this chapter distinguish between different "pure" approaches to conducting research in the management and the social sciences, the set is not exhaustive. One thing is certain, these strategies are not mutually exclusive. In fact, some of the better studies invoke two or more of the above approaches. A good example of this can be found in Tsafrir (1987). This work *bridges* multilevel optimization methods (Mesarovic, Macko, and Takahara 1970; Tarvainen 1981); and distributive justice theory, (Rawls 1971; Yaari 1981) while *structuring* the coordinative decision making for cooperation among independent agricultural cooperatives. Tsafrir *creatively applies* linear programming to optimizing resource allocation by each farmer (cooperative) as part of the iterative process of coordination. Lastly, he *validates* his methodology with data representing the fish-farming "branch" from several adjacent Israeli *kibbutzim* (cooperatives).

Often a researcher runs into a "stone wall." He or she sees the objective, but is methodologically stymied by his or her discipline. This most often occurs in the *ripple* type of research. As discussed in Chapters 8 and 9, it is an earmark of a mature discipline. Such hurdles are often overcome by *transfering technology* from other disciplines and/or by some *creative applications*, for example, borrowing knowledge from other disciplines and using it directly or by analogy. Some disciplines reach what appears to be a "dead end." Additional research, no matter how elegant in such arenas of knowledge, promises very little. By *bridging* this field with other disciplines, or by *embedding* all that is known in the field in a larger framework, one can open new vistas.

Individuals reared in the incremental approach to research are typically uncomfortable with the kind of unstructured problems one finds in the real world of management and/or consulting to decision makers. Moreover, in think-tank or creative-type settings, they are best suited for staff backup work. The same holds in the implementation phases of management-consulting studies.

The reverse is true for those with a track record of structuring ill-defined problems. Such people are often found among those who have successfully applied the structuring, the embedding, the bridging, and even the transfer-of-technology approaches. Another way of viewing the above is to recognize that the incremental types are essentially specialists, whereas the embedding and structuring types tend to be generalists to a much greater extent. As shown in Chapter 6, the solving of unstructured problems in the real-world environment as well as in many other mission-oriented studies requires generalist-type thinking or thinkers during the early project stages, for example, the feasibility study and the preliminary design stages. As one moves on to subsequent stages in the project life cycle (e.g., detail design, pilot program or protype construction, implementation/construction/production, etc.), the project team mix must have a greater proportion of the specialist-type skills, for example, statisticans, math and/or computer programmers, analysts of various kinds, manual writers, and the like.

CONCLUDING REMARKS

As indicated earlier in this chapter, the surest way of securing a publication in today's flagship management science journals, which are basically by and for the academic community, is to follow the ripple process. However, by not paying sufficient attention to the phenomenologic basis for our research, we "risk . . . having analytic development so far ahead of empirical observation and description . . . that we may not be developing the analytic tools that will be most helpful for modeling and studying actual phenomena" (Kaplan 1986). Both the structuring and the implosion or the validation processes are part of the roots of operations research management science; should we forget that and continue to inbreed in incremental ways, we are doomed to extinction as a profession. Moreover, should we do more of the embedding, bridging, and/or taxonomic type research, as stated at the outset of this book, we shall be buried in our own models. Finally, the earlier discussion of the prevalence of use of the incremental process in highly explored domains of knowledge, and the structuring approach in the "virgin" domains, implies that one can classify knowledge domains by stages of development. This hypothesis is explored in Chapters 8 and 9.

NOTE

This chapter is based on "On Alternative Strategies for Doing Research in Management and Social Sciences," which originally appeared in *IEEE Transactions on Engineering Management* 35(4): 215–21, November 1988.

REFERENCES

Anvari, Mohsen. 1979. "Retail Cash Collection and New Advances in Banking Industry." Ph.D. thesis, Department of Operations Research, Case Western Reserve University, Cleveland, Ohio.

Boles, J. N. 1955. "Linear Programming and Farm Management Analysis." *Journal of Farm Economies* 37:1–25.

Edie, L. S. 1961. "Car-Following and Steady-State Theory of Noncongested Traffic." *Operations Research* 9(1): 66–76.

Glaser, B., and A. Strauss. 1967. *The Discovery of Grounded Theory Strategies for Qualitative Research*. Chicago, Ill.: Aldine Publishing Co.

Harris, F. W. 1915. *Operations and Cost* (Factory Management Series) Chapter IV. Chicago, Ill.: A. W. Shaw Co.

Heady, Earl O., and H. C. Love. 1954. "Optimum Allocation of Resources Between Pasture Improvements, Crops and Other Investment Opportunities on Southern Iowa Farms." Bulletin 437, Agricultural Experiment Station, Iowa State University, Ames.

Hsu, Lie-Fern. 1987. "Economic Design of On-Line Inspection Plans in Advanced Manufacturing Systems." Ph.D. thesis, Department of Operations Research, Case Western Reserve University, Cleveland, Ohio.

Javad, Shahriar. 1980. "Multi-echelon Inventory Systems in Health Care Delivery Organizations." Ph.D. Thesis, Case Western Reserve University, Cleveland, Ohio.

Kaplan, Robert S. 1986. "Research Cultures in Managerial Accounting: Empirical Research." Plenary session paper, American Accounting Association annual meeting, New York, N.Y.

Lawrence, Stephen. 1987. "Production Scheduling to Maximize Net Present Value." Ph.D. thesis, Carnegie-Mellon University, Pittsburgh, Pa.

Mathur, Kamlesh, Harvey Salkin, Koichi Nishimura, and Susumu Morito. 1985. "Applications of Integer Programming in Radio Frequency Management." *Management Science* 31(7): 829–39.

Merton, R. 1949 and 1957. *Social Theory and Social Structure*. Glencoe Ill.: The Free Press.

Mesarovic, M. S., D. Macho, and Y. Takahara. 1970. *Theory of Hierarchical, Multilevel Systems*. New York: Academic Press.

Nahmias, Steven. 1982. "Perishable Inventory Theory: A Review." *Operations Research* 30(4): 680–707.

Rawls, J. 1971. *A Theory of Justice*. Cambridge, Mass.: Belknap Press.

Reisman, Arnold. 1968. "Unification of Engineering Economy: The Need and a Suggested Approach." *The Engineering Economist* 14(1): 1–24. (Also the American Society of Mechanical Engineers, ASME Paper 68, WA/MGT-9.)

————. 1971. *Managerial and Engineering Economics*. Boston, Mass.: Allyn and Bacon Publishing Company.

————. 1979. *Systems Analysis in Health-Care Delivery*. Lexington, Mass.: Lexington Books.

————. 1981. *Materials Management for Health Services*. Lexington, Mass.: Lexington Books.

————. 1987a. "Some Thoughts for Model Builders in the Management and Social Sciences." *Interfaces* (September/October).

————. 1987b. "Expansion of Knowledge Via Consolidation of Knowledge." Paper presented at the Second International Symposium on Methodologies for Intellegent Systems, Charlotte, N.C., October 14–18. Published in *ISMIS-87 Proceedings*, 159–72, ONRL-6417, Oak Ridge National Laboratory.

————. 1988. "Finding Researchable Topics Via a Taxonomy of a Field of Knowledge." *Operations Research Letters* 7(6): 295–301.

Reisman, Arnold, Raj Aggarwal, and Duu-Cheng Fuh. 1989. "Seeking Out Profitable Countertrade Opportunities." *Industrial Marketing Management* 18(1): 1–7.

Reisman, Arnold, Duu-Cheng Fuh, and Gang Li. 1988. "Achieving an Advantage with Countertrade." *Industrial Marketing Management* 17(1): 55–63.

Reisman, A., S. Kotha, L. Gonzaga, B. Kidd, and T. Murray. 1982. "IE's Find Ways to Improve Throughput, Worker Morale on a Firm's Wrap-Line." *Industrial Engineering* 14(9): 70–80.

Reisman, Arnold, and A. K. Rao. 1973. "A Generalized Scheme for Classification of Investment Models." In *Discounted Cash Flow Analysis: Stochastic Extensions*, 260–67. American Institute of Industrial Engineers, Monograph Series.

Sloane, William R., and Arnold Reisman. 1968. "Stock Evaluation Theory: Classification, Reconciliation, and General Model." *Journal of Finance and Quantitative Analysis* 3(2): 171–204.

Solomon, E., ed. 1959. *The Management of Corporate Capital*. Glencoe, Ill: Free Press.

Spitzer, M. 1961. "Solution to the Crew Scheduling Problem." Paper presented at the first AGIFORS symposium, October.

Stokes, George G. 1880. *Mathematical and Physical Papers*. Vol. 2, 1–7 and 36–50. Cambridge, England: Cambridge University Press.

Tarvainen, K. 1981. "Hierarchical Multiobjective Optimization." Ph.D. thesis, Case Western Reserve University, Cleveland, Ohio.

Tsafrir, A. 1987. "Coordination of Multilevel Optimization and Benefit Allocation in Agricultural Integrations." Ph.D. thesis, Department of Operations Research, Case Western Reserve University, Cleveland, Ohio.

United Nations Development Conference on Trade and Development (United Nations). 1986. "Countertrade." UNCTAD, GE. 86–56882/1770e, New York.

Wu, Chin-Yun A., Henry Co, and Arnold Reisman. 1988. "A Throughput Maximising Facility Layout Model." *International Journal of Production Research* 27(1): 1–12.

Yaari, M. E. 1981. "Rawls, Edgeworth, Shapley, Nash: Theories of Distributive Justice Re-examined." *Journal of Economic Theory* 24:1–39.

Chapter 3

Expansion of Knowledge Via Consolidation of Knowledge

INTRODUCTION

Yes, it is indeed possible to condense knowledge in a given field while significantly expanding it. This chapter addresses itself to the organization of knowledge—both new knowledge and existing knowledge. New knowledge is generated in various ways. Most researchers work in a realm that can be typed as the realm of specificity. That is, they work figuratively at the "bench level," discovering new phenomena, and uncovering or creating new processes. In the management sciences, they prove new theorems and develop more efficient algorithms. As discussed in Chapter 2, most often they expand knowledge incrementally by taking a problem of n dimensions for which a solution is known, and they find a solution for its $n + 1$ dimensional counterpart. However, a small minority of researchers are concerned with the classification of the specifics discovered or developed by others. They create taxonomies for the seemingly disjointed specifics. These contributors state the underlying principles, simplifying the assumptions and scope of the various specifics in comparable terms. Graphically, symbolically, or both, they vividly display the similarities and the differences among the various contributions, thus demonstrating the relationship of all contributions and the practical applications of each to the other. They provide a framework by which all of the existing knowledge can be systematically filed and therefore recalled efficiently and effectively. By providing what amounts to an aerial view—a picture of the "territory," as will be shown in Chapters 4 and 5—they often identify the voids in the literature. The higher the vantage point, the higher the platform from which the "picture" is taken, the greater is the territory that is encompassed by the resulting taxonomy. The greater the resolution of the classifier's "camera/film" combination, the more descriptive or detailed is the classification. As in cartography, there is a need for detailed topographies of local terrain, for example, the specific management science research areas. Similarly, there is a need for the more global views spanning a number of specifics and showing the gestalt, the structure, anatomy, or morphology, of a field of knowledge or a linkup across a number of seemingly disparate fields.

As indicated in Chapter 1, knowledge consolidation is a means to various ends, and it is also an end in itself. It is a means toward the end of more efficient and more effective teaching and learning of new or existing knowledge. It is a means toward the end of more efficient storage and more effective recall and/ or retention of knowledge. It is a means toward more efficient and more effective processes of research, leading to the yet unknown, to the design of the yet unavailable, and it is a means toward more efficient problem solving. It is applicable to problems of analysis, synthesis, instrumentation, or data collection and to problem solving. Lastly, applications of artificial intelligence and design of expert systems can be greatly enhanced by the kind of knowledge consolidation discussed in this chapter.

For those who are, or who aspire to be, generalists, this chapter attempts to provide a "road map" or a collection of "how-tos" for systematically representing what is known, albeit in a fragmented way, within a given field of knowledge. Distinctions between descriptive taxonomies and prescriptive generalizations are stated and illustrated in several realms of endeavor, thus providing the generalist a number of both approaches and role models.

The specialists will benefit from such work because it will facilitate their assimilation of knowledge, and even more importantly, it will give them perspective. Practitioners will benefit because the available literature will not be dominated by models that they find to be too specific or too esoteric to be widely useful or usable. When general models are developed, the specialists and/or practitioners can use them in a deductive fashion. Through simplification, they can deduce formulations for any specific problem. As discussed in Chapter 1, the inductive approach to deriving equations describing a particular realm of knowledge, phenomenon, objective, or system behavior is a more trying process, because it requires more creativity than the deductive approach. In the latter case, it is a matter of reducing a generalized formulation to one of its special cases by dropping the irrelevant terms and/or simplifying the relevant ones.

In terms of organizing knowledge, taxonomies provide a neat way for "pigeonholing" various contributions within the structure of a given field of knowledge. Efficiently and effectively, they show the similarities and the differences between contents of the various pigeonholes. Although the need to create taxonomies cannot be understated, there is a need for an even higher level of knowledge consolidation. The need is for knowledge generalization. A dichotomy? Not at all! By generalizing the works of others, it is possible to synthesize a field of knowledge, thus expanding it, sometimes by orders of magnitude. Generalized formulations that can be reduced to the specifics that are known provide the more global gestalt. Thus in one "fell swoop," one can significantly consolidate all that is known by embedding it in one general formulation. Almost by definition, such generalizations expand the embraced field both quantitatively and qualitatively. In Chapter 2 we discussed alternative strategies for this type of research.

As indicated earlier, descriptive classifications go a long way toward synthesizing a field of knowledge and even stimulating alternate schemes, strategies, theoretical and/or empirical model developments, and applications. However, the prescriptive generalizations, as powerful as they may be, fall short of the mark unless they are also accompanied by explicitly stated taxonomies that are theoretically rich yet typologically simple.

The subject areas comprising management science/operations research are ripe for the kind of integrations or generalizations described. The challenge to do this was sounded in Chapter 1. Here we discuss some different ways toward that end—in a taxonomic fashion, of course. Next we present the first cut at a taxonomy of taxonomies.

A TAXONOMY OF TAXONOMIES

The proposed *taxonomy of taxonomies* is shown in Figure 3.1. It has three Dimensions. Two of these are basic, namely those defining the end face of Figure 3.1. One edge of that face encompasses the factors P and D, where P symbolizes the fact that the work is prescriptive in nature and D symbolizes the fact that the work is descriptive in nature. The other edge encompasses the factors G and T, where G symbolizes the fact that the work offers a general model or equation(s) and T symbolizes the fact that the work is a classification or taxonomy. Thus, the term *TGDP* represents a case involving a taxonomy because T is present, a general model because G is shown, and it can serve both descriptive D and prescriptive P purposes. The Periodic Table of Chemical Elements is certainly a fine example of such a case.

Because taxonomies may assume several basic formats, Figure 3.1 provides the "third dimension," so to speak. The third edge represents subclassifications of the various taxonomies. More specifically if, and only if, a work can be classified as being a taxonomy (e.g., T is in the *TGDP* classification), then the work can further be described as being

t	a genealogy tree
v	an attribute vector description
a	an attribute acronym tableau
g	a geometric description
e	a statistical/empirical finding

Each of the above secondary classification descriptors, *t, v, a, g,* and *e,* are briefly discussed in the next section and are illustrated in the section that follows.

Figure 3.1
A Taxonomy of Taxonomies

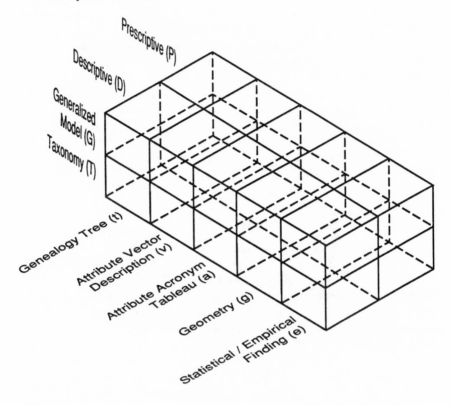

Genealogy Tree (*t*)

In this context, we are referring to a genealogy tree as a taxonomy following a traditional (rooted) tree-like structure starting with a single parent and having a multilayered hierarchy of descendants. Each descendant in this type structure can only have a single antecedent, as shown in Figure 3.2.

Attribute Vector Description (*v*)

This, in essence, is a classification scheme based on several parallel (rooted) genealogy trees, each typically shallow. In each tree there are but a few layers of descendants. The multiplicity of trees (a forest) indicates that the scheme is characterized as having a number of starting attributes. As in the genealogy tree each descendant can have but one antecedent. In other words, this kind of classification allows a specific work to be described by a vector of attributes and subattributes. This structure is shown in Figure 3.3. It can be shown that tax-

Figure 3.2
Genealogy Tree

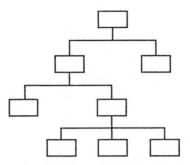

Figure 3.3
Attribute Vector Description

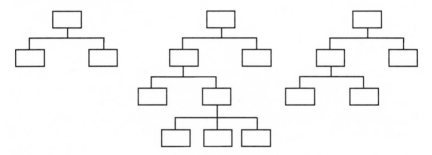

onomies using the matrix table formats are identical to or special cases of the attribute-vector-description format.

Attribute Acronym Tableau (*a*)

This form of classification recognizes the existence of a single general parent with a multilayer hierarchy of ever more specific descendants. This is implied by the ever smaller sized boxes as one moves downward from layer to layer. Moreover each descendant below the second layer may have multiple antecedents, as shown in Figure 3.4.

Geometry (*g*)

Physical and socioeconomic systems can often be described by the geometric format of their configurations. This is especially true of activity networks, such as in manufacturing of discrete products or in the processing of petrochemicals or of information. The most basic configurations, shown in Figure 3.5, are the

Figure 3.4
Attribute Acronym Tableau

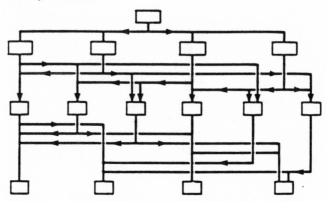

serial and the parallel processing formats. The most comprehensive configuration in this context is the general format.

Statistical/Empirical Findings (*e*)

Often a body of data becomes available or is gathered without an a-priori known theory, gestalt, or structure. Such is commonly the case in socioeconomic research, policy research, marketing research, and the like. In such situations, statistical methods can be brought to bear in search of patterns or in the testing of hypotheses. The resulting patterns thus classify the data. Methods such as regression analysis, factor analysis, cluster analysis, and a whole host of other pattern recognition tools are available to help in this regard.

SUMMARIES AND CLASSIFICATION OF SOME TAXONOMIC/INTEGRATIVE WORKS

As stated at the outset of this chapter, the taxonomy of taxonomies presented herein is a first cut. As such it's applicability and utility must be validated to satisfy the critics and the supporters alike. Fortunately Vogel and Wetherbe (1984, p. 5) provide us with the guidelines for such validations.

The key to taxonomy effectiveness rests on criteria of comprehensiveness, parsimony and usefulness. Obviously, to be effective, a taxonomy must represent the full spectrum of the research chosen for categorization. Thus, comprehensiveness is a necessary condition for effectiveness. It is, however, not sufficient. To further be effective, a taxonomy should be parsimonious.

It should not include unnecessary categories. Finally, to be considered effective, the taxonomy should be robust and generally useful. The categories should be reasonably, if not mutually exclusive, i.e., non-overlapping, reasonably distinct, meaningful, commonplace, and descriptive to allow utilization by a wide variety of interested persons.

Figure 3.5
Geometry-Based Classification

1. **Serial:** Each stage has at most one predecessor and successor

2. **Parallel:** Each stage is single with no predecessor or successor, but stages may share costs.

3. **Assembly:** Each stage has any number of predecessors, but at most one successor.

4. **Arborescent:** This is the opposite of the assembly structure; that is, each stage has a single predecessor but any number of successors

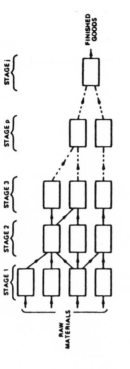

5. **Acyclic:** Each stage can have any number of predecessors and successors, but if stages are numbered as shown, a stage numbered j can only be successor of any stage p for $p < j$

6. **Cyclic or general:** No restriction on the relationship between stages. Feedback flows are permitted.

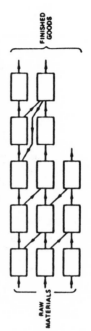

No one will deny that, in the context of the centuries-old tradition and track record of development enjoyed by chemistry and physics, the management sciences are relative upstarts. We, therefore, use examples from both of these "hard" sciences first, because they are, or should be, the role models for any emerging field. We next show examples from management science fields selected so as to demonstrate the full range of the *PDGT/tvage* taxonomy.

CHEMISTRY: THE PERIODIC TABLE

The best known taxonomic work is that attributed to D. I. Mendeleyev (1889) and known to us as the Periodic Table of Elements. Before the development of Mendeleyev's periodic table, the table we have all studied in high school and/ or in freshman chemistry, chemists knew of many seemingly unrelated elements. The periodic table set down, once and for all, the systematic interrelationship between the chemical elements. Therefore, it can be construed as a general model (theory) even though it is not expressed in equation form. Using the notation of the preceeding section, it can be classified by the symbol G because it represents a generalized theory unifying the state of knowledge. Over the years, it has certainly proven its mettle in prescribing what elements to look for by specifying their characteristic properties. Hence, it is both a prescriptive P and a descriptive D taxonomy T. In terms of format, it is an attribute vector description v. In summary, the periodic table can be dubbed as the *PDGTv* type of taxonomy.

Mendeleyev developed this chart by reflecting on the work of others, thus achieving a new synthesis that demonstrated a pattern and gave meaning to formerly unconnected elements. No one will deny that this table removed many burdens from the students of chemistry.

PHYSICS: THE NAVIER-STOKES EQUATIONS

Hydrodynamics is a study of fluids in motion. It addresses some of the basic laws of physics, namely the conservation of energy, of mass, and of momentum.

Fluids can flow within a pipe (this is one-dimensional flow), on top of a surface as is the case of rain waters flowing down our driveways (this is sheet or two-dimensional flow), or around an object like an aircraft in flight (this is three-dimensional flow). Moreover, the fluid can be compressible as are most gases, or incompressible as is water under normal flow conditions. Fluids can exhibit viscosity that is resistance to flow or can be assumed to be relatively free thereof. The latter are called ideal fluids. Good whisky is claimed to be such—"it goes down real smooth!" Lastly, the flow variables can change at any point in space over time, that is, unsteady flow; otherwise it is steady-state flow.

As shown in Figure 3.6, the three-dimensional (3), unsteady (U), viscous (V), compressible (C), or ($3UVC$) flow is the most general case imaginable. The rest

Figure 3.6
Taxonomy of Fluid-Flow Configurations

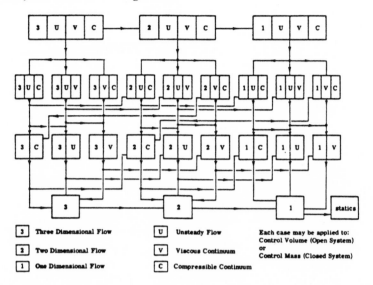

are all special cases, with fluid statics being the simplest (Taft and Reisman 1965).

The Navier-Stokes equations (Stokes 1880; Goldstein 1960) were derived to encompass the $3UVC$ case within each of the three basic conservation principles (e.g., those of energy, mass, and momentum). Any of the special cases of flow can be modeled by simplifying the general, or $3UVC$, model. Both Claude L. M. H. Navier and George G. Stokes must have had all of the special cases delineated in Figure 3.6 in mind back in the 1840s, but it does not appear that they ever stated so explicitly. In fact, a number of the special cases—for example, the Bernoulli (1738 and 1968) equation ($1VC$), or ($1V$)—have been developed independently and so they were taught for many generations (Vennard 1961; Binder 1959). The same can be said of the diffusion equation ($3U$), ($2U$), or ($1U$) (Taft and Reisman 1965), which first surfaced in the work of L. Bachelier (1900), but was not given the visibility it deserved until the work of A. Einstein (1906) and especially A. N. Kolmogorov (1931). Other speical cases of $3UVC$ represent the ''kernels'' of knowledge in such disparate fields as electromagnetics, thermodynamics, acoustics, magnetogasdynamics, heat transfer, lubrication, meteorology, electrical transmission, and so forth (Taft and Reisman 1965). Clearly the Navier-Stokes equations are prescriptive P, as they are descriptive D, and they are a general model G, but not explicitly, at least, a taxonomy. So, as they have been proposed, they can be described as the PDG case of $PDGT/tvage$. The $3UVC$ scheme shown in Figure 3.6, on the other hand, provides the Ta type taxonomy. Together they constitute the $PDGTa$ case of $PDGT/tvage$.

One cannot help but wonder whether the history of the above sciences and technologies might not have taken a different course had Navier and/or Stokes published some version of the $3UVC$ taxonomy.

OPERATIONS RESEARCH: INVENTORY-CONTROL THEORY

Inventory-control theory is one of the most extensively explored areas of operations research. Its roots go back to the Ford Harris (1915) EOQ formula. Yet, to date, the literature has not recorded any general formulation. This may be due to the fact that since the days of Harris, researchers in this field have been preoccupied with finding optimum solutions and hesitated to publish, or were kept from publishing any model for which they had no solution. However, because inventory-control theory literature is so vast, there is a need for a taxonomy. A classification of inventory-theoretic models is shown in Table 3.1. It is fairly self-explanatory.

The details of the taxonomy called $DOLRIPECTOMS$ are addressed in Reisman (1981). In summary, however, any model can be characterized by simply taking its appropriate identifier (for example, d_3, o_2, l_3, and so on) from each of the primary constituents (demand, ordering cycle, and so on) of Table 3.1 and constructing some special case of $DOLRIPECTOMS$ (for example, $d_1o_1l_2r_1i_1p_3e_2c_2t_1o_2m_1s_3$). In this way, both the student and the practitioner of inventory theory can categorize any proposed or existing model and easily specify its form, objectives, and built-in assumptions. This is clearly nothing but a descriptive D taxonomy T of the vector attribute v variety or a DTv case of $PDGT/tvage$.

FINANCE: VALUATION OF EQUITY SHARES

Until the mid 1950s, the theory of finance concerned with stock (equity) valuation was mostly descriptive in nature. Papers and books on the subject described the issues of concern using natural language enriched with numerical illustrations. Many hypotheses were thus discussed. Myron Gordon and Ezra Shapiro (Solomon 1959) offered one of the early mathematical models. This model assumed that a unit of stock issue should be valued at the present worth of the anticipated dividends discounted to perpetuity using the "the investors expectation rate." This was a landmark step in the development of a theory and was widely cited and reprinted.

A number of other models came in rapid succession—each was based on its own simplifying assumptions. Some of us personally witnessed the heated and publicly displayed antagonisms between the sages in the field at that time. In retrospect, much of the heat was simply the result of one model builder either not knowing or at best not agreeing with the simplifying assumptions used by another. One thing is sure, no one paid attention to a paper authored by a couple

Table 3.1
A Taxonomic Scheme for Classification of Inventory-Control Systems

Category	Level 1	Level 2	Level 3	Level 4	Code	Group
Demand	Deterministic		Static		(d_1)	D
			Demand		(d_2)	
	Stochastic		Stationary		(d_3)	
			Nonstationary		(d_4)	
Ordering Cycle	Continuous				(o_1)	O
	Periodic				(o_2)	
Lead-time	Zero				(l_1)	L
	Deterministic				(l_2)	
	Stochastic				(l_3)	
Stock Replenishment	Instantaneous				(r_1)	R
	Uniform				(r_2)	
Number of Items	Single				(i_1)	I
	Multi	Dependent			(i_2)	
		Independent			(i_3)	
Time Period	Single				(p_1)	P
	Multi	Finite Horizon			(p_2)	
		Infinite Horizon			(p_3)	
Number of Supply Echelons	Single				(e_1)	E
	Multi	General			(e_2)	
		Arborescence	General		(e_3)	
			Parallel		(e_4)	
			Series		(e_5)	
Item Characterization	Consumable				(c_1)	C
	Perishable				(c_2)	
	Reusable				(c_3)	
Treatment of Excess Demand	Backorder				(t_1)	T
	Lost Sale				(t_2)	
Objective of the	Cost Oriented				(o_1)	O
	Service Oriented				(o_2)	
Modeling	Exact				(m_1)	M
	Approximate				(m_2)	
Solution Method	Optimization				(s_1)	S
	Suboptimization				(s_2)	
	Heuristics				(s_3)	

From Reisman [1981]

of unknowns, a paper providing a general model and a taxonomy (Sloan and Reisman 1968) recognizing the fact that models in this area can be based on any one of a number of hypotheses as to the independent variables affecting the value of stock. All these hypotheses, it was shown, can be fitted in one of the following classifications:

1. The discounting of anticipated earnings to perpetuity approach.

2. The discounting of anticipated earnings to terminal date and discounting of anticipated terminal price approach.

3. The discounting of anticipated dividends to be received to perpetuity approach.

4. The discounting of anticipated dividends to a terminal date and discounting of the anticipated terminal price approach.

5. The discounting of anticipated net cash flow approach.

Most knowledgable writers have correctly pointed out that when properly formulated, approaches 1 through 4 above are equivalent, but this is not obvious, especially to the novitiate in the field. The purpose of the Sloane and Reisman (1968) paper was to present a general model accommodating all of the above hypotheses. Moreover, the model allowed for any or all of four methods of financing growth: (1) raising outside equity, (2) retaining earnings, (3) purchase of new equity shares by existing stockholders, and (4) debt.

The general model reduced to their present worths all independent variables involved in the possession of a share of stock. Mathematical relationships for all of the less complicated cases in stock evaluation were shown to be obtainable by merely dropping or simplifying certain terms in the general model. In this way, it was possible to cover all hypotheses and methods of growth financing in a systematic manner. The paper also provided a taxonomic scheme of the attribute-acronym-tableau variety similar to the $3UVC$ scheme shown in Figure 3.6.

Much like some publications before it (Reisman and Buffa 1962; Reisman, Weston, and Buffa 1966) and others since (Reisman and Rao 1973), that paper provided an algebraic statement general enough to unify an area of thought involving discounted cash flow analysis and, along with a taxonomic scheme, provided a means to show the similarities and the differences of the best known or state-of-the-art works. Moreover, each of the above papers delineated a number of special cases never before reported in the literature.

Each of the works cited in this section can be codified as belonging to the $PDGTa$ case inasmuch as they all have a general model (G) that can be used either in a prescriptive (P) or a descriptive (D) mode. Moreover, each provides the attribute-acronym-tableau (a) type of taxonomy.

MARKETING SCIENCE: TV VIEWING BEHAVIOR

Development of classification systems of television programs has been a major interest to marketing researchers as well as to networks. The study reported by Rao (1975) attempted to compare the classification schemes of television programs before and after removing the effect of prior knowledge on viewing behavior. Prior knowledge was measured in that study by two sets of variables: (1) socioeconomic, demographic, and television ownership characteristics of individuals and (2) variables describing the scheduling of the television programs. The method employed for forming program types was the same as that employed in past research, namely, factor analysis.

The above paper represents a taxonomy (T) that is descriptive (D) and is of the statistical/empirical finding variety (e). In other words, it is a DTe type of taxonomy. The literature abounds with DTe type taxonomies. These methodologies are often involved when there is no other unifying medium. This is typically the case in the early stages of development of a field of knowledge. Thus, these methodologies predominate in the marketing sciences and are often invoked in the various social sciences attempting to describe patterns of behavior. Moreover, these methods are now constructively used in artificial intelligence and in the construction of expert systems.

CONCLUDING REMARKS

The examples have been deliberately drawn from both the "hard" and the management sciences. No claim is made that these are the best examples. They have, however, served the intended purposes; they have illustrated the diversity of role models for knowledge consolidation and the robustness, logic, comprehensiveness, parsimony, and hopefully usefulness of the proposed taxonomy of taxonomies.

The anatomy and the morphology of the problem-solving processes discussed in Chapter 6 can serve as the basis for processes to be followed in creating future taxonomies and/or generalizations. The processes will have to be iterative. Each generalization should be viewed as a potential stepping stone for more global approaches, and each taxonomy can be either broadened or made more detailed. Lastly, and in addition to what has already been said, the potential pedagogical and the managerial benefits of taxonomies and generalizations are that they may suggest

New uses for older models.

The need for additional models.

The extent that such models are used in practice.

The types of enterprises using them.

The factors that enhance implementation and empirical success.

NOTES

This chapter is based on a paper by the same name. The paper was presented at the Second International Symposium on Methodologies for Intelligent Systems, Charlotte, N.C., October 14–18, 1987, and published in the *ISMIS-87 Proceedings*, Oak Ridge National Laboratory.

REFERENCES

Bachelier, L. 1900. "Théorie de la spéculation." *Ann. Sci. Ecole Norm.* 17:21–86.
Bernoulli, Daniel. 1738 and 1968. *Hydrodynamica*, Strasbourg: Sive de Viribus et Motibus Fluidorum Commentarii. (Published in English as *Hydrodynamics*. Translated by Thomas Carmody and Helmut Kobus, New York, 1968.)
Binder, R. C. 1959. *Fluid Mechanics*. 3rd ed. Englewood Cliffs, N.J.: Prentice-Hall.
Einstein, A. 1906. "On the Theory of the Brownian Movement." *Annals der Physik* 19:371–81, 289–306.
Goldstein, A. 1960. *Lectures on Fluid Mechanics*. London: Interscience Publishers.
Harris, Ford. 1915. *Operations and Costs*, Factory Management Series, 48–52. Chicago, Ill.: A. W. Shaw Co.
Kolmogorov, A. N. 1931. "Über die Analytischen Methoden in der Wahrscheinlichkeitsrechnung." *Mathematical Annals* 104: 415–58.
Mendeleyev, D. I. 1889. "The Periodic Law of the Chemical Elements (Faraday Lectures)." *Journal of the Chemical Society* 55: 643–56. (Reprinted in *Faraday Lectures*, Chemical Society 1928, *Lectures Delivered Before the Chemical Society*, London: Chemical Society, 1869–1928.)
Rao, Vithala R. 1975. "Taxonomy of Television Programs Based on Viewing Behavior." *Journal of Marketing Research* 12(3): 355–58.
Reisman, Arnold. 1971. *Managerial and Engineering Economics*. Boston, Mass.: Allyn and Bacon Publishing Company.
———. 1981. "Classification of Characteristics of Inventory-Control Problems." In *Materials Management for Health Services*, 240–43. Lexington, Mass.: Lexington Books.
Reisman, Arnold, and Elwood S. Buffa. 1962. "A General Model for Investment Policy." *Management Science* 8(3): 304–10.
Reisman, Arnold, and A. K. Rao. 1973. *Discounted Cash Flow Analysis: Stochastic Extensions*, 260–67. Norcross, Ga.: American Institute of Industrial Engineers, Monograph Series.
Reisman, Arnold, Fred J. Weston, and Elwood S. Buffa. 1966. "Beitrag Zu Einer Theorie der Optimalen Finanzstruktur." *Zeitschrift fur Betriebseirtschaft* 9 (January): 568–77.
Sloane, William R., and Arnold Reisman. 1968. "Stock Evaluation Theory: Classification, Reconciliation, and General Model." *Journal of Finance and Quantitative Analysis* 3(2):171–204.
Solomon, E., ed. 1959. *The Management of Corporate Capital*. Glencoe, Ill.: Free Press.
Stokes, George G. 1880. *Mathematical and Physical Papers*. Vol. 2, 1–7 and 36–50. Cambridge, England: Cambridge University Press.

Taft, Martin I., and Arnold Reisman. 1965. "The Conservation Equations: A Systematic Look." *Journal of Hydrology* 3(3/4): 161–79.

Vennard, J. K. 1961. *Elementary Fluid Mechanics.* 4th ed. New York: John Wiley and Sons Inc.

Vogel, Douglas R., and James C. Wetherbe. 1984. "MIS Research: A Profile of Leading Journals and Universities." *Data Base* (Fall): 3–14.

Finding Research Topics Via a Taxonomy of a Field of Knowledge

INTRODUCTION

In Chapter 1 we challenged workers in the management and social sciences to concentrate a bit more on research that is taxonomical, unifying, and/or generalizing in nature. In Chapter 3 we delineated a number of specific ways to structure classifications of knowledge. That chapter presented a taxonomy of taxonomies that distinguishes between the various descriptive taxonomies and those that are prescriptive in nature, for example, those that delineate the characteristics of research to be done or delineate each of the special cases of some general model, theory, or methodology. Various strategies for doing research in the management and social sciences are delineated in Chapter 2. These strategies ranged from the highly established and widely practiced incremental approach to the less common, but much more creative, big-leap-forward, or embedding, approach. That chapter also discussed the pros and cons of each approach from the researcher's point of view as well as from the vantage of the particular field of knowledge being investigated. In Chapter 5 we argue that knowledge in a problem-solving discipline or profession can be subdivided into three sectors: (1) empirical data or evidence, (2) theory or methodology, and (3) problems solved, or in need of solving. We then show how one can systematically identify the literature voids in each of these subsectors. Using a Venn type diagram we discuss the significance of each region, including those with and those without overlapping sectors.

In all four of the above mentioned chapters we hint at, discuss philosophically, and show symbolically that taxonomic studies can lead to researchable topics. In this chapter, we demonstrate how two good taxonomies, which were intended to describe and to classify the existing literatures in their field (Genest and Zidek 1986; Nahmias 1982), can be extended to systematically delineate existing gaps in the literature. Identification of such gaps is a step in identifying potential contributions to the corresponding field of knowledge.

Interestingly enough, the process suggested is relatively mechanistic. It is very doable and yet useful. A Ph.D. candidate may find this approach useful in pinpointing a manageable research topic, yet one that represents a potential contribution within his or her area of interest. A faculty member may find it useful in targeting his or her own research or in advising doctoral students. A manager of a research institute may find it useful in generating proposals for outside funding. A funding agency may find it useful to set priorities in deciding which proposals to fund or which specific Requests for Proposals to release. Lastly, all of the above can use this procedure to better match the motivational, behavioral, temperamental, expertise, and other characteristics of the researcher(s) and the requirements of the job as suggested in Chapter 2.

THE METHODOLOGY

In summary, the methodology calls for six steps:

1. Identify the factors, attributes, and/or characteristics that, in combination, describe the literature of a field of knowledge. Literature describing prior art in the discipline is often helpful in this step. Thus, survey articles, especially those using taxonomic approaches, such as Genest and Zidek (1986), Nahmias (1982), or Balinsky and Reisman (1973), should be considered as resource material. Often however, the prior art may be enriched by the taxonomy's designer who takes a panoramic view of the field of knowledge and recognizes that the factors identified may not completely circumscribe the domain of its potential knowledge. Such a recognition can lead to significant extensions and expansions of the state-of-the-art boundaries of a field of knowledge. Examples of such expansions are shown in Chapters 16 and 17 and in Sloane and Reisman (1968) and Reisman and Rao (1973).

   Any one contribution to the literature (published paper, dissertation, study report, etc.) should of course be uniquely describable by a subset of the attributes chosen. The union of such a subset with that describing another contribution will delineate their commonalities, similarities, or overlaps and the remainder would then describe the differences. It is indeed possible to have sets of subattributes in various kinds of hierarchies, as shown in Chapter 3.

2. Assign a unique symbol to each of the above attributes and any subattributes. Such symbols may represent the existence or nonexistence of the corresponding attribute in the model or methodology described. Alternatively, the symbol may take on specific values if the attribute is described by some continuum. Lastly, the general symbol may be replaced by some specific as is the case in queueing theory where the $M/M/1$ queue is a special case of the $X/Y/m$ taxonomy. It is desirable, but not necessary, to develop an acronym involving the above sets of symbols, as shown in Chapters 3, 16, and 17.

3. Manually, or using a computer, enumerate all combinations of the above symbols/attributes.

4. Manually, and/or using a computer, prune out from the above set all of the combinations that intuitively make no sense in the context of the field. Clearly, steps 3 and 4 can be combined, especially if the enumeration is performed by a computer.

5. Using a thorough literature review, and the above classification, assign reference numbers to those cells for which literature exists. The remaining cells provide an address for potential research.

6. Consider a research problem from the surviving cells in step 5 based on social, political, institutional, and/or economic priorities or on the expertise, temperament, and/or objectives of the researcher.

ILLUSTRATIVE APPLICATIONS

Two literature review articles representing two disparate fields of knowledge were chosen to illustrate the application and the potential of the methodology. The articles were chosen because of the large number of papers they each review and because the review results are presented in a taxonomic format.

Illustrative Example 4.1

Christian Genest and James V. Zidek (1986, pp.114, 128) address the literature concerned with "aggregating a number of expert opinions which have been expressed in some numerical form in order to reflect individual uncertainty vis-a-vis a quantity of interest." They also provide "a taxonomy of solutions," which they use as a "framework for a survey of recent theoretical developments in the area." Each of some ninety papers is abstracted and classified according to "the approach which it adopts as well as the sort of opinions that it considers." Their taxonomy is based on

The Approach Adopted

AT: Axiomatic treatment (especially with regard to group consensus belief formation)

BU: Bayesian updating of opinion (in the presence of a decision maker)

CI: Consensus reached iteratively (group interaction)

DM: Decision making aspects are stressed (e.g., considerations of utilities are included)

RC: Concerned with the reconciliation of probability assessment (involves only one individual)

UB: Use of bargaining theory to reach a joint decision

Expression of Opinions

C: Cumulative distribution functions

D: Probability density functions

L: Odds ratios or log odds

M: Probability measures

P: Discrete probabilities

Moreover, the abbreviation **AL** is used when a paper is concerned with the somewhat different problem of resource allocation. The above are clearly the attributes Genest and Zidek considered necessary and sufficient to describe their subject matter and they used these symbols to classify—show the similarities and the differences, among each of the ninety papers surveyed. Exhibit 4.1 shows a representative page of their paper.

Theirs is a major contribution for novitiates as well as for seasoned researchers or practitioners in this field. It is an excellent example of a *descriptive* taxonomy (*D*) of the attribute vector (*v*) variety. Hence, in terms discussed in Chapter 3, this can be classed as a *TDv* case of taxonomies. However, it falls short of being *prescriptive* because, as can be seen in Exhibit 4.1, the paper merely classifies the existing literature according to one or more attributes involving the approach adopted and one or more attributes representing expression of opinion. To round out the example, Exhibit 4.2 shows an entry with *multiple* attributes involving the expression of opinion.

The six Genest and Zidek attributes comprising the approach-adopted dimension can be shown to result in $2^6 - 1 = 63$ unique combinations. Moreover, the five attributes comprising the expression-of-opinions dimension result in thirty-one combinations. These two sets of factors represent a two-dimensional classification matrix having 1,953 unique cells. Clearly, some of these are conceptually meaningless, such as those involving both **C** and **L**. After pruning the set down to include only what we consider defensible combinations, the list remains large—numbering 210, as shown by the nonempty cells in Table 4.1. Furthermore, the table indicates that the 90 papers abstracted and classified by Genest and Zidek have addressed only 22 of the 210 feasible subject categories. These are represented by the double asterisk entries. The remaining 190 (single asterisk) cells of Table 4.1 represent voids in the literature and, therefore, areas of potential research. Surely there is the possibility that some work has been done in one or more of these categories and has not been picked up by Genest and Zidek (1986) in their review of the literature.

Illustrative Example 4.2

Steven Nahmias (1982) provides a review of and a taxonomy for the perishable inventory theory literature. His review is organized as follows:

  I. Fixed Life Perishability
    1. Deterministic Demand
    2. Stochastic Demand
      a. Optimal Policies for a Single Product
      b. Approximately Optimal Policies for a Single Product

Exhibit 4.1
A Sample of Genest and Zidek's Paper Classifications and Abstracts

ACZEL, J. (1984). On weighted synthesis of judgments. *Aequat. Math.* 27, 288-307.

AT: L Although the author provides some new evidence in favor of the logarithmic opinion pool in cases where the experts judgments are expressed in the form of odds, this paper should be viewed primarily as a contribution to the theory of functional equations. Aczel's joint results with Saaty (1983) and Alsina (1984) are generalized to the case where experts are not treated symmetrically. An extra hypothesis is added which guarantees that the aggregating function is locally sensitive to each of the individual opinions. The potential readers must expect mathematical hurdles such as cancellative semigroups.

ACZEL, J. and ALSINA, C. (1984). Characterizations of some classes of quasilinear functions with applications to triangular norms and to synthesizing judgments. *Methods Oper. Res.* 48 3-22.

AT; L The functional equations solved here are motivated by and generalize those which werestudied in Aczel and Saaty (1983). However, this article says very little about the pooling problem per se.

ACZEL, J., KANNAPPAN, P.L., NG, C.T. and WAGNER, C.G. (1981). Functional equations and inequalities in rational group decision making. *General Inequalities 3: Proceedings of the Third International Conference on General Inequalities*, Oberwolfach.

AT; AL, P Reformulation of the results exposed in two previous papers by Aczel and Wagner (1980, 1981), but with resolution of the case in which nly two resources are to be allocated. This corresponds to the situation faced when the underlying probability space is not tertiary.

ACZEL, J., NG, C.T. and WAGNER, C.G. (1984). Aggregation theorems for allocation problems. *SIAM J. Alg. Disc. Meth.* 5 1-8.

AT; AL, P This fourth collaborative paper between Aczel and Wagner drops the "consensus of rejection" hypothesis (the ZPP condition (3.3)) This leads to a generalized linear opinion pool of the form (3.7) for allocation problems. See also Genest (1984).

ACZEL, J. and SAATY, T.L.(1983). Procedures for synthesizing ratio judgments. *J. Math. Psych.* 27 93-102.

AT; L By assuming that the influence of each individual opinion can be "separated" (condition (5.1)) and that the experts can be treated symmetrically, the authors characterize a large class of aggregating functions for odds ratios (line (5.3)). All the formulas they present obey the reciprocal property $f(x,...,x) = f(1/x,...,1/x)$ and preserve unanimity. When an additional homogeneity requirement is imposed, the symmetric geometric mean emerges as the unique solution.

ACZEL,J. and WAGNER, C.G. (1980). A characterization of weighted arithmetic means. *SIAM J. Alg. Disc. Meth.* 1 259-260.

AT; AL, P Axiomatic derivation of weighted arithmetic means within the context of group allocation of resources. When the "resource" is a probability mass, the authors' so-called k-allocation property amounts to saying that pooling probability distributions must yield a probability distribution. The other axioms used are equivalent to the SSFP and the ZPP, i.e., conditions (3.2) and (3.3).

ACZEL, J. and WAGNER, C.G. (1981). Rational group decision making generalized: the case of several unknown functions. *C.R. Math. Rep. Acad. Sci. Can.* 3 139-142.

AT; AL, P Sequel to the above paper in which the same result is derived under a weaker assumption that reduces to the WSFP, condition (3.5), when probability distributions are pooled.

AGNEW, C.E. (1985). Multiple probability assessments by dependent experts. *J. Amer. Statist. Assoc.* 80 343-347.

BU; D The Bayesian updating model of Winkler (1968) is extended to account for situations in which the experts are providing assessments about several random variables. When assessment errors have a mutivariate normal density, the posterior distribution depends only on a weighted average of the experts' stated means. Special cases of interest are those in which the individual's distributions are dependent but the random variables are not, and vice versa.

AUMANN, R.J. (1976). Agreeing to disagree. *Ann. Statist.* 4 1236-1239.

BU; P Formalizes the idea of common knowledge and uses this definition to prove a theorem asserting that if two people have the same prior, and if their posteriors for an event are common knowledge, then these posteriors are equal. "Might be considered a theoretical foundation for the reconciliation of subjective probabilities" (p. 1238). See also Geanakoplos and Polemarchakis (1982), as well as Shafer (1983).

BACHARACH, M. (1972). *Scientific Disagreement.* Unpublished manuscript, Christ Church, Oxford.

AT, CI, DM; D This penetrating essay articulates some of the philosophical and psychological assumptions underlying the theory of consensus, whether it be concerned with probabilities or with utilities. After criticizing past proposals for the resolution of difference of opinion, the author sets up a general model describing the structure of individual beliefs and their interplay within a group. An iterative method of "Bayesian dialogue" (cf. also Bacharach, 1979) ensues and questions of convergence are examined. It is shown, among other things, that the consensus is a logarithmic opinion pool with equal weights when disagreement between the experts is uniquely attributable to different observations.

Exhibit 4.2
Expression of Opinion

GENEST, C., MC CONWAY, K.J. AND SCHERVISH, M.J. (1986). Characterization of
externally Bayesian pooling operators. *Ann. Statist.* 14(2), 487-501, June.

AT;P,D Basically, This is an extension of the result contained in Genest,
C. (1984). A characterization theorem for externally Bayesian groups.
Ann. Statis. 12(3), 1100-1105.

Externally Bayesian pooling operators are characterized without
resorting to any regularity condition whatsoever. A condition is given
under which the generalized linear opinion pool (3.14) emerges.

    c. LIFO Inventory Systems

    d. Multiproduct Models

    e. Multiechelon Models

II. Random Lifetime Models

    1. Periodic Review Models

    2. Exponential Decay

III. Queueing Models with Impatience

IV. The Application of Perishable Inventory Models

V. Areas for Further Research

He further points out that the literature is divided according to whether the first in, first out (FIFO) or the last in, first out (LIFO) issuing policy is invoked. He reviews and classifies some seventy-five papers based on the above organizing scheme.

For the purpose of this example, we suggest a slight rearrangement of the classification. Specifically, Table 4.2 delineates twelve factors that pretty much capture the essence of Nahmias's organizing outline. As indicated in Table 4.2, the factors in each pair are mutually exclusive; that is, a model is based either on the FIFO or the LIFO discipline. Moreover, the demand for product is assumed or treated as being deterministic or stochastic and so forth. Thus, six of these factors, one from each pair, should uniquely delineate a model for perishable inventory management. This results in $2^6 = 64$ unique descriptions. These are shown in Table 4.3.

Table 4.3 further shows that most of the work in perishable inventory theory up to the date of Nahmias's review focused on both optimal and heuristic solutions (OS, HS) to ordering and allocation problems (OM, AM) with the FIFO issuing policy on a single product (SP) with fixed product lifetime (FL) and stochastic demand (SD), deterministic demand (DD) being a special case of stochastic demand.

Table 4.1

A Taxonomy of the Literature on Rational Group Decision Making: Combining Probability Distributions

	C	D	L	M	P	D,P
AT	**	**	**	**	**	*
BU	*	**	*	*	**	**
CI	**	*	*	*	**	
DM	*	**	*	*	**	
RC	*	*	**	*	*	
UB		*				
AT,CI	*	*	*	*	**	**
AT,BU	*	*	*	*	*	*
AT,UB	*	*	*	*	*	
BU,CI	*	*	*	*	**	*
UB,BU	*	*	*	*	*	*
AT,DM	*	**	*	**	*	*
BU,DM	*	*	*	*	**	*
DM,UB	*	*	*	*	*	
CI,DM	*	*	*	*	**	
BU,RC	*	*	*	*	**	*
CI,RC	*	*	*	*	*	
DM,RC	*	*	*	*	*	
AT,RC	*	*	*	*	*	*
AT,BU,CI	*	*	*	*	*	*
AT,UB,DM	*	*	*	*	*	
AT,BU,DM	*	*	*	*	*	*
AT,BU,UB	*	*	*	*	*	
AT,CI,DM	*	**	*	*	*	*
BU,CI,DM	*	*	*	*	*	*
BU,CI,RC	*	*	*	*	*	*
BU,DM,RC	*	*	*	*	*	*
BU,DM,UB	*	*	*	*	*	
CI,DM,RC	*	*	*	*	*	
AT,BU,RC	*	*	*	*	*	*
AT,CI,RC	*	*	*	*	*	*
AT,DM,RC	*	*	*	*	*	*
BU,CI,DM,RC	*	*	*	*	*	*
AT,BU,CI,DM	*	*	*	*	*	*
AT,BU,CI,RC	*	*	*	*	*	*
AT,BU,DM,RC	*	*	*	*	*	*
AT,CI,DM,RC	*	*	*	*	*	*
AT,BU,CI,DM,RC	*	*	*	*	*	*

**Models as considered by Genest and Zidek (annotated *bibliography*) *Statistical Science* 1986, vol. 1.

Not much work has been recorded dealing with multiple product models. Models with random lifetimes are also few. Moreover, there are few models that deal with the LIFO issuing policy. Perhaps the reason is that the FIFO issuing policy is usually the optimal issuing policy because it minimizes expected outdating cost without a corresponding increase in other costs. However, Nahmias does point out that when newer units yield higher utility (e.g., foods), and

Table 4.2
Factors for Classifying Perishable Inventory Models

FACTORS	ACCRONYM	
FIFO issuing policy	FIFO	} *
LIFO issuing policy	LIFO	}
Stochastic product demand	SD	} *
Deterministic product demand	DD	}
Fixed product lifetime	FL	} *
Random product lifetime	RL	}
Single product	SP	} *
Multiple product	MP	}
Ordering model	OM	} *
Allocation (multiechelon) model	AM	}
Optimal solution method	OS	} *
Heuristic solution method	HS	}

*   Mutually exclusive

customers are free to pick units on the shelf, then the result is, in fact, a LIFO policy. Because of the LIFO/FIFO dichotomy, this too is an attribute vector (v) taxonomy and as proposed, it is strictly descriptive (D). Hence, in terms of Chapter 3, it can also be designated as a *TDv* case.

CONCLUDING REMARKS

In this chapter we have shown how taxonomies intended to systematically describe the state of knowledge in a given field can be almost mechanistically transformed into an identification and delineation of gaps in the literature and hence a specification of potential research topics. The history of science is replete with examples where such approaches have accelerated the rate of knowledge generation. The best known of these is, once again, the Periodic Table of Chemical Elements. As stated in Chapter 3, Dmitri I. Mendeleyev (1889) organized the prior art in a taxonomic fashion and then proceeded to delineate the gaps (e.g., descriptors of elements yet to be discovered). Alternatively, as indicated in Chapter 3, there are examples where the progress of a science was retarded by the lack of a taxonomy.

This methodology, it should be emphasized, does *not* address domains of

Table 4.3
Taxonomy of Perishable Inventory Models

FIFO,DD,FL,SP,OM,OS;	***	LIFO,DD,FL,SP,OM,OS
FIFO,DD,FL,SP,OM,HS	***	
FIFO,DD,FL,SP,AM,OS	***	
FIFO,DD,FL,SP,AM,HS	***	
FIFO,DD,FL,MP,OM,OS	**	
FIFO,DD,FL,MP,OM,HS	**	
FIFO,DD,FL,MP,AM,OS	*	
FIFO,DD,FL,MP,AM,HS	*	
FIFO,DD,RL,SP,OM,OS	**	
FIFO,DD,RL,SP,OM,HS	**	
FIFO,DD,RL,SP,AM,OS	*	
FIFO,DD,RL,SP,AM,HS	*	
FIFO,DD,RL,MP,OM,OS	*	
FIFO,DD,RL,MP,OM,HS	*	
FIFO,DD,RL,MP,AM,OS	*	
FIFO,DD,RL,MP,AM,HS	*	
FIFO,SD,FL,SP,OM,OS	***	
FIFO,SD,FL,SP,OM,HS	***	
FIFO,SD,FL,SP,AM,OS	***	
FIFO,SD,FL,SP,AM,HS	***	
FIFO,SD,FL,MP,OM,OS	**	
FIFO,SD,FL,MP,OM,HS	**	
FIFO,SD,FL,MP,AM,OS	*	
FIFO,SD,FL,MP,AM,HS	*	
FIFO,SD,RL,SP,OM,OS	**	
FIFO,SD,RL,SP,OM,HS	**	
FIFO,SD,RL,SP,AM,OS	*	
FIFO,SD,RL,SP,AM,HS	*	
FIFO,SD,RL,MP,OM,OS	*	
FIFO,SD,RL,MP,OM,HS	*	
FIFO,SD,RL,MP,AM,OS	*	
FIFO,SD,RL,MP,AM,HS;	*	LIFO,SD,RL,MP,AM,HS

*** Much has been done

** Some has been done and good area for further research

* Hardly anything has been done and room for original research

knowledge where existing literature (e.g., the prior art) needs revisiting. Needs for such revisiting may be due to theoretical gaps identifiable through inconsistent findings, weak results, methodologically bound conclusions, or in general where the quality of past research is questionable.

In structuring the taxonomies used in both examples of this chapter we relied essentially on the state-of-the-art boundaries defining each field. In fact, for the Genest-Zidek example we used the authors' own set of attributes. We made no attempt, in either example, to create new dimensions for the respective fields of knowledge. However, depending on how *visionary* one is *in choosing the attributes* comprising the taxonomy, one can limit the identified voids to the state-of-the-art boundaries defining the field of knowledge or one can *significantly expand* such boundaries.

It should be noted that the method described here will well serve the many who prefer to work within the existing confines or boundaries of the field of knowledge. Researchers interested in major breakthroughs, such as those who creatively merge disparate disciplines and/or create a new realm of study, will have to create a set of attributes that meaningfully describe the field of knowledge being envisioned in order to gain the benefits of this methodology.

NOTE

This chapter is based on the paper "Finding Researchable Topics Via a Taxonomy of a Field of Knowledge," which appeared in *Operations Research Letters* 7(6): 295–301, December 1988.

REFERENCES

Balinsky, W., and A. Reisman. 1973. "A Taxonomy of Manpower—Educational Planning Models." *Socio-Economic Planning Sciences* 7(1): 13–17.

Genest, C., and J. V. Zidek. 1986. "Combining Probability Distributions: A Critique and an Annotated Bibliography." *Statistical Sciences* 1(1): 114–48.

Mendeleyev, D. I. 1889. "The Periodic Law of the Chemical Elements (Faraday Lectures)." *Journal of the Chemical Society* 55:634–56. (Reprinted in *Faraday Lectures*, Chemical Society 1928, *Lectures Delivered Before the Chemical Society*. 1869–1928. London: Chemical Society, 1869–1928.)

Nahmias, S. 1982. "Perishable Inventory Theory: A Review." *Operations Research* 30(4): 680–707.

Reisman, A., and A. K. Rao. 1973. "A Generalized Scheme for Classification of Investment Models." In *Discounted Cash Flow Analysis: Stochastic Extensions*, 260–67. Novcross, Ga: American Institute of Industrial Engineers, Monograph Series.

Sloan, W. R., and A. Reisman. 1968. "Stock Evaluation Theory: Classification, Reconciliation, and General Model." *Journal of Finance and Quantitative Analysis* 3(2): 171–204.

Chapter 5

A Systems Approach to Identifying Knowledge Voids in Problem Solving Disciplines and Professions

INTRODUCTION

As important as it is to know what is known about a field of knowledge, it is equally important, even critically so, to know what is not known. As important as it is to classify, codify, and/or unify the existing knowledge, it is equally important to classify, codify, and thereby specify what needs to be discovered, collected, found, developed, and/or solved. As stated in earlier chapters, Dmitri I. Mendeleyev (1889) led the way in this regard. By reflecting on the work of others he classified, codified, and thereby unified a major portion of the chemistry of his day. But he did more. The voids in his periodic table specified what was yet to be found. Some of these voids exist to this day. Although they defy discovery, they are real voids in knowledge, nevertheless.

In the context of problem solving, irrespective of the discipline or profession involved, knowledge can be described along a three- dimensional continuum. One of these dimensions concerns the availability of empirical data—that is, the empirical grounding of knowledge. The other dimension concerns the existence of the theory and/or methodology necessary to address the problems of concern. The last dimension deals with the extent to which the problems of concern have been solved, or at least have been addressed, and so recorded in the literature of the discipline or the profession involved. On reflection, it should be recognized that the preceding chapter addressed the literature voids issue based on only this last dimension, that is, the problems solved.

Using a systems approach, this chapter explores the *three-dimensional continuum of knowledge* depicted in Figure 5.1. This exploration suggests a framework whereby the status of the knowledge base of a given profession or discipline can be documented in a taxonomic format. More importantly, however, the framework allows one to efficiently, yet systematically, go about documenting the existing knowledge voids, be they essentially in the realm of data unavail-

Figure 5.1
A Systems Approach to Identifying Knowledge Voids in a Given Problem-Solving Discipline or Profession

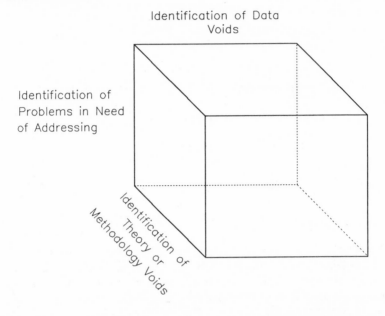

ability, inadequacy of methodology/theory, or of problems that have yet to be addressed.

Using a Venn diagram, Figure 5.2, one can somewhat differently describe knowledge availability along the three-dimensional spectrum to illustrate the state of knowledge in a given field. If the circles are used to circumscribe the availability of knowledge in each of the three categories (i.e., data, theory, and problems solved or to be solved), then the region represented by the union of all three circles, labeled region A, represents what might be called the "best of all worlds." Namely, the problems have been solved using the most appropriate theory or methodology. Moreover, the solutions have been validated using real-world data. There is very little that one can do to improve this subset of knowledge. However, as discussed in Chapter 2, such knowledge can be used as a springboard for solving other problems by analogy or for expanding theory or methodology using the embedding approach.

The confluence of the data and the problem circles, region B, is the next best situation, inasmuch as the problem solutions are well grounded with real-world data, albeit the theory, or especially the methodology used, may have fallen short of what might be considered best. For example, computer-aided simulation is often used on a "cut and try" basis. This methodology is invoked because the state-of-the-art of mathematical optimization methods do not allow finding

Figure 5.2
A Venn Diagram Classification of Knowledge Availability in a Given Problem-Solving Discipline or Profession

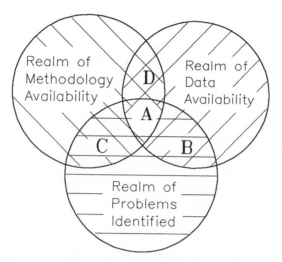

Region A: "Best of all worlds."
Region B: "Grounded" Solutions to problems
      using less then perfect methodology
      or theory   — — >   methodology voids.
Region C: Theoretical Solutions to problems
      — — >   data voids.
Region D: Grounded theory in search of
      problems.

the "global optimum" solution without having to bend the problem formulation beyond reasonableness so as to fit methodological constraints. This clearly identifies voids in the methodology.

Region *D* represents the existence of methodological tools and grounded theory in search of a problem. The remaining areas of each of the three circles, respectively, represent theory or methodology that has progressed on its "own steam" beyond the realm required for solving problems identified to date, data that were collected in anticipation of need for problem solving or for theoretical developments, and problems identified but not addressed, or problems defying solution.

The remainder of this chapter discusses and illustrates the systems approach to identifying knowledge voids in each of the three dimensions (data, theory, or methodology voids), and we shall return to the issue of problems in need of being addressed.

DATA VOIDS

The U.S. national education statistical base shall serve as the contextual setting for illustrating the systems approach to identifying data voids.

In forecasting the supply and demand of highly trained human resources at the national level, it must be recognized that people flow through an educational network that starts at kindergarten and ends in postgraduate education. The upper reaches of this network exhibit many branches and even some feedback loops. Network models used in such forecasting require people flow data, in addition to many socioeconomic and political considerations (Reisman et al. 1986).

The example that follows derives from a National Center for Educational Statistics (NCES) sponsored manpower-planning project conducted at Case Western Reserve University (CWRU), having as its objectives:

1. Forecasting the supply and demand of teachers for grades kindergarten through 12.
2. Forecasting the number of bachelors, masters, and Ph.D.'s graduating each year over the next decade.

During the initial stages of the project, several highly disaggregated models were developed to track the flows of people into and through the educational system network. Figure 5.3 illustrates one of the network flow models that was considered. This model was established without regard to data availability. It was based on the Bolt et al. (1965) model, a forerunner to the Reisman-Taft (1972) network model originally proposed by Reisman (1966).

The model requires as input school-age populations. Each cohort is then *pushed* through the lower network levels, and in its upper reaches, it is *pulled* by job availabilites and other socioeconomic factors.

During the course of the project, extensive efforts were made by the project team to determine where and how the data required for the model in Figure 5.3 could be collected. Among the agencies contacted were the NCES, National Research Council (NRC), National Academy of Science (NAS), National Science Foundation (NSF), Bureau of Labor Statistics (BLS), Bureau of the Census (BC), National Education Association (NEA), Institute of International Education (IIE), U.S. Department of Defense, U.S. Department of Justice, U.S. Department of State, John Mitner & Associates, Association of American University Professors (AAUP), and the departments of education in a number of states. These agencies were truly helpful and generous with data they had in hand. On some occasions, if the data were found to be nonexistent within the agency's files, referrals to other agencies or organizations were made.

The study findings are best illustrated by Figure 5.4. This happens to be an incidence matrix representation of the network flow model shown in Figure 5.3. A zero (0) or one (1) entry in this matrix denotes the existence of a population flow between the two nodes identifying the respective cells. Cells left blank in Figure 5.4 clearly delineate node pairs that are not connected in the network

Figure 5.3
The Education and Use of Human Resources: A Highly Deaggregated Network Flow Model

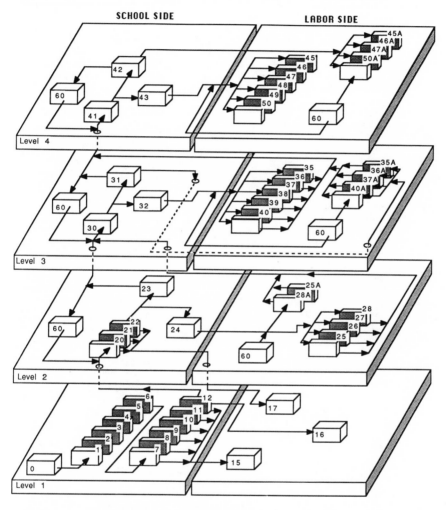

model. What is most interesting is that the fairly exhaustive search for data, indicated earlier, still left most of the connected node pairs devoid of data. These are marked by zeros (0) in Figure 5.4. Conversely, the one (1) entries represent data that are available.

The project did not attempt to segregate educational disciplines (e.g., science versus humanities) or professions (e.g., engineering versus law), and within the teacher model, no attempt was made to distinguish between specialties (e.g., science versus mathematics versus physical education). This kind of segregation in the data is needed to aid in the formulation of national level policy. The

Figure 5.3A
Network Node Legend

Node No.	Node Description	Node No.	Node Description
0	Kindergarten and nursery schools	40	Not in labor force with master's degree and certification
1-12	Grades 1 to 12		
15	High school dropouts	35A	College teachers with master's degree without certification
16	High school labor force (with at most a high school diploma)	36A	Government employees with master's degree without certification
17	College dropout		
20	Freshmen in college	37A	Industry employees with master's degree without certification
21	Sophomores in college		
22	Juniors in college	40A	Not in labor force with master's degree without certification
23	Seniors in college		
24	Teacher certification program	41	First year in Ph.D. program
25	College labor force (with at most a college degree) with certification	42	Final year in Ph.D. program
		43	Teacher certification program
26	Elementary school teacher labor force with certification	45	University teachers with Ph.D. degree and certification
27	High school teacher labor force with certification	46	Government employees with Ph.D. degree and certification
28	Not in labor force with certification	47	Industry employees with Ph.D. degree and certification
25A	College labor force without certification	48	Elementary school teachers with Ph.D. degree and certification
28A	Not in labor force without certification	49	High school teachers with Ph.D. degree and certification
30	First year in master's degree program	50	Not in labor force with Ph.D. degree and certification
31	Last year in master's degree program		
32	Teacher certification program	45A	University teachers with Ph.D. degree without certification
35	College teachers with master's degrees and certification	46A	Government employees with Ph.D. degree without certification
36	Government employees with master's degrees and certification	47A	Industry employees with Ph.D. degree without certification
37	Industry employees with master's degrees and certification	50A	Not in labor force with Ph.D. degree without certification
38	Elementary school teachers with master's degrees and certification	60	Foreign inflow and outflow of students and workers
39	High school teachers with master's degrees and certification		

project served to illustrate the data voids in national education statistics (Reisman et al. 1986). In terms of the taxonomy of taxonomies discussed in Chapter 3, this is a *TDPg* type taxonomy because it uses a geometric format describing a network of student flows (*g*) to both describe data needed (*D*) and to prescribe (*P*) data voids.

APPLICATION VOIDS

Planning the development of human resources also serves as the contextual setting for using the systems approach in identifying the unsolved problems in a given area.

The literature has recorded many models dealing with manpower (human

Figure 5.4
Data Needs Versus Data Availability Matrix: Education and Use of Human Resources Network Model

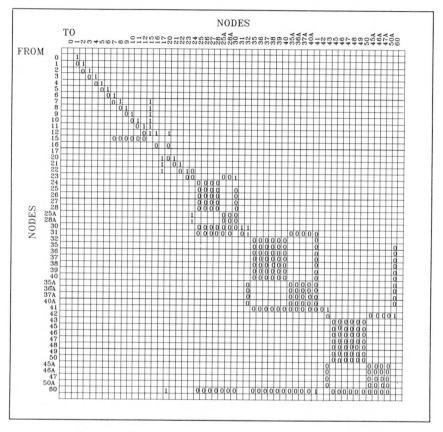

Refer to Figure 5.3A legend for node descriptions.

resources) forecasting and planning. Khalas and Gray (1976), Hayne and Marshall (1977), Huckfeld (1973), Kwak et al. (1977), Milkovich et al. (1972), Pollack-Johnson et al. (1990), Reisman et al. (1973), Weber (1971), and Ikem and Reisman (1990) are but a sampling. The approaches used by the various authors are disparate. Reisman, Song, and Ikem (1991) present a taxonomy for manpower planning and forecasting methodologies. They then classify the landmark developments in this field. The taxonomic scheme is also applied to unifying the models in consideration of the methods and the decision factors used for forecasting and/or planning. It allows for the most complex model structure, containing all the factors considered germane in the existing literature, and it pinpoints the characteristics of problems (models) that have gone unsolved or at least unreported in the literature. The approach to this work was based on Reisman and Buffa (1962), Reisman and Taft (1968), and Balinsky and Reisman (1973).

Manpower planning can be performed under four principal assumptions regarding the quality of knowledge pertaining to the future. These are certainty, risk, uncertainty, and ignorance. Irrespective of the quality of knowledge, planning must be preceded by forecasting of the future states or events. The forecasting effort required depends largely on the level of knowledge regarding the states of the future. For example, when certainty about the future is assumed, the forecasting effort required is trivial because there can be but one outcome to a given set of decisions. Under conditions of "risk," the outcomes are assumed to fall into a probability distribution of which the shape and therefore the parameters are known. Under the assumption of uncertainty, the outcomes are presumed to depend on various scenarios of the future. The feasible scenarios must first be delineated and assigned a probability of occurrence. This can be done by panel consensus or by the judgment of an expert. In any case, it is a subjective input.

The forecast of outcomes, given the future states of events, is most valuable to the planning effort because it provides a basis for the justification of any planning decisions to be made. The idea here is that the value of any manpower plan is a function of the quality of the forecast on which it is based. Although this measure of a plan may be true, it is pertinent to add here that the value of knowledge from even the most sophisticated forecasting techniques cannot be fully realized unless, of course, the results of such forecasting techniques can be effectively applied in the manpower-planning process. Manpower planning has become sufficiently sophisticated that the forecasting and the planning functions have come to be recognized as integral parts, supportive of one another, of the manpower planning process. Two papers by Fildes (1979, 1985) provide an excellent review of forecasting methods in general. Some of these methods can, for instance, be used to forecast the parameters needed in a manpower forecast.

The underlying philosophy in developing the taxonomy for research in the combined forecasting and planning of manpower has been

1. To identify the important factors that have been, and might be, considered in manpower forecasting and planning models.

2. To show that all existing models can be classified as subcases of an acronym representing the general model envisioned. The classification for each subcase can be obtained by merely dropping certain terms or writing appropriate subscripts in the general acronym. In this manner it is possible to delineate most, if not all, manpower forecasting and planning models in a systematic fashion.

The classification scheme having been developed, it was used next to codify the landmark models in the literature. Lastly, it was shown that this approach can also be used to delineate those models that are yet to be developed, that is, the heart of this discussion. In terms defined in Chapter 3, this is a *TDPv* case taxonomy.

Definition of terms used in the taxonomy

H	symbolizes the length of the planning horizon considered by the methodology: short range (H_s), medium range (H_m), and the long range (H_l). Short range is a horizon of less than one year, medium range is roughly one to ten years, and long range is more than ten years into the future.
L	symbolizes the level of planning: national (L_n), regional (L_r), state (L_s), and institutional or company (L_i).
A	symbolizes the level of aggregation: high (A_n) and low (A_l). A high level of aggregation is characterized by a single category (single profession) and/or high level of geographic lumping (e.g., national or regional lumping). A low level of aggregation is concerned with multiple categories (multiple professions) and/or smaller units of geographical, or sectoral lumping.
W	symbolizes the basic approach used: objective (W_o), subjective (W_s), and mixed (W_m). Objective methods seek patterns or relationships between variables based heavily on historical "hard" data. Subjective methods rely primarily on qualitative or "soft" data, such as judgments/opinions of experts or consumers regarding information or anticipation of future events. Mixed methods combine the objective and subjective methods in such a way that quantitative subjective estimates on parameter values which are changing due to external factors (e.g., technology, manpower constraints, economy and political realities, etc.) are obtained.
P	symbolizes the purpose of the model: optimization (P_o), policy evaluation (P_e), and forecasting (P_f). Optimization models for manpower planning match the forecasted or projected manpower supply with manpower demand in an optimal fashion. Policy evaluation models measure the impact of alternate assumptions about manpower policies, demand levels, and transition probabilities in the demand process. Forecasting is simply concerned with demand and/or supply forecast.
I	symbolizes the assumed impetus for people movement within the system: push (I_p), pull (I_e), and mixed (I_m). Education of youngsters in a system based on compulsory education is assumed to be a push flow, for example a Markovian (Haggstrom 1971) type model because the students are "pushed" through the system. Recruitment and/or promotion in a work force, on the other hand, are assumed to be pull flows, for example a renewal (Weber 1971) type model. Manpower planning models sometimes contain mixed flows; for example, part of the pipeline is push type (e.g., students in elementary schools) and part is pull (e.g., students graduating from doctoral programs and entering the work force).

These six symbols, *HLAWPI* with the appropriate subscripts, represent the common factors used in the development of manpower forecasting and planning models as reported in the literature. They are therefore used as a basis of the classification. Other factors that are included in some manpower forecasting and planning models but not in all models are described next.

F	symbolizes the fact that feedback (closed) loops are incorporated in the model. Closed loops allow outflows to reenter a particular sector of the model. Conversely, models without feedback loops are unidirectional. These latter models allow people to feed forward or transfer from one sector to another, but in one specified direction.
N	symbolizes the fact that mathematical nonlinearities are allowed in the model. Therefore, those models that include any functional representation (or tabular representation), other than those that can be expressed as linear functions, are classified as nonlinear.
M	symbolizes the fact that multiple variates are incorporated in the model. Univariate models are based on extrapolation of manpower trends, whereas multivariate models incorporate structural changes and/or environmental circumstances.
C	symbolizes the cross-sectional structure of the system at a given time. The common feature of all cross-sectional models is that historical data prior to the given time is not required by these models, whereas longitudinal models require an historical time series database.
S	symbolizes the stochastic nature of the model. If all or some of the flows (e.g., recruitment, attrition, promotion, and transfer) are controllable and deterministic, then it is not necessary to have a stochastic model. Voluntary attrition is almost always not controllable and probabilistic, but promotion may be controllable and deterministic in accordance with manpower policies.
T	symbolizes the time-dependent behavior (nonstationarity) of the model. If a system or organization operates over a long period of time with the same expansion rate and recruitment and promotion policies and if the attrition rates do not change, the proportion of people in each grade will reach an equilibrium value. Although in practice one would never expect to reach equilibrium, it is often possible to get quite close to an almost stable system by suitable temporary changes in recruitment (and also possibly early retirement schemes).

The Taxonomy Scheme, *HLAWPIFNMCST*

The most general model that can be conceived includes all of the above factors. It is symbolized by the acronym $H_hL_lA_dP_pI_fFNMCST$, where the general subscripts take on specific meanings (e.g., h can be s, m, or l, etc.). This model is conceived to explicitly consider the length of the planning horizon, the level of planning, the level of aggregation, the basic approach applied to the model, the purpose of the model, and structural considerations such as feedback loops, nonlinearities, multivariates, stochastic nature, and time dependent behavior (nonstationarity). The less complicated models are symbolized simply by deleting the symbols represented by capital letters and/or by specifying the subscripts in

HLAWPIFNMCST. For example, a model described as having a long-range planning horizon, directed at a national level of planning, high level of aggregation, using objective methods, optimization, push flows, and having a stochastic nature would be the $H_lL_nA_hW_oP_oJ_pS$ subcase of *HLAWPIFNMCST*. Should it also contain nonstationarity, then the model would be the $H_lL_nA_hW_oP_oJ_pST$ subcase of *HLAWPIFNMCST*. Since every model must contain some planning horizon, level of planning, level of aggregation. methodology, purpose of the model, and impetus for people movement, every subcase of *HLAWPIFNMCST* must contain the symbols *HLAWPI* with the appropriate subscripts. However, if a particular model is applicable to all levels of *H, L,* or *A,* respectively, then the subscript is omitted. For example, if a model is applicable to all lengths of the planning horizon (e.g., short, medium, and long), then no subscript appears next to *H*.

As stated earlier, the taxonomy developed was intended to classify manpower forecasting and planning models. Landmark models which appeared in the literature were summarized and classified using the resulting scheme. The classification showed, in an efficient manner, the similarities and the differences of all models considered. Moreover, this scheme can also be used to pinpoint voids in the literature and therefore areas for future research, as discussed in Chapter 4 and shown by an examination of the blank entries in Table 5.1.

METHODOLOGY VOIDS

Many models for planning human resources attempt to address policy issues in the most optimum manner, for example, Balinsky (1970), Charnes et al. (1971), Grinold (1976), Grinold and Marshall (1977), Grinold and Stanford (1974), and Ikem and Reisman (1990). To be sure, others use less mathematical but more realistic techniques, for example, Weber (1971) and Michenzi (1974). Mathematical optimization is therefore used as the contextual setting for identifying methodology voids.

Chapter 17 unifies a broad, although not exhaustive, arena of mathematical programming. The approach involves development of a general mathematical problem formulation, which is shown to reduce, in a deductive manner, to each of the major subfields of mathematical programming. Furthermore, a taxonomy is provided for classifying each of the special cases. Lastly, the premiere algorithms for solving each of the cases are duly indicated and referenced. Again, by classifying the existing literature using the taxonomy provided, one can identify voids in the methodology (Pollock and Reisman 1988).

Following the approach of Reisman and Buffa (1962), Sloan and Reisman (1968), and more recently of Brockett and Golden (1987), Chapter 17 formulates a general single objective mathematical programming (MP) optimization problem (e.g., its objective function and constraint set) and then proceeds to show how this formulation can be reduced to each of the typical mathematical programming formulations, for example, linear programming (LP), integer programming (IP),

Table 5.1
Taxonomy of Forecasting and Planning Models

Authors*	Length of Planning Horizon H	Levels of Planning L	Level of Aggregation A	Basic Approach W	Purpose of Model P	People Movement I	Feedback F	Non-Linear N	Multi-Variate M	Cross-Section C	Stochastic S	Non-Stationarity T
Bolt,Koltun & Levine [2]**	long range	national	high	objective	policy evaluation	mixed	x					
Reisman [22]	long range	national	high	objective	policy evaluation	mixed	x	x	x			
Reisman, Dean et al. [29]	long range	regional	high	mixed (objective& subjective)	forecasting	push		x	x		x	
Charnes, Cooper and Neihaus [3]	medium	institution company	low	objective	evaluation	push			x		x	
Hayne and Marshall [14]	long range	national	low	objective	evaluation	push			x		x	
Grinold & Stanford [12]	medium	institution company	high	objective	optimization	push		x	x			
Kwak, Garrett & Barone [17]	short	institution company	high	objective	forecasting	push			x		x	
Kahalas & Gray [16]	medium	institution company	low	objective	optimization	mixed			x			
Clowes [4]	medium	institution company	low	objective	evaluation	mixed		x	x		x	
Grinold [11]				objective	optimization	push			x		x	
Weber [33]		institution company	low	objective	evaluation	mixed			x		x	x
Reisman & Taft [31]	long range	national	high	mixed (objective & subjective)	forecasting	mixed	x	x	x		x	x
Young & Vassiliou [34]	long range	institution company	low	objective	evaluation	pull		x	x		x	
Milkovich, Annoni and Mahoney [20]	long range	national	high	mixed (subjective & objective; two seperate models)	forecasting	mixed			x		x	
Haggstrom [13]	long range	national	high	mixed (objective & subjective)	forecasting	push	x					
Dean, Reisman & Rattner [7]	long range	national	high	mixed (objective & subjective)	forecasting	mixed	x		x			

* The articles included represent an illustrative sampling of the literature.
** The bracketed numbers correspond to the Reference section of the paper.

nonlinear programming (NLP), and so forth. The chapter also suggests a taxonomic scheme based on classifications of the structures of the objective function and that of the constraints, the types of variables, and the number of constraints involved. Lastly, the chapter suggests the premiere algorithms for solving each of the special cases of the general formulation. Clearly, the special cases are quite broad in their own right (e.g., LP, IP, NLP, etc.)

Although this has not been done, the taxonomy developed in Chapter 17 provides the basis for developing a matrix similar to that of Table 5.1 and those in Chapter 4 as well as in the many references cited throughout this book. Once again a thorough review of the existing mathematical programming literature along with the above mentioned matrix will identify voids in this realm of knowledge. Hence, it is a *TGDPv* category taxonomy, using terms defined in Chapter 3.

CONCLUDING REMARKS

This chapter has further reinforced the essence of Chapter 4. We have shown how taxonomies intended to systematically describe the state of knowledge in a given field can be almost mechanistically transformed into an identification and delineation of gaps in the literature and hence a specification of potential research topics. As indicated before, the history of science is replete with examples where such approaches have accelerated the rate of knowledge generation and our ability to teach and/or recall such knowledge.

It should once again be emphasized that this methodology does *not* address domains of knowledge where existing literature (e.g., the prior art) needs revisiting. Needs for such revisiting may be due to theoretical gaps identifiable through inconsistent findings, weak results, methodologically bound conclusions, or in general where the quality of past research is questionable.

The taxonomies in each of the examples cited were essentially based on the state-of-the-art boundaries defining the respective fields of knowledge. In this chapter, as in Chapter 4, no attempt was made to create new dimensions for the respective fields. Once again, by the *choice of attributes* comprising the potential taxonomy, one can either limit or expand the state-of-the-art boundaries defining the field of knowledge.

This method will serve those who prefer to work within the existing confines or boundaries of a field of knowledge. However, researchers interested in major breakthroughs, such as those who creatively merge disparate disciplines and/or create a new realm of study, will have to exert some vision and creativity in choosing the parameters so as to get the maximum benefits from this approach.

NOTE

This chapter is based on a paper by the same name. It appeared in *Knowledge in Society: An International Journal of Knowledge Transfer* 1(4): 67–86, Winter 1988–89.

REFERENCES

Balinsky, W. 1970. "Some Manpower Planning Models Based on Levels of Educational Attainment." Ph.D. diss., Department of Operations Research, Case Western Reserve University, Cleveland, Ohio.

Balinsky, W., and A. Reisman. 1972. "Some Manpower Planning Models Based on Levels of Educational Attainment." *Management Science* 18(12): B-691–B-705.

———. 1973. "A Taxonomy of Manpower Educational Planning Models." *Socio-Economic Planning Science* 7(1): 13–17.

Bolt, R. H., W. L. Koltun, and O. H. Levine. 1965. "Doctoral Feedback into Higher Education." *Science* 148 (May): 918–28.

Brockett, P. L., and L. L. Golden. 1987. "A Class of Utility Functions Containing All the Common Utility Functions." *Management Science* 33(8): 955–63.

Charnes, A., W. W. Cooper, and R. J. Niehaus. 1971. "A Generalized Network Model for Training and Recruiting Decisions in Manpower Planning." In *Manpower and Management Science*, 115–30. D.J. Bartholomew and R. Smith, eds. Lexington, Mass.: Lexington Books.

Clowes, G. A. 1972. "A Dynamic Model for the Analysis of Labor Turnover." *Journal of Royal Statistical Society* 135 (2): 242–56.

Dean, B. V., A. Reisman, and E. Rattner. 1971. "Supply and Demand of Teachers and Supply and Demand of Ph.D.'s 1971–1980." Unpublished paper, Weatherhead School of Management, Case Western Reserve University, DE Contract nos. DEC-0-71-0957 and DEC-0-71-0958.

Fildes, R. 1979. "Quantitative Forecasting—The State of the Art: Exptrapolative Models." *Journal of the Operations Research Society* 30(8): 691–710.

———. 1985. "Quantitative Forecasting—The State of the Art: Econometric Models." *Journal of the Operations Research Society* 36 (7): 549–80

Graham, R.L., E. L. Lawler, J. K. Lenstra, and Kan A. H. G. Rinnooy. 1979. "Optimization and Approximation in Deterministic Sequencing and Scheduling: A Survey." *Annals of Discrete Mathematics* 5:287–326 .

Grinold, R. C. 1976. "Manpower Planning with Uncertain Requirements." *Operations Research* 24(3): 387–99.

Grinold, R. C., and K. T. Marshall. 1977. *Manpower Planning Models*. New York: North Holland.

Grinold, R. C., and R. E. Stanford. 1974. "Optimal Control of a Graded Manpower System." *Management Science* 20(8): 1201–16

Haggstrom, G. W. 1971. "The Growth of Graduate Education in the Post-Sputnik Era." Unpublished paper prepared for April 1971 conference of the Association of American Universities.

Hayne, W. J., and K. T. Marshall. 1977. "Two Characteristic Markov-type Manpower Flow Models." *Naval Research Logistics Quarterly* 24:(2) 235–55.

Huckfeldt, V. E. 1973. "A Classification Structure for Models." In "A National Planning Model for Higher Education." Ph.D. diss., Department of Operations Research, Case Western Reserve University, Cleveland, Ohio.

Ikem, F., and A. Reisman. 1990. "An Approach to Planning for Physician Requirements in Developing Countries Using Dynamic Programming." *Operations Research* 38(4): 607–18.

Kahalas, H., and D. A. Gray. 1976. "A Quantitative Model for Manpower Decision Making." *OMEGA, The International Journal of Management Science* 4(6): 685–98.

Kwak, N. K., W. A. Garrett, Jr., and S. Barone. 1977. "A Stochastic Model to Demand Forecasting for Technical Manpower Planning." *Management Science* 23(10): 1089–98.

Mendeleyev, D. I. 1889. "The Periodic Law of the Chemical Elements (Faraday Lectures)." *Journal of the Chemical Society* 55: 634–56. (Reprinted in *Faraday Lectures, Chemical Society 1928, Lectures Delivered Before the Chemical Society*, London: Chemical Society, 1869–1928.)

Michenzi, A. 1974. "Analysis of Feedback Models of Higher Education Degree Production." Ph.D. diss., Department of Operations Research, Case Western Reserve University, Cleveland, Ohio.

Milkovich, G. T., A. J. Annoni, and T. A. Mahoney. 1972. "The Use of the Delphi Procedures in Manpower Forecasting." *Management Science* 19(4): 381–88.

Pollack-Johnson, B., B. V. Dean, A. Reisman, and A. Michenzi. 1990. "Predicting Doctorate Production in the USA: Some Lessons for Long-Range Forecasters." *International Journal of Forecasting* 6:39–52.

Pollock, G., and A. Reisman. 1988. "Unification of a Class of Single Objective Mathematical Programming Problems." Technical Memorandum #641, Department of Operations Research, Case Western Reserve University, Cleveland, Ohio.

Reisman, A. 1966. "A Population Flow Feedback Model." *Science* 153(3731): 88–91.

Reisman, A., and E. S. Buffa. 1962. "A General Model for Investment Policy." *Management Science* 8(3): 304–10

Reisman, A., B. V. Dean, V. Esogbue, V. Aggarwal, V. Haujalgi, P. Lewy, and J. S. Gravenstein. 1973. "Physician Supply and Surgical Demand Forecasting: A Regional Manpower Study." *Management Science* 19(12): 1345–54.

Reisman, A., P. H. Ritchken, B. Pollack-Johnson, B. V. Dean, E. S. Escueta, and G. Li. 1986. "On the Voids in US National Education Statistics." *Journal of Economic and Social Measurement* 14(4): 357–65.

Reisman, A., M. H. Song, and F. Ikem. 1991. "A Taxonomy of Manpower Forecasting and Planning." In *Socio-Economic Planning Sciences* 25(3): 221–31.

Reisman, A., and M. I. Taft. 1968. "On the Generation of Doctorates and Their Feedback into Higher Education." *Socio-Economic Planning Science* 2, 2, 3 and 4(12): 53–60.

Sloane, W. R., and A. Reisman. 1968. "Stock Evaluation Theory: Classification, Reconciliation, and General Model." *Journal of Finance and Quantitative Analysis* 3(2): 171–204.

Weber, W. L. 1971. "Manpower Planning in Hierarchical Organizations: A Computer Simulation Approach." *Management Science* 18(3): 119–44

Young, A., and C. G. Vassiliou. 1974. "A Non-linear Model on the Promotion of Staff." *Journal of Royal Statistical Society, A* 137(4): 584–95.

Alternative Strategies for Real-World Problem Solving and Mission Oriented Research

INTRODUCTION

In Chapters 1–5 we challenged the management science research community to do more work that is integrative and unifying in nature. We then proceeded to show the various strategies and how-to's for doing this. In these discussions, we assumed that the reader has made the transformation from textbook-type problem solving to the initially unstructured and often ill-defined problems of research, be it pure or applied. Experience shows that for some this transformation is not part of a natural progression. Yet, it is necessary. Textbook problems are typically well defined and efficiently stated. They typically provide all the data needed to solve the problem—no more, no less. The methodology needed to solve the problem is provided in the chapter or chapters that precede the problem statement. Moreover, the methodology usually follows a straightforward sequence of operations, which typically lead to a unique solution.

Unfortunately, in research the above paradigm does not apply except for some cases that can be handled using the incremental research strategy. Never does the above paradigm apply in real-world problem solving. In both of these settings, the problems are ill defined, if they are defined at all. Typically, the data needs to be collected and the environment in which it resides often has much "noise" surrounding the "signal." The methodology needed to arrive at the goal is rarely prescribed, in fact, it must often be borrowed from other disciplines as discussed in connection with the bridging or the transfer-of-technology strategies of Chapter 2. Certainly in the case of real-world problem solving, and to a lesser extent in research, there is *not* a unique answer.

Because of the above similarities between research and real-world problem solving, and because the distinctions are not all that clear, especially in the case of mission-oriented research, we next address alternative strategies for problem solving.

Figure 6.1
Schematic of the Conventional Strategy

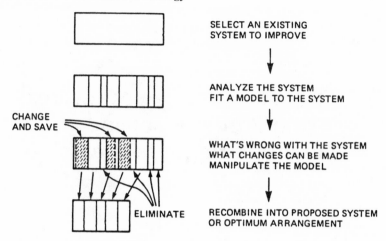

SELECT AN EXISTING
SYSTEM TO IMPROVE

↓

ANALYZE THE SYSTEM
FIT A MODEL TO THE SYSTEM

↓

WHAT'S WRONG WITH THE SYSTEM
WHAT CHANGES CAN BE MADE
MANIPULATE THE MODEL

↓

RECOMBINE INTO PROPOSED SYSTEM
OR OPTIMUM ARRANGEMENT

From-Bottom-Up Approach

The conventional strategy for problem solving usually involves the following steps:

1. Identify the problem or an existing system that is to be improved.

2. Gather all kinds of information that may conceivably be relevant to the problem at hand.

3. Break the problem down into smaller manageable units and/or divide the existing system into components. Design a model or a conceptual scheme that describes the problem or system. The model chosen should relate to as many of the available facts or characteristics of the system as possible. The model thus is a representation of reality, albeit crude at times.

4. Manipulate the model to modify, save, or eliminate various components or to change the relationships among them. These manipulations provide alternative solutions to the problem or offer redesigns of the existing system.

5. The modifications that appear to minimize the original problem or that tend to provide the most improvement to the existing system are combined to form the recommended solution or are installed in the existing system.

This strategy is at times referred to as the "from-bottom-up approach" inasmuch as it moves toward improvement from the base that exists, as shown in Figure 6.1. For example, in the redesign of a curriculum, the process consists essentially of changing a textbook, providing some new problems, perhaps introducing new audiovisual equipment, or starting up some new topics within existing courses. When all these changes have been implemented, it is assumed that the redesign of the curriculum is completed.

It should be observed that what is called a conventional strategy here is, in reality, the type of strategy used in most real-world problem solving. In research, one is often seeking a generalization, law, or theory to unify a series of facts. Thus, in doing research one often proceeds in an *inductive* manner. In problem solving and design, on the other hand, one often proceeds using a *deductive* process. Here a specific answer is sought that can be deduced from the generalizations, theories, laws, or principles produced by research. When the conventional strategy is used to solve problems of design, it rarely produces a breakthrough. The solution process tends to focus attention on what is wrong with the existing system rather than on what the system might be like. In research, such a methodology tends to move the investigator to finding where a favorite technique may be applied rather than to the investigation of what problem really needs solving. It causes people within the system to be defensive. Furthermore, this strategy makes inefficient use of human resources by making people accumulate much information that is irrelevant to the problem and by having them design or redesign components that, from a long-range point of view, may not even be required. It is for these reasons, among many others, that another strategy is recommended by Nadler (1967).

From-Top-Down Approach

The strategy for problem solving that Nadler argues for he calls the IDEALS concept. The word IDEALS is an acronym for ideal design of effective and logical systems. According to Nadler (1967), "the IDEALS concept is the systematic investigation of contemplated and present work systems to formulate, through the IDEALS system's concept, the easiest and most effective systems for achieving necessary functions." In the ideal system's strategy, the best system possible is designed, and then this information is used as the guide in developing the recommended solution. In this way, the information developed by designing the ideal system is utilized to provide much better recommended solutions, and the actual redesigned system is more amenable to changes that will bring it into greater conformity with the ideal system.

A graphical illustration of the IDEALS concept is presented in Figure 6.2. The cone in Figure 6.2 illustrates a hierarchy of systems and some appropriate relationships between them. The present system, which usually consists of many components or units, may be conceptually and physically modified, simplified, and refined in the direction of a theoretical ideal system, as indicated in Figures 6.1 and 6.2. During this process, the present system can be imagined as becoming more and more "ideal." One quantifiable measure of the degree to which a given system is ideal can be represented quantitatively by its cost per unit. The cost of a system is usually expressed in dollars, but this context implies a somewhat more general idea. Here, the cost is taken to mean the allocation of all types of resources, such as money, personnel, time, energy, and information. The cost per unit of output is a measure of the degree to which the system

Figure 6.2
Application of Gerald Nadler's Ideals Concept to the Design or Redesign of a Curriculum

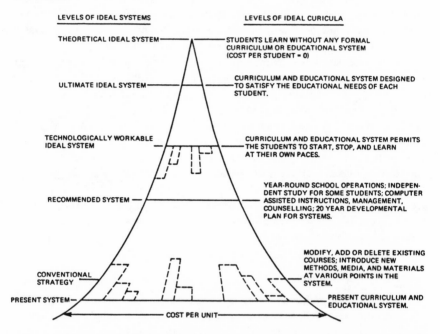

performs its intended function. In the cone of Figure 6.2, the distance between the sides of the cone is equivalent to the cost per unit of output. As the system becomes more ideal, its cost per unit decreases until, in the limiting case (which one can never hope to achieve), the cost per unit of the theoretical ideal system is zero.

Between the base of the cone, representing the existing system, and the tip or vertex, representing the theoretically ideal system, there exists the ultimate ideal and the technologically workable ideal. The ultimately ideal system cannot be attained with existing technology, resources, and the like, yet it shows a direction to strive for. The technologically workable ideal system, on the other hand, with some "downward" modifications necessitated by the realities of life in one or more components, can be built, installed, and/or implemented. Nadler concludes his argument by saying that this from-top-down strategy always yields better solutions than the conventional strategy.

The Iterative Approach

As indicated in Figure 6.3 and in Reisman and Kiley (1973), Reisman and de Kluyver (1972), and the like, the process of problem solving can, and perhaps should, be viewed as being *iterative*. One starts at the "bottom," learning about

Figure 6.3
The Problem-Solving Spiral Model

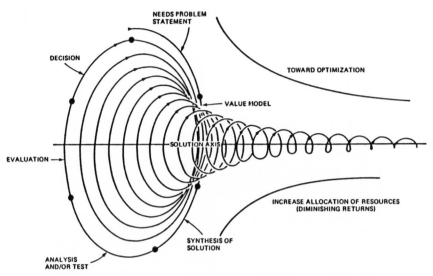

the real system via a systems description, as discussed in Reisman (1979). Without getting bogged down in the process of collecting information and data, one should reflect and create an ideal to strive for, albeit imaginary. The process of iteration between these two, for example, from-bottom-up and from-top-down approaches, is then the optimum approach to problem solving; that is, it allows the problem solver to be able to ''see the forest without getting bogged down with the trees,'' on the one hand, and it provides a basis for a solution that is meaningful and implementable, on the other. Chapter 8 of Reisman (1979) deals further with this subject as does Reisman and de Kluyver (1972).

The iterative approach allows the analyst to develop a model based on understanding the system, which in turn might be based on some preliminary estimates of data. When such estimates are made by the people closest to the operating issues involved, the estimates may in fact be very close to the actual data.

Having formulated a model and estimated the data for the variables and/or the system parameters, it is possible to manipulate the model to test its sensitivity, and thereby that of the system, to the precision of the data inputs. Whenever such analysis indicates a high sensitivity of outputs or behavior to the numbers used, an area of clear payoff for data collection has been established. Inversely, whenever such sensitivity is not indicated, then the estimates, albeit crude, can stand as is—why spend time, effort, or energy collecting data that are relatively useless. Yet the from-bottom-up, or traditional, approach to problem solving indicates this very process. Consequently, it often results in much useless data, coupled with little or no data to which the system is highly sensitive.

Figure 6.4
Stages of the Problem-Solving Process

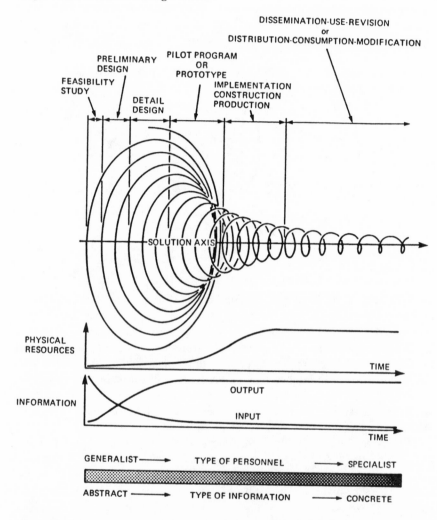

The problem-solving process is depicted as a spiral in Figure 6.3. Each loop describes one iteration in the process; its phases are described as the identification of the problem (need), resulting in the problem statement; the development of a value model; synthesis of solutions, analysis and testing; evaluation of the results; and a decision whether to iterate, that is, to modify the problem statement, the value model, and the like, or to stop the process.

Recognizing that the axis of the spiral represents time, the loops of Figure 6.4 can be grouped into stages of the project life cycle. Thus the first iteration or two represent the feasibility study. This stage typically responds to the question, Is the project feasible from the technological point of view? If it is technologically feasible then the question of economic feasibility often follows.

If the feasibility is established, then the preliminary design stage follows. This in turn leads to detail design, and in turn to pilot programs or prototype construction, and so on. Figures 6.3 and 6.4, respectively, describe the anatomy and the morphology of the problem-solving project life cycle.

This representation further suggests the iterative nature of the process, converging over time to the desired solution. As with most converging processes, criteria are needed to decide when to stop the process. Thus, the spiral illustrates the effect of the law of diminishing returns in problem solving.

As is shown also in Figure 6.4, one often needs little in terms of physical resources during the initial stages of the project but this need increases in time as one starts to require computer time and/or laboratory facilities and the like. The same trend describes information output. As time moves on, the progress reports provide computational results, data, and so forth, and are followed by the final report, instructions for use, and other documentation. The reverse is true of information input requirements. It is high initially and then declines.

Lastly, and perhaps most significantly, Figure 6.4 shows that initially complex and/or unstructured projects require a generalist mentality—people who can structure the right problem the right way, and people who can cull out the signal and abstract it into some form of model. Such abilities are often hard to come by. Our educational system turns out the specialists (e.g., statisticians, mathematicians, computer programmers, etc.) who are needed to an ever greater extent as the project life cycle draws to completion.

NOTE

This chapter is based on A. Reisman and C. de Kluyver, "Strategies for Implementing Systems Studies," in *Implementing Operations Research/Management Science* by R. Schultz and D. Slevin, chapter 14, New York: American Elsevier Publishing Co., 1975; A. Reisman and C. de Kluyver, "Evaluation and Implementation of Systems Studies: Some Philosophical Comments," *Proceedings of the International Symposium of Systems Engineering and Analysis*, vol. 1, October 23–27, 1972, Purdue University; and on A. Reisman, *Systems Analysis in Health-Care Delivery*, chapters 7 and 8, Lexington, Mass.: Lexington Books, 1979.

REFERENCES

Nadler, G. 1967. *Work Systems Design: The Ideals Concept*. Homewood, Ill.: Irwin.

Reisman, A. 1979. *Systems Analysis in Health-Care Delivery*. Lexington Mass.: Lexington Books.

Reisman, A., and C. de Kluyver. 1972. "Evaluation and Implementation of Systems Studies: Some Philosophical Comments." *Proceedings of the International Symposium on Systems Engineering and Analysis*, Vol. 1, Invited Papers, October 23–27, Purdue University.

Reisman, A., H. Emmons, C. de Kluyver, T. George, P. Darukhanavala, F. Staub, B. V. Dean, M. Lin, J. Rasmussen, and J. Gravenstein. 1974. "Anesthesiology Manpower Planning Study Phase III, Final Report." Technical Memorandum #332, Department of Operations Research, Case Western Reserve University, January.

Reisman, A., and M. Kiley. 1973. *Health Care Delivery Planning*. New York: Gordon and Breach.

Schultz, L., and D. P. Slevin, eds. 1975. *Implementing Operations Research/Management Science*. New York: American-Elsevier.

—————————————————————————————

Chapter 7

Formal Aids to Creativity
and Synthesis

INTRODUCTION

The process of creativity or synthesis is not as favored by management science professors or by authors as are the tools of analysis. Yet, as discussed in Chapter 2, the various strategies of doing research require various degrees of creativity. The structuring and embedding strategies place the greatest demands on creative thinking, whereas the incremental process requires the least. Creativity is also required in the problem-solving process, discussed in Chapter 6. Typically, this process requires among its various phases (for example, problem definition, establishment of a value model, data collection, analysis and test) a phase that stands alone in that it calls for creativity on the part of the problem solver. In this phase, it is necessary to synthesize alternative solutions, configurations, approaches, and so on. Consequently, this chapter summarizes the various formal aids to creative thinking.

A number of useful methods for stimulating the generation of imaginative and novel solution alternatives have been discussed in the literature. Some of the major approaches, together with pertinent information about each of them, is presented in Table 7.1. Each method is discussed briefly in the following sections.

Solo Ideation

The most common method of synthesis is known as "solo ideation," namely, the generation of ideas by individual people. Good ideas are the result of intense mental effort, natural curiosity, broad experiences, patience, and persistence. A considerable amount of courage is required to leave the beaten path and risk mistakes. In this context, the old adage "nothing ventured, nothing gained" is certainly applicable. Perhaps the most distinctive characteristic of human beings that distinguishes them from other species is their ability to learn from their

Table 7.1
Formal Methods of Synthesis

Name of Method	Number of People Required	Types of People Required	Typical Tools Required	Major References
Solo Ideation	1	Problem solver	Notebook and pencil	A.F. Osborn (1963)
Checklisting	1 or more	Problem solver	Pencil and paper; lists of features, improvements, and questions	
Brainstorming	6 to 12	Mostly specialists, some amateurs Interdisciplinary group and one expert on the problem	Chalkboard and chalk; or tape recorder Tape recorder or stenographer	G.C. Beakley H.W. Leach J.J. Gordon (1967)
Morphological or Matrix Analysis	1 or more	Almost any type of person	Heuristics, "Monte Carlo" techniques using random number generators with digital computers	M.S. Allen (1962)
Analogies Physical Model Conceptual Model Direct Analogy Role-playing	1 or more	Imaginative, highly experienced, uninhabited, interdisciplinary people	Fabrication shop Analog, digital, hybrid computers. Similar problem solutions. Imaginative and artistic personnel. Broad literary background.	M. Weinberg (1975)

mistakes and from the experiences of others. Human history is a saga of trial-and-error learning. It is usually necessary to accumulate many facts and ideas and to try a great many different combinations of them before a satisfactory solution to a complex problem is obtained.

The time required to produce a solution alternative can be significantly shortened by keeping a notebook handy and writing down all facts and pertinent ideas as they surface. The reason for this is that in attempting to verify a scientific hypothesis, it is necessary to make many careful observations and to record them. It then becomes possible to systematically analyze and correlate this information with a minimum of repetitious effort. When a problem involves many variables, there is a tendency for the human mind to consider only a small handful of these over and over again. Many potentially good combinations, configurations, or alternatives are unintentionally ignored. The process of making information explicit by writing it down is therefore mandatory.

There is another reason for utilizing a pencil and paper while generating fresh viewpoints or alternatives. VonFange (1959, p. 41) has stated this reason as follows:

In all of our efforts to uncover ideas it is very important that we record each one as quickly as it occurs. An idea is a fleeting thing, and is quickly replaced by other thoughts. It frequently happens that we become so enthusiastic over its import that we begin to visualize all of the ramifications in its application. After one or two minutes, thoroughly sold on its value, we set out to record the idea itself, but all we can remember is the last application that we thought of—the idea itself is lost. Most creators, having experienced this frustration too often, always have a pad and pencil handy.

New combinations of ideas or components can be achieved by a process of association—by utilizing similarity, contrast, and contiguity. If, for example, one is trying to devise ways of solving the traffic and parking problems on a large urban campus, one might look around for similar situations on other campuses. By contrast, one might consider how parking problems are solved in downtown shopping areas, railroad depots, or outdoor movie theaters.

One way to recall worthwhile concepts and ideas having high creative potential is to apply the principle of "contiguity" (proximity or nearness). An individual tends to remember events, facts, and dates more easily if they occur near the time of some unusual important event—a birth, death, graduation, wedding, flood, car accident, and so forth. It is possible to take advantage of this fact by preparing a list of major personal experiences that occur each year. Then, when a situation that demands new ideas is encountered, a focus on each major experience will bring a recall in greater detail of the many minor events and concepts that occurred at about the same time as the major experience. The half-forgotten events, concepts, and ideas can be compared and contrasted with the task presently under consideration. Written reports and records can be very helpful if they are available at the time the creative act is being done.

When one finds it hard to muster good ideas after trying the aforementioned techniques, it can become necessary to resort to the "good listener" method. This approach is to try to explain the problem to someone who does not understand in depth what is being done but is willing to lend a sympathetic ear and occasionally ask some pertinent questions. In attempting to communicate the complexities of the problem, the problem presenter offers one explanation after another in the hope that the listener will show some comprehension. Suddenly it is found that the explanations and analogies have made the problem, as well as some promising solutions, quite clear. One's boss, colleague, or mate might have to tolerate the inconvenience, but the problem solver has made progress in the synthesis process.

Checklisting

The process of synthesizing new ideas or solutions to problems can be long and arduous. During the period of time when one is consciously and unconsciously working on some really creative idea, hundreds of ideas and combinations of ideas are considered, in a process that may take months or even years. Most of these ideas are discarded before they are even written down, because of intuitive feelings that they are too expensive, impractical, or perhaps too new. If all ideas were to be recorded as they are thought up, it would be possible to then compare them and select the one that, on an overall basis, appears to offer the most promise.

One simple way to ensure that a major consideration or variable is not over-looked in the deliberations is to develop a *checklist*. In the field of health services, checklists can be used for various purposes. For instance, if one were trying to assess the behavior of a patient, it would be helpful to have a checklist of various behaviors that the patient might exhibit. In the training field, Ryans (1960) offers a checklist of negative teacher behaviors such as:

partial

autocratic

aloof

restricted

harsh

dull

stereotype

apathetic

unimpressive

evading

erratic

excitable

uncertain

disorganized

inflexible

pessimistic

immature

narrow

The usefulness of such a list is greatly improved with the provision of a checklist of positive teacher attributes at the other end of the spectrum. Such a list would consist of such behaviors as fair, democratic, responsive, understand-ing, kindly, and so on.

Another type of checklist, developed by Osborn (1963), is used to stimulate new ideas when one is attempting to design physical objects or procedures. Osborn's checklist consists of a number of "idea-spurring" questions which one might ask:

1. Put to other uses? New ways to use as is? Other uses if modified?
2. Adapt? What else is like this? What other ideas does this suggest? Does past offer parallel? What could I copy? Who could I emulate?

3. Modify? New twist? Change meaning, color, motion, sound, odor, form, shape? Other changes?

4. Magnify? What to add? More time? Greater frequency? Stronger? Higher? Longer? Extra value? Plus ingredient? Duplicate? Multiply? Exaggerate?

5. Minify? What to subtract? Smaller? Condensed? Miniature? Lower? Shorter? Lighter? Omit? Streamline? Split up? Understate?

6. Substitute? Who else instead? What else instead? Other ingredient? Other material? Other process? Other power? Other place? Other approach? Other tone of voice?

7. Rearrange? Interchange components? Other pattern? Other layout? Other sequence? Transpose cause and effect? Change pace? Change schedule?

8. Reverse? Transpose positive and negative? How about opposites? Turn it backward? Turn it upside down? Reverse roles? Change shoes? Turn tables? Turn other cheek?

9. Combine? How about a blend, an alloy, an assortment, an ensemble? Combine units? Combine purposes? Combine appeals? Combine ideas?

Brainstorming

There are a number of group techniques that can be utilized to stimulate the imaginations of people delving into a specific problem situation. The underlying idea behind these techniques is the generation of as many ideas as possible during a specific period of time. It has been shown that those sessions that produce twice as many usable ideas usually include twice as many "good" ideas (VonFange 1959; Osborn 1963; Hueter 1966). This is an example of a case where the quality of the output is directly proportional to the quantity of the output. One idea leads to another, and this one, in turn, forms the basis for still other ideas and combinations of ideas. One of the most familiar, and most utilized, techniques is known as "brainstorming."

Although people may engage in brainstorming individually, the usual situation is for a small group of willing, compatible people to meet in a room where interruptions and distractions are prohibited. In order to enable each person to express his or her own ideas, a relatively small group, consisting of from six to approximately fifteen people, is invited to the brainstorming session. However, for some types of problems, the armed forces has held brainstorming sessions that utilized up to one hundred people. A capable group leader is used to encourage stimulating comments that are directed toward positive suggestions about solutions to a stated problem situation. All ideas and suggestions of the group are listed in a key-word form on a blackboard, which is exhibited for all to see. If ideas are being generated very rapidly by a large group and it is difficult to record all of them, the use of a tape recorder is sometimes necessary.

Since the major objective of a brainstorming session is to produce as many creative ideas as possible, it is necessary to stimulate an atmosphere that is conducive to imaginative thinking. The type of relaxed atmosphere that we seek resembles one similar to a "bull session." Most people have at some time participated in small, impromptu groups dreaming up ways to play a trick on someone else. They have experienced the delight of proposing an outlandish scheme, having it immediately topped by someone else, and then presenting a more outlandish trick themselves. The "can you top this" atmosphere usually results in ideas that are truly ingenious, brought into existence as a direct result of the mutual support and encouragement pervading the group. The following items represent a brief summary of some of the major ideas regarding brainstorming.

1. State the problem in basic terms, with only one focal point. Break down complex problems into problems specific enough to be brainstormed. Instead of asking "What are some of the short-range objectives (potential activities and projects) of a proposed new department of community medicine?" use four separate problems: "What are some of the short range objectives of (a) the surrounding community, (b) the faculty of that new department, (c) the university, and (d) the students?

2. The basic aim of brainstorming is to pile up a quantity of alternative ideas. Therefore, the problem must be one that lends itself to many possible answers. Do not ask the type of questions that require a decision, such as, "What is the best time to start the fundraising campaign?" Brainstorming can only produce alternative ideas; it cannot make a decision.

3. Criticism is ruled out. Do not find fault with, or stop to explore, any idea. Judgment is suspended until a later screening or evaluation session. Allowing yourself to be critical at the time you are being creative is like trying to get hot and cold water from one faucet at the same time—ideas are not hot enough; criticism is not cold enough; the results are tepid.

4. Freewheeling is welcome. Reach for any kind of idea, no matter if it seems remote at the time. The wilder the ideas, the better. Even offbeat, impractical suggestions may "trigger" in other panel members practical suggestions that may not otherwise occur to them.

5. Quantity is wanted. The greater the number of ideas, the greater the likelihood of winners. It is easier to pare down a long list of ideas than to puff up a short list. Successful brainstorming requires adherence to a goal—either a quantity of ideas or a time period (for instance, two hours). At first, ideas will appear fast and easily, but during the last half hour it is possible that very few ideas will be generated. It is likely that the last ideas that are achieved after all the obvious alternatives and ideas have been exhausted are the ones that are unique and creative. Originality is often achieved by thinking hard and uncritically for a little longer than normally about available alternatives.

6. Combinations and improvements are sought. In addition to contributing ideas of their own, panel members should suggest how suggestions by others can be turned into better ideas, or how two or more ideas could be combined into a still better idea. Since there is no evaluation of the soundness of any of the ideas, none of the participants feels restricted except in purpose. It is, of course, necessary for the group leader to provide the support and encouragement necessary for uninhibited thinking.

The major advantage of using brainstorming lies in the fact that it usually produces a very large number of potentially useful ideas in a relatively short period of time. VonFange (1959, p. 51) pointed out that "two engineers had spent over a month in conceiving and accumulating 27 embryonic solutions to a difficult control device problem. When they were finally prevailed upon to conduct a brainstorming session, a group of eleven young engineers with no intimate acquaintance with the details of the problem came up with every one of these ideas plus many others in a short 25 minute session." The major disadvantage of this technique is that evaluation of the ideas and follow-up developments are difficult to accomplish, since the group procedure results in combined suggestions of several different individuals. No one feels strongly committed to, or directly associated with, any of the results. When the results are subjected to later analysis and criticisms, there is no one with enough personal involvement to defend and develop them further for application. By avoiding the motivation, persistence, and commitment aspects of the creative-thinking procedure of individuals, brainstorming loses a significant portion of its value to users. It can augment, but not replace, individual thinking.

There are a number of pitfalls that might be avoided in setting up a brainstorming session:

1. Failure to indoctrinate the panel in the technique of brainstorming.
2. Failure to get support of at least one of the supervisors, department heads, or administrative personnel.
3. Overselling the technique before having results to show.
4. Failure to orient the problem properly or make it specific enough.
5. Failure to evaluate the ideas creatively.
6. Failure to take action on the best idea.
7. Failure to report to panel members what action is taken on ideas.
8. Selling the use of brainstorming as a substitute for individual thinking. It is a supplement.

Synectics

As brainstorming proved its value as a group technique, some people attempted to improve group effectiveness. William J. J. Gordon (1961) developed an approach, suggested by Nicholson (1956) and quoted in VonFange (1959, p. 45)

Mr. Gordon was in charge of the design-invention group of Arthur D. Little, Inc.—a firm which, among other things, develops new products for industry. Once a week he gathered with a group of engineers to work out radically new solutions to client problems. The solutions were reached in sessions conducted along unique, but apparently workable lines. The Gordon technique has two distinguishing characteristics:

The group attacks the underlying concept of the problem, rather than the problem itself. For example, if a new principle for a can opener is wanted, the group leader introduces the general subject of opening. When the client desires a new workshop item, the subject of hobbies is raised. When a cutting device is wanted, the subject of severing is introduced. Underlying concepts are explored at length, and subjects are examined from many angles—social and economic as well as mechanical.

Out of these sessions have come a number of radically new ideas, including construction methods, cutting devices, pumps and other tools. Participants—most of them engineers— claim that *concentrating on the underlying concept has two advantages. It prevents early closure on the problem.* That is, it keeps participants from thinking they have already seen the obvious answer.

It *encourages radical applications of old techniques.* For example, when one client wanted a new type of lawnmower and the subject of severing was discussed, participants went so far afield as to consider the principle of the acetylene torch. Had the specific objective of a lawnmower been considered, in all likelihood, their minds would never have made such a leap, Mr. Gordon says. An average Gordon session frequently requires an entire morning and afternoon of discussion. (emphasis added)

The Gordon technique, then, does not merely generate answers to a specific problem, it also provides training of thought. The methodology can be useful not only in the design and development of engineered products, but also in many applications related to the management of the health services. Some problems may involve planning; others, budgeting. Some problems may involve curriculum design counseling and so forth. If the problem should happen to be "How can we park more cars closer to the center of the office and clinic space?" the team leader might state only a key word, storage. The team then generates all types of ideas on storage. Later, the leader reveals the specific problem and the ideas already generated are then creatively fitted to the problem.

In the early 1960s, William J. J. Gordon became chairman of a corporation called Synectics, Inc., which provided the vehicle for carrying on intensive research in "the integration of diverse individuals into a problem-stating and problem-solving group" (1961).

The synectics process is essentially a complicated way to make the strange seem familiar and the familiar seem strange. It assumes that creative group thinking is directly analogous to the creative-thinking process in individual human beings. Furthermore, it assumes that there are specific principles and character-istics of the creative-thinking process that can be described, and that are similar in all fields of endeavor, whether in the sciences or the arts. Although at the present time synectics is a rather complicated procedure, a summary of the major features of this approach can be found in Edel (1967, pp. 104–105).

A Synectics group is formed to include *six or seven carefully selected experts* such as a physicist with interest in psychology, an electromechanical engineer, an anthropologist with interest in electronics, a graphic artist with a background in industrial engineering, and a sculptor with some background in chemistry. Their method of study is as follows:

1. Formal group sessions are *aimed at problem identification and problem solving*. These sessions produce concepts which are criticized, researched and implemented, using the Synectics process.

2. Obstruction arising in the implementation phases leads to short informal sessions.

3. When a formidable block stands in the way, then formal sessions are brought to bear.

4. Recording tapes are made of formal sessions and reviewed to examine group work process and to indicate sources of new insights in invention problems to be solved.

The synectics process has nine phases, which are identified as follows:

1. *Problems as given.* A statement of the problem to those responsible for its solution; implies a labyrinth of interconnected assumptions which may or may not be correct.

2. *Making the strange familiar.* Concentrated analysis will uncover elements not previously revealed; contrary elements need to be brought out into the open.

3. *Problem as understood.* Various atomistic bits of information about a problem are isolated for examination; concludes the digestion of the problem as given.

4. *Operational mechanisms.* Analogies or metaphors are developed, which are relative to (and evoked by) the problem as understood; some conceptual fingerholds developed.

5. *The familiar made strange.* A conscious attempt to achieve a new look by distorting, inverting, or transposing the everyday ways of looking and responding; a fundamental step for disciplined creative thinking.

6. *Psychological states.* The mind's attitude attains the states of involvement, detachment, deferment, speculation and commonplaceness which are most conducive to create activity.

7. *States integrated with problem.* The most pertinent analogy is conceptually compared with the problem as understood, which liberates the problem from its old rigid form.

8. *Viewpoint.* Potential new viewpoints are effectively extended into actual technical insights.

9. *Solution or research target.* The viewpoints are reduced to practice in terms of testing the underlying principles.

Synectics has been successful in *effective creative thinking* for inventions. They claim that *a well-trained group can compress into a few hours the kind of semiconscious mental activity which might take months of "incubation" for a single person.* Also, individual daring for higher psychological changes is enhanced by direct group interpretations and help. The salaries of many experts are expensive to maintain, however.

A number of improvements in Synectics group operations have been developed in types of group leadership, selection of experts, implementation with model building and refinement of its theory and hypothesis. There research continues and other forms of applications are being tried. [emphasis added]

Since synectics recommends viewing problems from various analogous situations, its use can be envisioned in the design of new facilities, equipment, processes, and procedures. Facilities design presents a multitude of problems that must be overcome if the facilities are to withstand intensive usage and irregular demand patterns. In these cases, the synectics participant tries to imagine himself or herself as the personality of the facility to be designed, such as a hospital floor, the intensive care unit, the clinic, the automatic coffee dispensing machine, the automatic dollar bill changer, and the heavily abused dining room tables and chairs. The participant might ask himself "What would be my reaction if I were any of the aforementioned objects?'' In this way, these objects take on strange appearances and actions, and many of the difficult design concepts become more comprehensible. By direct extension, the synectics approach can be used in the development of new procedures for processing patients through a clinic or in developing new teaching methods for a variety of different students and course objectives. It should be noted that a major factor in the success of this technique resides in the group leader's ability to make the team members reconcile seemingly unrelated ideas into new and useful physical objects, programs, procedures, and policies.

The major drawbacks of this method appear to be that the participants must have some experience and training before they can use it effectively, and the fact that synectics takes a considerable amount of time before it comes to grips with a given problem. In contrast with the brainstorming approach, which produces ideas rather quickly, synectics does it at a slower rate. In the solution of real problems, it is recommended that both methods be used when appropriate and possible. Synectics, like brainstorming, provides a vehicle for the involvement of a number of people in the creative process. As discussed in Reisman (1979), this in itself is a very useful aspect of the process.

Morphologic Analysis

Thus far the discussion has concerned various ways of generating new ideas, attributes, checklists of questions, and other new raw material for the synthesis process. In most nontrivial problems, there is usually far more information than is comprehensible. There are an enormous number of combinations of ways in which lists of ideas can be combined to form new configurations—hence *morphologic analysis* (Allen 1962).

Morphologic analysis usually starts with a broad and general statement of the problem. All the major dimensions, or all the independent variables, of the desired system are then listed. Each independent variable may have a number of subvariables or subdivisions. A number of useful procedures have been developed for generating all the possible combinations of the subvariables to form potential solutions to a problem. Some of these methods are illustrated by the following example.

Suppose one is faced with the problem of designing an examination to be given to students who are taking a course in a training program. As seen in Table 7.2, there are numerous items that must be taken into consideration in the design of a test. One initial question that might be asked is ''What are the objectives of the test?'' For simplicity, let there be three major objectives: (1) recognition of the material, (2) reconstruction of the material, (3) application of the material in new situations. These three objectives can be considered subdivisions or subvariables of the variable known as ''objectives.'' If the objectives were the only variable that were to be considered in design of the test, then there are a number of different combinations of objectives that might be used. A test

Table 7.2
A Morphologic Approach to the Design of a Test

Parameter A Objectives	Parameter B Type of Test	Parameter C Type of Student	Parameter D Type of Question
Recognition of Material	Open Book	Above Average	True or False
Reconstruction of Material	Closed Book	Average	Completion
Application of Material in New Situations	Oral	Below Average	Multiple Choice
Recognition, Reconstruction	Open, Closed	Above, Average	Essay
Reconstruction, Application	Closed, Oral	Average, Below	Matching
Recognition, Application	Open, Oral	Above, Below	Outlining of Ideas or Procedures
Recognition, Reconstruction Application	Open, Closed, Oral	Above, Average, Below	Only Short Answers

could be designed that uses any one of the three objectives, any two of the three objectives, or all of the objectives. If all the logical combinations of objectives were considered, there would be a total of seven possible tests that could be designed:

$$\{1\} \ \{2\} \ \{3\} \ \{1,2\} \ \{2,3\} \ \{1,3\} \ \{1,2,3\}$$

It is obvious, then, that more ideas can usually be generated by considering all the combinations on a list than by considering all the pairs of items on the list.

The total number of combinations is equal to all the ideas taken one at a time, plus all the ideas taken two at a time, plus all the ideas taken three at a time, plus all the ideas taken r at a time, plus all of the ideas taken all n at a time.

Let C_r^n equal the number of possible combinations of n ideas taken r at a time:

$$C_r^n = n!/(n - r)!r!$$

Therefore, the total number of c_T of possible combinations on the list is

$$C_T = C_1^n + C_2^n + C_3^n + \cdots + C_r^n + \cdots + C_n^n$$

Utilizing this formula to calculate the total number of possible combinations for the list having three items (objectives), this is

Table 7.3
Two-Dimensional Morphologic Table

Objectives	Type of Test - Dimension (2)						
Dimension (1)	1	2	3	1,2	2,3	1,3	1,2,3
1	1	2	3	4	5	6	7
2	8	9	10	11	12	13	14
3	15	16	17	18	19	20	21
1,2	22	23	24	25	26	27	28
2,3	29	30	31	32	33	34	35
1,3	36	37	38	39	40	41	42
1,2,3	43	44	45	46	47	48	49

OBJECTIVES	TYPE OF TEST
1 = Recognition	1 = Open book
2 = Reconstruction	2 = Closed book
3 = Application	3 = Oral examination

$$C_T = 3!/(3 - 1)!1! + 3!/(3 - 2)!2! + 3!/(3 - 3)!3!$$
$$= 3 + 3 + 1$$
$$= 7$$

Now to make the problem slightly more complicated, suppose that in addition to consideration of the objectives of the test, one also wants to consider the type of test to be given, namely, whether it should be an open-book, closed-book, or oral examination. Thus, there is a new *independent variable*, which might be called "type of test." Just as in the case of the objectives, there are even possible combinations of tests that result from these three new subdivisions. The two independent variables or dimensions define $7 \times 7 = 49$ different possible tests that can be given to the students. It is a relatively simple matter to verify that this is indeed the case by drawing a simple table such as Table 7.3.

It can be seen that each of the cells in Table 7.3 has been numbered so that it can be identified. So 44 represents a closed-book examination in which the objective is to test a student for recognition, reconstruction, and application. This combination represents a test that is given quite often in most schools. However, combination 1, which requests recognition of the material while using an open book, is a combination unlikely to be used. A careful study of each of the cells in the morphologic table reveals some combinations that have either been ignored or quickly dismissed in the past or were never thought of by the majority of people designing tests. A morphologic table enables the conscious acceptance or elimination of any of the possible combinations that exist.

The foregoing morphologic approach can readily be extended to the case of three dimensions. A third dimension can be introduced by taking into consideration the type of student who will be examined. They can be classified as (1) above average, (2) average, or (3) below average. For the sake of simplicity,

Figure 7.1
Three-Dimensional Matrix for Design of a Test

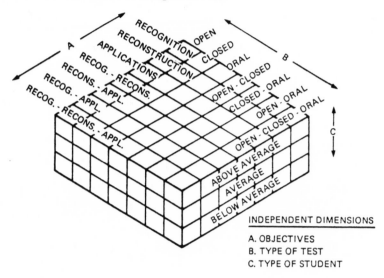

INDEPENDENT DIMENSIONS

A. OBJECTIVES
B. TYPE OF TEST
C. TYPE OF STUDENT

assume that the examination will be given to any one of the three types of students just mentioned, and not to combinations of such students. Thus the possibility of giving the examination to a "mixed" group of students will be ignored. Given this assumption, all the logical combinations of the subdivisions, or subvariables, of each dimension, are shown graphically in the three-dimensional matrix of Figure 7.1. Utilizing only these three dimensions, the total number of tests that can be constructed is $7 \times 7 \times 3 = 147$. However, if the possibility of mixed classes were included, then there would have been seven subdivisions of the "type of student" rather than three—the total number of possible tests would then rise to 343.

Another example of the morphologic approach is represented by the need for improved quantitative analyses of teaching methods. The methods of teaching can be characterized in many different ways, and the following approach is presented merely as an illustration of the complexity in this area. Roe (1963) has stated that the corpus of knowledge of teaching methods can be viewed in three dimensions: (A) relation of the structuring to the students and teachers, (B) relation to the structure of the specified course content, and (C) relation to the behavioral aspects of the students. Some of the possible elements along each dimension are illustrated in Figure 7.2. Theoretically, interactions between elements in one dimension and elements in another dimension should lead to the filling of each cell with a brief description of a particular teaching method. One of the cells, for example, would describe a teaching method that is characterized by a large lecture class in which the socratic (Taft 1964) method is used to

Figure 7.2
Teaching Methodology in Three Dimensions

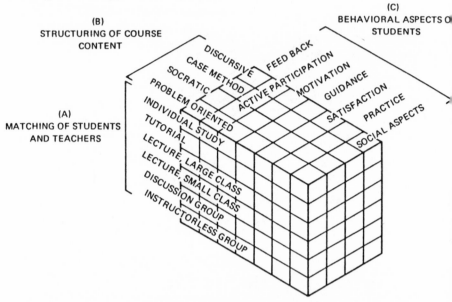

structure the course content, and in which there is active participation on the part of the students. In general, it is difficult to obtain hard data that describe each one of the cells in the morphologic matrix. In the experimental literature on teaching methodology, statements are usually made regarding the elements in one of the dimensions only. Dimension C, which is related to the behavioral aspects of the student, has been summarized by McKeachie (1961) and Tyler (1960). The other dimensions have been discussed by Roe (1963). Gage's book (1963), a basic reference on teaching methodology, cites other models and approaches to this complex area.

At this point, it should be rather obvious that when thinking of the three dimensions related to this problem, one might be able to think of four, five, or more dimensions. For instance, a fourth dimension might be added to the teaching methodology by considering the behavioral aspects of the teacher. The rather simple extension of thinking to more than three dimensions, unfortunately, is not accompanied by an equally simple graphical representation of all the possible logical combinations. Allen (1962) has developed a method for handling more than three variables. Beakley and Leach (1967, p. 411) have summarized the major steps in this methodology as follows:

Step 1: Get the feel for the general problem area. Read all available material concerning the problem, marking or otherwise identifying all ideas that appear to be of any possible significance, or without making any immediate evaluation. Talk with as many people as possible who are parts of the problem in any way. Take careful notes.

Step 2: Type all of the ideas collected in step 1 on 2- by 3-inch cards, with the 3-inch side horizontal.

Step 3: Lay the cards on a table in blocks of twelve—three cards wide and four cards high. Leave about one quarter of an inch between individual cards, and one inch between blocks of cards. This arrangement has worked out to be the best of many different plans.

Step 4: Read the cards over four or five times, as quickly as you can. All of the ideas presented will be retained in your mind permanently, most of them in your subconscious. We shall make intuitive use of these "submerged" ideas during the process of setting up the total problem.

Step 5: Go away from the cards for at least half an hour, taking great pains to occupy your conscious mind so completely that it will not be thinking about the cards. Your subconscious mind will continue to work diligently on the problem, and with much higher efficiency than it could if your conscious mind simultaneously is criticizing every new idea proposed by your intuition.

Step 6: Return to the cards and again study them. You will now notice that certain of the cards appear to be friendly to one another—just friendly—and may easily be collected into congenial groups. If you had started with five hundred cards you might wind up with from twenty to thirty of these friendly groups. Now write a descriptive title card for each group (use a distinctive color) and place a rubber band around the group.

Step 7: Treating each of the groups of cards now as a single element, continue synthesizing the groups into a still smaller number of groups, until you finally come to no more than seven groups. Again, write a descriptive card for each of these final groups. These are the fundamental elements of the problem, which are commonly called parameters. (This number seven was not an arbitrary assumption, but is in recognition of the proven psychological fact that seven elements is the maximum that the human mind can consider efficiently at one time in a single group.)

Step 8: Analyze the cards of each parameter into not more than seven subgroups, called components. The original groupings as found in step 6 will often turn out to be components, but sometimes other arrangements will appear more suitable.

Step 9: Type the parameters, and their components, in columns.

Step 10: Cut the pages up into strips of one parameter each. Then paste the strips on pieces of thin cardboard of the same size as the paper strips. Make a simple device to hold the slides. You are now ready to take a look at the real, the total, problem.

In order to generate new combinations, it is merely necessary to slowly move each strip (representing each parameter) up and down and to note the changing relationships and new solutions that are suggested by the new patterns. If every strip were to be moved up or down into seven different positions, the total number of tests that become available is $7 \times 7 \times 7 \times 7 = 2,401$. It should be noted that what has been called here a dimension, or an independent variable, has been termed by Allen (1962) a "parameter."

When some time and effort have been expended in this type of morphologic analysis, one begins to realize that a particular combination contains other combinations within it, and this can lead to the isolation of yet another variable or parameter. Although it is conceptually a simple matter to add additional parameters to the four already shown, it becomes very difficult, both from a physical and a psychological viewpoint, to manipulate all the information that can be generated by this method. Fortunately, there now are some statistical, heuristic, and computing tools available to enable the problem solver to tackle these more complicated situations (Allen 1962).

Heuristics

In a given problem, as the number of variables, their subdivisions, and their corresponding combinations grows, ways and means must be sought to reduce the total number of combinations in order to facilitate their manipulation. The foregoing illustrations indicate that when only four variables and only about three subdivisions are present for each variable, there are literally thousands of logical possible solutions. One rather common approach to reducing the deluge of information that is generated involves the use of heuristics. A *heuristic* is a "rule of thumb" procedure that may help to solve a given problem.

The most obvious usable heuristic is to intensively investigate each and every combination that is generated. This procedure will certainly produce at least one acceptable solution, but one might run out of time and money long before trying all the possibilities. For example, considering all the possible ways in which only twenty items or subdivisions could be combined would require the investigation of $2^{20} - 1$ possible solutions. Here, for example (1,2,7) is the same combination as (2,7,1) or (7,1,2), and hence all three are counted as one possibility.

However, the number of solutions can be immediately cut down by the imposition of some of the constraints enumerated earlier in the statement of the problem. Thus, in considering the design of a test, one could recognize that all the classes contained a mixture of students with different capabilities. Recognition of this constraint effectively eliminates "type of student" as one of the parameters in the problem. Similarly, one could recognize that there is only a limited time available to give the test, and therefore might discard the possibility of using essays on the test. Because of manpower considerations, one may wish to consider testing the student with only "short answer" problems. In this manner, one can eliminate a considerable number of items on the morphologic chart, and hence reduce the total number of potential examinations. Roe (1963) has developed a very powerful heuristic that can reduce a very large problem to one of manageable proportions in a matter of minutes. In essence, his approach requires starting out with or assuming one particular solution to the problem. It is reasonable to expect that if a formal statement of the problem has been made, including such things as available resources and constraints and criteria, one would have a pretty good picture in mind of what an acceptable solution should be like. Returning to the illustrative problem of designing a test, the administrator can refer to the morphologic chart (Table 7.2) and select one subdivision from each of the four parameters, composing, in this way, one acceptable test. Suppose that a test in anatomy is to be designed for a class of honor nursing students, and that the duration of the test is to be approximately forty-five minutes. One acceptable test can be characterized by selecting one subdivision for each parameter. Thus there might be reconstruction of material, closed-book examination, completion type of examination, and above average type of students.

This set of attributes may not exactly describe the test that is wanted. At this point each of the parameters should be reviewed in determining whether the subdivision or attribute that is selected, corresponding to that parameter, is really the best one available. In this case, one must consider only the other six items on the list and compare them with the items selected. Perhaps one or two other equally suitable items will be found on the list. The point is that, at most, there will be seven items for each of the four lists that will be evaluated, requiring only twenty-eight comparisons. This approach, then, yields, at most, a handful of potentially useful alternatives rather than the consideration of the 2,401 different tests. It should be realized that the power of this tool is directly proportional to one's ability to recognize a potentially good solution when one sees one.

The foregoing approaches are satisfactory for the synthesis activity in everyday problems. A number of important and highly complex problems, however, are not amendable to such relatively simple syntheses procedures. Some of the problems might be:

1. The layout of school facilities to minimize walking distances between buildings, minimize costs, maximize functional relationships, and conform to all building codes and governmental regulations.

2. The simultaneous scheduling of courses, students, faculty, and facilities subject to the constraints of available resources, satisfaction of the desires and preferences of students and faculty, and maximization of the efficiency of school operations.

3. Allocation of resources (money, equipment, facilities, personnel, and information) among competing departments, schools, and/or school activities.

4. Optimal sequencing of courses, topics, or items so as to maximize the students' overall mastery of the subject matter at the time of graduation, and to maximize the student retention of the subject matter for long periods after graduation.

These types of problems have so many dimensions, with so many subdivisions for each dimension, that the number of possible solutions becomes astronomical. In such cases, one is forced to resort to large computers in order to store the vast amounts of information related to the problems. Furthermore, various algorithms have been, and are being, developed for finding acceptable and sometimes optimal solutions to the given problem.

In the present context, an *algorithm* is defined as a formal procedure that, if followed to the end, will lead to a solution of the problem. This does not imply that an algorithm produces an "optimal" solution. As was mentioned earlier, some criteria for judging an acceptable solution can be set up, and then a computer can be programmed to try all the possible combinations of the variables and select the one that satisfies all the criteria. When the number of combinations runs into the thousands or even millions, it is possible to use this type of algorithm. However, as is often the case, the number of alternatives that must be considered, if an exhaustive search is to be made, runs into numbers like ten raised to the twentieth power (10^{20}). Even if one had a computer that was capable of inspecting one million alternatives per second, the computer would have to work on the problem for millions of years before it would have tried all the alternatives. It is obvious that more powerful algorithms must be used in such cases.

NOTE

This chapter essentially replicates Chapter 6 of A. Reisman, *Systems Analysis in Health-Care Delivery*, Lexington, Mass.: Lexington Books, 1979.

REFERENCES

Allen, M. S. 1962. *Morphological Synthesis*. Englewood Cliffs, N.J.: Prentice-Hall.

Beakley, G. C., and H. W. Leach. 1967. *Engineering—An Introduction to a Creative Profession*. New York: MacMillan.

Edel, H. D., Jr., ed. 1967. *Introduction to Creative Design*. Englewood Cliffs, N.J.: Prentice-Hall.

Gage, N. L., ed. 1963. *Handbook of Research on Teaching*. Chicago, Ill.: Rand-McNally.

Gordon, William J. J. 1961. *Synectics*. New York: Harper and Row.

Hueter, J. N. 1966. "Creativity-Choice or Chance?" *The Journal of Industrial Engineering* 17(10): 505.

McKeachie, W. J. 1961. "Understanding the Learning Process." *Journal of Engineering Education* 51: 405–8.

Nicholson, S. 1956. "Group Creative Thinking." *Management Record* 18(7): 234–237. The National Industrial Conference Board.

Osborn, A. F. 1963. *Applied Imagination*. New York: Scribner.

Reisman, A. 1979. *Systems Analysis in Health-Care Delivery*. Lexington, Mass.: Lexington Books. 311 pages.

Roe, A. 1963. "Preliminary Draft for the Panel on Teaching Methods." In *Report to the Conference on Honors in Engineering*, Appendix VII, 163. Boulder, Colo.: University of Colorado.

Ryans, D. G. 1960. *Characteristics of Teachers*. Washington D.C.: American Council on Education.

Taft, M. I. 1964. "The Socratic Method: Extrapolation to Engineering Education." *Journal of Engineering Education* 54(10): 346–49.

Tyler, R. W. 1960. "The Evaluation of Teaching." *Journal of Engineering Education* 50: 863–65.

VonFange, E. K. 1959. *Professional Creativity*. Englewood Cliffs, N.J.: Prentice-Hall.

Weinberg, G. M. 1975. *An Introduction to General Systems Thinking*. New York: Wiley-Interscience.

Part III

Some Philosophical Considerations

Part III of this book attempts to provide both an historical and philosophical background to the challenges of Part I and the how-tos of Part II.

Chapter 8 invokes Rostow's theory of economic development, the kinetics of chemical reactions, and the principles of technology forecasting to address, by analogy, the stages of knowledge development in management science. It shows that different strategies (discussed in Chapter 2) dominate research at the various stages of its development. Lastly, it relates the stages to the level of knowledge accumulated and the relative difficulty of teaching/learning the accumulated knowledge.

Chapter 9 reviews some concepts from the history and philosophy of science and applies them to examining the stages of development reached by some theoretical OR/MS subdisciplines and by several applications areas.

An attempt is made to create an epistemologic context for the recent debate regarding the state-of-the-art of OR/MS and implications for its future.

Chapter 8 _____

On Stages of Knowledge Growth in the Management Sciences

INTRODUCTION

In *The Stages of Economic Growth*, W. W. Rostow (1971) synthesized much factual as well as anecdotal information and produced a theory explaining the path leading toward industrialization of national and/or regional economies. It appears that there exists an analogy between the stages of economic growth, as theorized by Rostow, and the growth of knowledge in a given field. This chapter reviews the growth stages of management science using the Rostow framework. We further elaborate on the subject by showing that there exist analogies between the stages of OR/MS knowledge growth and the kinetics of chemical reactions. Moreover, the empirically based theory of forecasting technological developments is also invoked to discuss the subject from yet another point of view. We then relate the various research strategies delineated in Chapter 2 (Reisman 1988a) to the stages of knowledge growth, and show their contributions to the challenges of expanding as well as consolidating knowledge articulated in Chapters 1 and 3 (Reisman 1987a, 1987b). Lastly, we elaborate on the relative ease or difficulty of teaching/learning the field at each stage.

ROSTOW'S STAGES OF ECONOMIC GROWTH

Following is a summary of Rostow's five stages of economic growth.

The Traditional Society

Economic structure is developed within limited production capability based on pre-Newtonian science and technology, and on pre-Newtonian attitudes toward the physical world.

A central fact about a traditional society is that it is characterized by a ceiling on the level of attainable output per head. The value system of such a society is generally geared to what might be called a long-run fatalism. Many of the Third World countries (e.g., Uganda, Haiti, etc.) are still in this stage. Some countries have regional or economic sector pockets that are in this stage, while the rest of the economy is much more advanced. India is a good example.

The Preconditions for Takeoff

The preconditions for takeoff are developed in a clearly marked way as the insights of science begin to be translated into new production in both agriculture and industry. Western Europe experienced this in the late seventeenth and early eighteenth century, while Taiwan and South Korea went through this stage in the 1950s.

Among preconditions is the radical shift in the society's effective attitude toward fundamental and applied science, toward the initiation of change in production technique, toward the taking of risk, and toward the conditions and methods of work. The essence of transition can be described legitimately as a rise in the rate of investment to a level that regularly, substantially, and perceptibly outstrips population growth. The modern sector can—and often should—be built in part on capital items for agriculture. A high proportion of total investment must go into transport and other social overhead outlay.

The Takeoff Stage

The takeoff is defined as requiring all three of the following related conditions:

1. A rise in the rate of productive investment from, say, 5 percent or less to over 10 percent of national income.
2. The development of one or more substantial manufacturing sectors with a high rate of growth.
3. The existence or quick emergence of a political, social, and institutional framework that exploits the impulses to expanding the modern sector and the potential external economy effects of the takeoff. These are the conditions that give growth an on-going character.

Takeoff requires existence and the successful activity of some group in the society that is prepared to accept innovation. The group must come to perceive it to be both possible and good to undertake acts of capital investment. Taiwan and South Korea in the 1960s are again good examples.

The Drive to Maturity

The stage of maturity is defined as the stage in which an economy demonstrates capacity to move beyond the original industries that powered its takeoff and to absorb, and efficiently apply widely the most advanced fruits of available technology. This is the stage in which an economy shows that it has the technological and entrepreneurial skill to produce if not everything, at least anything that it chooses to produce.

In terms of sectoral development, the drive to maturity sees the industrial process differentiated, with new leading sectors gathering momentum to supplant the older takeoff sectors where deceleration has increasingly slowed the pace of expansion. This stage has a long interval of sustained but at times fluctuating progress. Japan has experienced the drive to maturity in the 1960s and 1970s.

Age of Mass Consumption

In this stage, the leading sectors shift toward durable consumer goods and services. Real income per head has risen to a point where large population segments gain command over consumption and the consumption transcends basic food, shelter, and clothing. Also, the expansion of consumption levels emphasizes quality and goes beyond the basics (e.g., food, shelter, and clothing) and into mass consumption of durable consumer goods and of services.

The structure of the working force has changed in ways that increased not only the proportion of urban to total population, but also the proportion of the population working in offices or in skilled factory jobs. The balance of attention of the society has shifted from supply to demand, from problems of production to problems of consumption, and of welfare in the widest sense.

The national interest at this stage is not only the pursuit of national welfare—the use of the powers of the state to achieve human and social objectives—but also the pursuit of external power and influence (i.e., the allocation of increased resources to military and foreign policy). Israel has passed through all of the above stages during its forty years of existence as a State.

We next show the parallelism between summaries of Rostow's five stages and the growth of management sciences.

STAGES IN THE DEVELOPMENT OF KNOWLEDGE IN MANAGEMENT SCIENCE

The "Traditional Society"

Before the invention of sewing machines and following the industrial revolution in the eighteenth century, the techniques in managing production were intuitive.

The myth of management in this stage led to a value system best described as fatalism. Success or failure was considered the will of God. Man in charge was considered but a representative of God. The laws of nature's changes were imitated by people in managing planting of crops. The Chinese lunar calendar reflects this in relating seasonal changes to the planting of crops.

The Preconditions for Takeoff

The preconditions for takeoff in the economic sector brought about a managerial class that focused on production. Elaborating on the discussion of historical roots in Chapter 1, Adam Smith (1776), a Scottish economist, first wrote about economic advantages that can be secured from the division of labor. Charles Babbage (1832), a mathematician and inventor of the early digital computer refined the division of labor issue and related it to compensation (e.g., pay scales). According to Babbage, efficiency was the major objective of managing the factors of production. Robert Owen (1815) recognized that maximum productivity was attained only through cooperation of management and labor. F. W. Taylor (1919), almost a century later, progressed toward his philosophy of management through a gradual elaboration of techniques for analyzing and measuring elementary processes. Taylor then developed time study and claimed that it was possible to obtain the fundamental objective of scientific management, namely "high wages with low labor cost."

In this stage, the name *scientific management* was used instead of *management science*. The basic approach was to apply scientific study in managing the factors of production and related issues, such as personnel administration, wage administration, organization, time and motion study, and planning and control of production. Mathematical analysis of managerial decision making is traced to this period with the introduction of the economic lot size equation by Harris (1913). Although the preconditions for takeoff of management science, as we know it today, existed in the 1930s (McCloskey 1987a), the real takeoff stage began in the 1940s.

Disciplines such as operations research, systems analysis, industrial engineering, optimization, and stochastic processes are all outgrowths of the more aggregated movement to introduce a "science" base to the practice of management.

The Takeoff Stage

The takeoff stage in the development of management science can be marked by the latter years of World War II. During this period, the Allies gathered a group of scientists and engineers and challenged them to apply scientific techniques in locating the preciously few radar sites, deciding flight patterns for RAF pilots in search of German U-boats, planning logistics of the Normandy invasion, and the like (McCloskey 1987b, 1987c; Miser 1989; Morse 1986). The experiences gained were refined and applied in the field of industrial management following the war's end. In this stage, not only efficiency but also effectiveness was considered in the applications of management science.

Requirements for the takeoff stage of economic growth (conditions 2 and 3, as stated earlier) have their counterparts in knowledge takeoff stages. Specifically, in an emerging area of management science, these are, respectively, recording one or more significant applications; proving a new, novel, and powerful way of addressing old problems; and the existence or quick emergence of a political, social, and institutional framework. All of these emerged rather quickly following Robert McNamara's introduction of Program Planning Budgeting System (PPBS) to the U.S. government.

The shift from military applications to the industrial world provided the major momentum for takeoff of management science. The other major environmental factor was the need for Western Europe's recovery after the war. Before the 1960s, world economics were so prosperous that everyone was tempted to create new ways of doing business in order to exploit the impulses of modern scientific management. This enabled the incursions of management science into marketing, financial management, and managerial economics to survive and thrive in the world of management.

The Drive to Maturity

The drive to maturity stage in development of the management sciences is evident following the 1960s. This can also be marked by Robert McNamara's taking office as the U.S. secretary of defense. Integration of management science in government is illustrated in his use of PPBS for regulating the defense budget. Besides the shifting of objectives from efficiency to effectiveness, the objectives of optimization are also changed to the pursuit of satisfactory solutions. As it is stated in describing economic growth at this stage, the technological and entrepreneurial skills are able to manage anything that they choose to manage, if not everything.

The drive to maturity in management science also has sectoral characteristics, with new leading sectors gathering momentum to supplant the older leading sectors. Here the sectors can be classified as military, industry, government, public service and/or health care applications. We have seen from much evidence that a new idea or technology developed in one sector will be soon applied to other sectors. A semi-stochastic decision process developed in solving machine replacement problems can be applied to the movement of coronary patients within a hospital. The cross-sector application symbolizes the stage of drive to maturing in the development of management sciences as well as economic growth. Similar statements can be made in the more theoretical (e.g., methodological) aspects of management science. For example, theoretical developments in integer programming, quadratic programming, and nonlinear programming took off in the 60s while the earlier leading takeoff sector (i.e., linear programming) experienced a decelerated rate of growth in knowledge (theory), albeit its applications and calculational capability continued to expand.

The Age of Mass Consumption

This stage could be better labeled *maturity*. It is maturity in both the positive and the negative sense of the word. It is positive in that much of the terminology, philosophy and methodology has permeated other disciplines and professions and is fairly widely accepted and used in decision making (Wagner 1988). It is incorporated in M.B.A. curricula and taught in many disciplinary graduate programs. It is negative because much of the institutional infrastructure (e.g., the graduate programs, the professional societies, and especially the landmark journals) have become inbred (Ackoff 1987). They concentrate on research based on established paradigms, work that is essentially logic-deductive rather than grounded in reality. As elaborated on in Chapter 9, it is negative because it moves with extreme reluctance into uncharted territories, be they methodology or applications oriented (Reisman 1987c).

As stated earlier, in the age of mass consumption the economy goes beyond the basics (e.g., food, shelter, and clothing) and into mass consumption of durable consumer goods and of services and the balance of attention of the society shifts from supply to demand. One could argue that the bulk of management scientists have analogously refocused attention from addressing problems of import to running organizations—from the shop-floor "nut and bolt" logistical problems to a preoccupation with strategic problems, theoretical constructs, and with algorithms. This represents a shift from focusing on the *demand* of real world problems needing to be solved, to a focus on the *supply* of techniques in search of problems. The latter too, is an analogy, albeit in reverse.

STAGES OF DEVELOPMENT ANOMALIES

A faulty *paradigm* can, at times, bog down economic development. This is currently poignantly displayed as each of the formerly *communist* societies are moving from *centrally planned* to *market driven* economies. Similarly, the wrong paradigm can bog down development of a field of knowledge. Soviet biology was mired for decades because of the Stalin supported dogma created by a man called T. D. Lysenko (Joravsky 1970). According to B. M. Cohen (1976, p. 347)

Joseph Stalin himself picked T. D. Lysenko to be the "green thumb" on the steel fist of the hoped-for rapid industrialization of agriculture. This kept Soviet agricultural science in turmoil during the 1930's and put it in a strait jacket during the 1950's.

To be sure, the course of management sciences has not been set by any one, Stalin or Lysenko. Rather, the dominant paradigm evolved over the years. The results of this evolution, however, have engendered much debate and some consternation. The question as to what constitutes "good" operations research (Ackoff 1979a, 1979b, 1987; Blumstein 1987; Dando and Bennett 1981; and Sadler 1978) has yet to be resolved. For example, this author recently ran into the following logic: "*Countertrade/Barter* is negotiation. Negotiation is Game Theory. If Game Theory is not used then all this work is *not* Operations Research." Such logic surfaced among colleagues in connection with doctoral theses dealing with attempts to structure countertrade, a practice that encompasses

Figure 8.1
Stages of Knowledge Accumulation

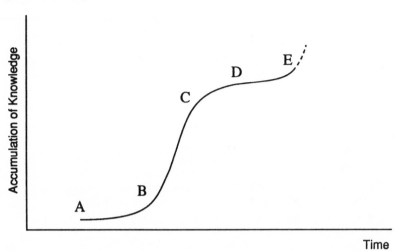

30 percent of world trade and is growing (World Bank 1986). More importantly this logic surfaced in the editorial review process of flagship management science journals (Reisman 1987c).

It is left for the reader to judge the impact of the paradigm illustrated above on our ability to rationalize and create knowledge pertaining to so pervasive a field of practice as is the case of countertrade (barter). Clearly the impact of such a paradigm on operations research itself must also not be overlooked.

ANALOGY BETWEEN KNOWLEDGE GROWTH AND THE KINETICS OF CHEMICAL REACTIONS

The growth of knowledge in a given field can also be likened to a chemical reaction. Hence, the rate of knowledge growth is like the rate of a chemical reaction. Figure 8.1 represents a relationship between the accumulation of knowledge and time. Consequently, the slope of this curve at each point represents the rate of knowledge growth at that specific point in time.

For chemical reactions to proceed or for a field of knowledge to grow, a driving force is needed. Driving forces may be external or internal. The external forces are controllable. For chemical reactions, the external forces can be the environmental, for example, the temperature, the pressure, and/or the concentration of reactants. In terms of knowledge growth, the external forces can be considered as the number, creativity, and energy of the people involved. New ideas or knowledge introduced (transferred) from other disciplines, environmental incentives, and so forth also tend to drive development of ideas. Researchers often produce more when armed with more money, better equipment, or an influx of quality resources. External crises such as a war, an epidemic, and the like also tend to accelerate the creation of knowledge.

Internal forces, on the other hand, are not controllable. Such is the case in chemical reactions. Different reactions have different specific reaction rates. The extent of a reaction, at a point in time, basically determines the rate at that time. Specifically, the reaction rate is determined by the amount of reactants left, the amount of products produced and how far the system is from its equilibrium point. In the growth of knowledge, the nature of the knowledge and the attainment of a "critical mass" of investigators in a certain field basically determines the growth pattern of that field of knowledge. The growth rate often depends on how well the field has been developed, the amount or the kind of knowledge already known, and how far it is from the upper limit of what *can* be known in the field as that field is defined or bounded at the time. Generally speaking, when a reaction is initiated or a field of knowledge takes off, the rate is quite high. When the reaction reaches the equilibrium point or the field of knowledge becomes mature, the rate is very low.

Reflecting on Figure 8.1, at the very beginning the driving forces are very weak. There are few workers trying to understand and bring structure to a new arena. They have few, if any, supporters or individuals interested and knowledgeable with whom they can "bounce around ideas." Much of the work is *empirical* in nature. The "reaction" rate is fairly slow. This is the pretakeoff stage. As time goes on and some investigators persist and show good results an abrupt turn occurs (*B*). All the necessary and sufficient conditions for the "reaction" to be carried out are in place. Man has gained enough knowledge in that field to excite others to enter and to provide a base for rapid development. Much of the *structuring* work has been done. From *B* to *C* the "reaction" proceeds at high rates, knowledge at this stage accumulates rapidly. A large quantity of knowledge is developed in that field, hence, the takeoff stage is reached.

Gradually the "reaction" slows down. In a similar way the pace of accumulation of knowledge slows down as shown from *C* to *D*. The law of *diminishing returns* seems to apply. Creating additional basic knowledge or making new discoveries becomes more and more difficult. This is the stage when most of the research is based on the *ripple* or *incremental strategy*. However, point *C* is not a distinct division between period *B–C* and period *C–D*. Just as the chemical reaction does not suddenly slow down, neither does the growth of knowledge. The birth, growth, and maturation of search theory, discussed in the following chapter, demonstrates this hypothesis.

During the period *C–E*, the "reaction" reaches an equilibrium, and reaction rate is close to zero. Correspondingly, the knowledge in that field has been almost fully developed. A paradigm (the dominant theory or model of the field) is well established and accepted. It seems difficult to add anything new to that field of knowledge. Further progress at this period can be made either by exerting greater effort or by making a breakthrough. It is just like a chemical reaction that has reached an equilibrium. Extensive external influences must be applied to the system, such as more heat or more pressure.[1] Under these circumstances a new reaction takes place because something new has been added to the system. That something new could be a catalyst, which originates a new reaction composed of some or all of the old reactants, or some new compound, which reacts on the original reactants. Point *E* marks this turn. The dashed line starts the next cycle. In terms of the growth of knowledge, there is a revolution or paradigm shift in that field of knowledge. It results from some new mode of thinking or from a *transfer of technology*, for example, knowledge introduced from other fields.

ANALOGY BETWEEN KNOWLEDGE GROWTH AND TECHNOLOGICAL DEVELOPMENTS

Technological forecasting deals with the change patterns of the characteristics (such as performance or function) of a certain technical approach or a technology—a series of technical approaches which perform the same function.

Martino (1983) defines *technological forecasting* as "a prediction of the future characteristics of useful machines, procedures, or techniques." (p. 2) The above definition is a synthesis of definitions for *technology* and for *forecast*. *Webster's Seventh Collegiate Dictionary* defines *technology* as "the totality of the means employed to provide objects necessary for human sustenance and comfort." Martino accepts this definition with a proviso that the notion of *objects* "include not only goods but services."

"Thus technology here will mean the tools, techniques, and procedures used to accomplish some desired human purpose; that is, technology is not restricted to hardware only but may include know-how and software." Martino goes on to emphasize further that not all technology is science based. Much of it is still an art based on practical experience. He then cites Webster's definition of *forecast*, "to calculate or predict (some future event or condition) usually as a result of rational study and analysis of available pertinent data." (p. 1)

In many aspects, there are similarities between research on knowledge growth in a certain field and technological forecasting for a certain "technical approach or technology." First, they both use growth curves to represent the different stages in the development of the object of study.

In technological forecasting, the growth curve is the performance of a technology or the performance of a technical approach versus time. Figure 8.2 demonstrates this notion using historical data describing the transition of the U.S. Merchant Marine fleet from sail (wind) to mechanical power. The form of power propelling the ships is the "technology" or "technologic approach" demonstrated by this figure. In knowledge growth, the growth curve is the knowledge accumulated in a certain field versus time.

Figure 8.3 demonstrates the time lag between the development of a concept

Figure 8.2
Percentages of the U.S. Merchants Using Mechanical Power (adapted from Martino 1983)

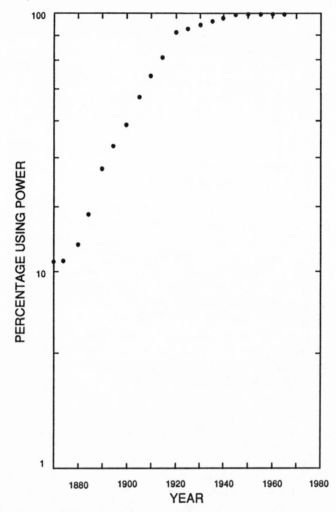

and its application. Attempts to similarly show time lags between major mile-stones in development of management science theory/methodology and their applications proved to be somewhat problematic. We seem to have experienced a bipolar distribution of such lags. Many of the theories/methodologies having arisen out of a real-world need are applied almost contemporaneously. Such was the case in linear programming, dynamic programming, and the like. However in some cases, such as in game theory, good real-world applications demonstrating prescriptions that led to action are hard to find. To be sure, game theory has been used widely in a descriptive mode and as an interesting pedagogical

Figure 8.3
Time Between the Development and Application of Advanced Composites to Aircraft

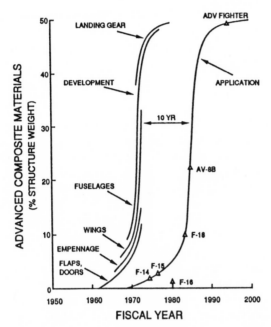

Source: Adapted from Hadcock 1980.

tool. Even the widely accepted assumption that game theory was actually used in altering a major World War II decision, as implied in a landmark publication on the subject (Haywood 1954), is now being seriously questioned (Ravid 1990).

Growth curves in both technology development and knowledge accumulation follow the same basic pattern. As stated earlier, in the growth of knowledge, at the early period of development, the growth rate is small. After a certain period of preparation, the rate increases. Gradually, the growth is slowed down, approaching its equilibrium state. In technological forecasting, Martino (1983, pp. 53–54) pointed out, "history seems to show that when a technical approach is new, growth is slow owing to initial difficulties. Once these are overcome, growth in performance is rapid. However, as the ultimate limit is approached, additional increments in performance become more difficult, and growth again becomes slow."

Another similarity is that a breakthrough may occur in both of the growth processes—the growth of knowledge in a field and the growth of a technology. Martino (1983, p. 129) defines a breakthrough in technology forecasting as "an advance in the level of performance of some class of devices or techniques, perhaps based on previously underutilized principles, that significantly transcends the limits of prior devices or techniques. This definition has several implications.

One is that simply moving up the growth curve of an established technical approach does not qualify as a breakthrough. Another is that the predictable limits of a specific technique must be surpassed by the breakthrough.'' Hence, the nature of a breakthrough in both cases is the same.

Considering the interlinkage between knowledge and technology, these similarities are expected. Technology can be considered as a form of knowledge that is based either on practical experience or on scientific theory. Knowledge in a certain field involves many technologies, each having a characteristic growth curve. The growths of several different technologies may contribute to the growth of knowledge in a given field. The growth of knowledge, in turn, provides knowledge bases for the development of new technologies.

All of these interactions between knowledge and the technologies in a field should be reflected in the growth curve of knowledge. But knowledge does not consist of technologies alone. Therefore, its growth curve is not simply the sum of all the growth curves of the technologies involved in that field. Furthermore, at different stages of knowledge growth, the closeness of the correlation between technology and knowledge differs. At an early period, knowledge in a certain field is hardly developed. Technologies are mostly empirical. Growth curves of technologies have little influence on the growth curve of knowledge. As time goes on, technologies become more and more science based. The growth curves of technologies contribute more and more toward the growth curve of knowledge in that field.

In technological forecasting, people have tried to describe the growth curve of a technical approach or the trend of a technology quantitatively. Different mathematical models have been used. The most frequently used models are exponential in nature (Martino 1983; Cetron 1969).

As mentioned above, the growth of knowledge involves the growths of many different kinds of technologies, but knowledge is not merely a bundle of technologies. Therefore, it is very difficult to represent the curve of the growth of knowledge in a field quantitatively by using a single mathematical formula or a combination of several formulas. The growth curve of knowledge is the sum of many growth curves or trends of technologies, pure theories, and all other notions considered as knowledge in that field.

STAGES OF GROWTH AND STRATEGIES OF RESEARCH

The stages of knowledge growth can be related to the dominant type of research strategy used. The alternative research strategies have been explored in Chapter 2 (Reisman 1988a). The choice of strategy can be considered as both a cause and effect. The state of knowledge at a given stage requires certain kinds of strategies for further development. On the other hand, the application of those strategies results in the advent of the corresponding stage of knowledge growth.

At the preliminary period of knowledge growth in a certain field, from A to B in Figure 8.1, most areas in that field of knowledge are unexplored. A subject area in the *traditional society stage* is untouched by OR/MS, albeit it may be practiced widely. Barter and countertrade (Reisman, Li, and Fuh 1988) was in such a stage prior to the mid 80s. The dominant strategy for *preconditions to takeoff* is to learn from what the practitioners say and do. Defining the key variables, and especially the key parameters, dominates the research being done. As discussed in Chapter 9, the classical period of search theory (Stone 1989) represents a good example of this stage in an OR/MS subdiscipline.

Research in such settings was labeled the *structuring process*[2] in recognition of the fact that the process requires observation and documentation of the institutional phenomena, such as the flow and the processing of resources such as materials, energy, money, people, information, and the like; the decision disciplines; and so forth (Reisman 1988a). This is the stage from which paradigms evolve. Lastly, the process requires the structuring or abstracting of observations in the form of meaningful parameters and/or models. Clearly the models can take on mathematical, statistical, or conceptual (graphical and/or computer-aided) formats. As discussed in Chapters 4 and 5, often this process expands knowledge through generalization and/or by finding and specifying voids in the literature (Reisman 1988b, 1988c). Much of the quantitative social science structuring research is still statistical in nature. That is, empirical data are subjugated by one or several pattern-seeking methodologies such as cluster, discriminant, or factor analysis, or by the relationship-seeking regression techniques. This strategy typically requires much effort and produces new knowledge at a relatively low rate.

During the modeling era, often part of the *takeoff stage*, from *B* to *C* in Figure 8.1, the strategies used involve either the transfer of technology or the creative application modes.[3] The former generates knowledge by transferring technology from another, even a disparate discipline, by analogy, while the latter applies technology from another discipline directly to the field in question. Both strategies could bring about rapid changes in the knowledge of the field studied. New applications of the various optimization methods fall in this category. Thus the early applications of linear programming in agriculture (Boles 1955; Heady and Love 1954) fall in this category. The structuring strategy, mentioned earlier, is also very prevalent at this stage of development. Moreover, the theories or models that emerge from the structuring process need to be validated. Hence, the *empirical validation strategy* is used to verify theories or models by collecting empirical data. This tends to contribute more to the consolidation of knowledge than to the generation of knowledge.

On the other hand, once the drive to maturity gets going the ripple strategy dominates. Such is currently the case in many OR/MS subdisciplines, especially those emphasizing *algorithm development*. This stage is characterized by very intensive and highly technical work in a well-structured and sharply bounded field of knowledge.

As discussed in Chapters 1 and 3, during the life cycle of any subdiscipline, it is both possible and necessary to do some research on the research being done.

This can be termed *meta research* and it goes beyond the usual literature reviews. It attempts to unify and consolidate the literature (Reisman 1987a, 1987b). During the classification and generalization stages, the dominant approaches involve the bridging strategy, the embedding strategy, and the empirical validation approach discussed in Chapter 2.

The embedding and the bridging strategies tend to unify knowledge. Applications of these strategies push the growth of knowledge in a certain field into the stage featuring the unification of knowledge.

As implied earlier the pace of the knowledge growth is greatly slowed down in the steady-state stage from D to E in Figure 8.1. Achievements result from greater effort. Here the ripple strategy dominates. The knowledge system is well established, the paradigm is well developed and progress is typically highly technical and not significant. There are hardly any breakthroughs.

Occasionally a breakthrough does occur after the growth of knowledge in a field has stagnated for some time. The strategies used to make this breakthrough could be some of the strategies used in the periods of rapid growth and of unification of knowledge, such as embedding strategy, bridging strategy, and transfer of technologies strategy. These are basically creative in nature. In the process of unifying knowledge (Reisman 1987b, 1988b, 1988c; Cooper 1988, 1989), or looking for inner links among different bodies or domains, as discussed in Chapter 9, people can be inspired to think differently and in fact challenge the paradigms of the day.

STAGES OF GROWTH AND DIFFICULTY OF MASTERING THE KNOWLEDGE BASE

Figure 8.4 relates the state of knowledge in any management science discipline to that discipline's stage of development. Furthermore, the graph superimposes some "measure" of difficulty of mastering the then current state of knowledge. During the structuring era much data and/or anecdotal information is gathered and, as indicated earlier, the key variables and the key parameters are identified or defined. As more information comes in, due to the disjoint nature of such information, the difficulty of mastering what is known goes up exponentially. It is much like what chemistry was before Mendeleyev's invention of the periodic table. Prior to that development, neophytes were obliged to learn, by rote, the characteristics of each chemical element known to science of the day. The periodic table[4] showed the structure, or the gestalt. That domain of chemistry became forever much easier to learn. Many fields in the social sciences are still in the pre-Mendeleyev stage.

During the next stage, the observations are abstracted in the form of models. The models can take on mathematical, statistical, or conceptual (graphical and/ or computer-aided) formats. The models at this stage are rather specific to a well-circumscribed event, phenomenon, or practice and they appear to be quite

Figure 8.4
Stages of Knowledge Growth Versus Difficulty of Mastering the State of Knowledge

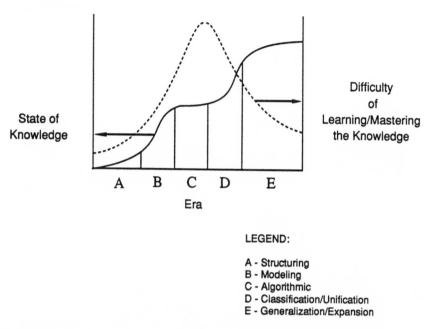

State of
Knowledge

Difficulty
of
Learning/Mastering
the Knowledge

A   B   C   D   E

Era

LEGEND:

A - Structuring
B - Modeling
C - Algorithmic
D - Classification/Unification
E - Generalization/Expansion

disjoint one from the other. The difficulty of learning and especially mastering the knowledge base keeps going up on an exponential track.

During the *algorithmic stage* much activity is consumed by developing computational methods for obtaining solutions to the specific models established earlier. This activity typically generates little in terms of new knowledge about the field but does create much literature, and hence ever increasing difficulty of mastering the subject matter.

In the next stage, some researchers attempt to unify much if not all of the work that preceded in the earlier stages through various modes of literature reviews and classifications. From this point on, the difficulty of mastering the knowledge base declines and with each such classification/unification/generalization of the knowledge base it becomes ever easier to learn the subject much like is the case in post-Mendeleyev chemistry.

For some time, people have connected the concept of entropy of a system with the ignorance, the incompleteness of information about that system (Denbigh and Denbigh 1985; Brillouin 1962; Tribus 1969), or the lack of information about the detailed structure of the system (Angrist and Hepler 1967). If we define the knowledge base of a field (e.g., its literature) as the "system," then all efforts directed at unifying, classifying, and systematizing that knowledge tend to decrease that system's entropy. Hence, the knowledge becomes more trans-

Figure 8.5
Knowledge Organization Versus Stages of Growth

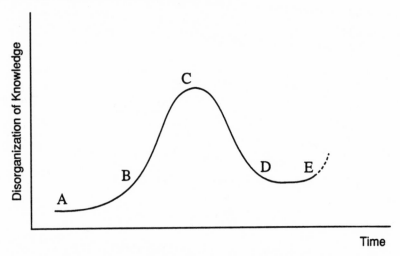

mittable, and easier to learn. Moreover, what is learned is less disjoint for it is part of a clear pattern, or gestalt.

Finally, by embedding the knowledge base in generalized models and/or theories, the knowledge base is expanded while at the same time its mastering becomes ever easier.

There is a similarity between Figures 8.4 and 8.5. Actually, the difficulty of learning/mastering the knowledge does directly depend on how well the whole knowledge system in the field is organized. The more systematic the knowledge is, the easier it is for one to learn or master that knowledge.

Recognizing the situation of MS/OR in this respect, Herbert Simon, in his keynote address at the Fourteenth International Meeting of the Institute of Management Sciences held in Mexico City in 1967, challenged management scientists "to unify, systematize, and thereby consolidate their knowledge or face the possibility of being buried in (their) own models." Although much consolidation of MS/OR knowledge has taken place since 1967, this challenge is still relevant and timely.

NOTES

This chapter is based on the paper "On Stages of Knowledge Growth in the Management Sciences," by Arnold Reisman and Xiaomei Xu, forthcoming in *IEEE Transactions in Management*, 1991.

1. Only for reactions that absorb heat (endothermic reactions) and reactions in which the volume decreases.

2. See Chapter 2.

3. See Chapter 2.

4. It should be noted that the periodic table has, for close to a century, also served as a sort of road map pinpointing the unknown.

REFERENCES

Ackoff, R. L. 1979a. "The Future of Operational Research is Past." *Journal of Operational Research Society* 30(2): 93–104.

———. 1979b. "Resurrecting the Future of Operational Research." *Journal of Operational Research Society* 30(3): 189–199.

———. 1987. "OR: A Post Mortem." *Operations Research* 35(3): 471–74.

Angrist, S., and I. Hepler. 1967. *Order and Chaos—Laws of Energy and Entropy*. New York: Basic Books, Inc.

Babbage, Charles. 1832. *On the Economy of Machinery and Manufacture*. London: Knight.

Blumstein, Alfred. 1987. "The Current Missionary Role of OR/MS." *Operations Research* 35(5): 926–29.

Boles, J. N. 1955. "Linear Programming and Farm Management Analysis." *Journal of Farm Economies* 37(1): 1–25.

Brillouin, L. 1962. *Science and Information Theory*. New York: Academic Press, Inc.

Cetron, Marvin J. 1969. *Technological Forecasting: A Practical Approach*. New York: Gordon and Breach Science Publishers.

Cohen, B. M. 1976. "Some Insights into the Application of Science to Agriculture in the Soviet Union." *Economic Botany* 30(4): 347–59.

Cooper, C. M. 1988. "Organizing Knowledge Syntheses: A Taxonomy of Literature Reviews." *Knowledge in Society* 1(4): 104–26.

———. 1989. "Meta-Analysis and the Integrative Research Review." Paper presented at the meeting of the Operations Research Society of America/The Institute of Management Sciences, New York, October.

Dando, M. R., and P. G. Bennett. 1981, "A Kuhnian Crisis in Management Science?" *Journal of Operational Research Society*, Vol. 32, pp. 91–103.

Denbigh, K. G., and J. S. Denbigh. 1985. *Entropy in Relation to Incomplete Knowledge*. Cambridge, Mass.: Cambridge University Press.

Hadcock, Richard N. 1980. "The Cautious Course to Introducing New SDM Technology Into Production Systems." *Astronautics and Aeronautics* March: 31–33.

Harris, F. W. 1913. "How Many Parts to Make at One Factory." *The Magazine of Management* 10(2): 135–36.

Haywood, O. G., Jr. 1954. "Military Decision and Game Theory." *Operations Research* 2(4): 365–85.

Heady, E. O., and H. C. Love. 1954. "Optimum Allocation of Resources Between Pasture Improvements, Crops and Other Investment Opportunities on Southern Iowa Farms." Agricultural Experiment Station, Iowa State University, Ames IA, Bulletin 437.

Joravsky, D. 1970. *The Lysenko Affair*. Cambridge, Mass.: Harvard University Press.

Martino, Joseph P. 1983. *Technological Forecasting for Decision Making*. 2nd ed. New York: North-Holland Publishers.

McCloskey, Joseph F. 1987a. "The Beginnings of Operations Research: 1934–1941." *Operations Research* 35(1): 143–52.

————. 1987b. "British Operational Research in World War II." *Operations Research* 35(3): 453–70.

————. 1987c. "US Operations in World War II." *Operations Research* 35(6): 910–25.

Miser, Hugh J. 1989. "The Easy Chair: What Did Those Early Pioneers Have Uppermost in Mind, Model Building or Problem Solving?" *Interfaces* 19(4): 69–74.

Morse, P. M. 1986. "The Beginnings of Operations Research in the United States." *Operations Research* 34(1): 10–17.

Owen, Robert. 1815. *Observations on the Effect of the Manufacturing System*. London: R. & A. Taylor.

Ravid, Itzhak. 1990. "Military Decision, Game Theory and Intelligence: An Anecdote." *Operations Research* 38(2): 260–64.

Reisman, A. 1987a. "Some Thoughts For Model Builders in the Management and Social Sciences." *Interfaces* 17(5): 114–20.

————. 1987b. "Expansion of Knowledge Via Consolidation of Knowledge." Paper presented at the Second International Symposium on Methodologies for Intelligent Systems, Charlotte, N.C. *ISMIS- 87 Proceedings*, 159–72, ONRL-6417, 7. Oak Ridge National Laboratory.

————. 1987c. "Where Have We Lost Our Way." *OR/MS Today*, October, p. 7.

————. 1988a. "On Alternative Strategies for Doing Research in the Management and Social Sciences." *IEEE Transaction on Engineering Management* 35(4): 215–21.

————. 1988b. "Finding Researchable Topics Via a Taxonomy of a Field of Knowledge." *Operations Research Letters* 7(6): 295–301.

————. 1988c. "A Systems Approach to Identifying Knowledge Voids in Problem Solving Disciplines and Professions: A Focus on the Management Science." *Knowledge in Society: The International Journal of Knowledge Transfer* 1(4): 67–86.

Reisman, A., G. Li, and D. C. Fuh. 1988. "Achieving an Advantage With Countertrade." *Industrial Marketing Management* 17(1): 53–63.

Rostow, W. W. 1971. *The Stages of Economic Growth: A Non-Communist Manifesto*. Cambridge, England: University Press at Cambridge.

Sadler, P. 1978. "OR and the Transition to a Post-Industrial Society." *Journal of Operational Research Society* 29(1): 1–9.

Smith, A. 1776. The Wealth of Nations. London: McMillan and Co.

Stone, L. D. 1989. "What's Happened in Search Theory Since the 1975 Lanchester Prize?" *Operations Research* 37(3): 501–6.

Taylor F. W. 1919. *Principles of Scientific Management*. New York: Harper and Brothers.

Tribus, M. 1969. *Rational Descriptions, Decisions and Designs*. New York: Pergammon Press.

Wagner, H. M. 1988. "Operations Research: A Global Language for Business Strategy." *Operations Research* 36(5): 797–803.

World Bank. 1986. *Annual Report*. Washington, D.C.: The Bank.

Chapter 9 _____

Toward an Epistemology of OR/MS

> If we could first know where we are, and wither we are tending, we could better judge what to do. . . .
>
> A. Lincoln

INTRODUCTION

In "OR: A Post Mortem," Russ Ackoff (1987) traces "the devolution of Operations Research from its original state as a *market-oriented* profession through the stage of *output-orientation* to its current state of *input-orientation*." He classifies professionals at these stages as follows.

Input-oriented professionals "are defined by the physical and intellectual instruments (for example concepts, theories, tools, techniques and methods) that their members employ to solve problems." Among the examples he cites for input-oriented professionals are statisticians, computer programmers, accountants, and now operations researchers.

Output-oriented professionals are "defined by their products—by the kind of problems they solve." He goes on to point out that these types of professionals "generally employ a wider variety of instruments than do input-oriented professionals but contribute less to the development of such instruments." As examples of output-oriented professionals he suggests designers of incentive systems, production- and inventory-control systems, management information systems, and the like.

Market-oriented professionals are "defined by the class of users they address. They attempt to deal with as many as possible of the problems that their users have. Such professionals use a wider range of instruments and consult with a wider range of input-oriented technicians and output-oriented specialists than professionals of the other two types. They are generalists in the same way that general practitioners (GP's) of medicine who treat anyone who is ill, whatever the illness, are generalists. GP's frequently use medical specialists. For example, input-oriented technicians such as anesthesiologists.''

In that article Ackoff also traces the devolution of OR/MS in the decades following World War II and correlates this devolution with the changing needs of U.S. industry, the inbreeding of faculty teaching OR/MS subjects, and the concomitant inbreeding of OR/MS journals. He concludes his article, ''the field's introversion drove it into a catatonic state in which it died mercifully but it is yet to be buried.''

This rather pessimistic view of OR/MS on the part of one of the field's academic founders and longtime practitioners is counterbalanced by Alfred Blumstein's article ''The Current Missionary Role of OR/MS'' (1987). Blumstein, a former president of both ORSA (The Operations Research Society of America) and TIMS (The Institute of Management Science), takes a much more positive view of OR/MS. While acknowledging that ''those who function merely as mechanical optimizers'' may have ''problems keeping up with the normal course of evolution of OR/MS,'' he suggests that ''those who view themselves as modelers, particularly if they have developed scope, flexibility, and a tolerance for ambiguity'' will enjoy ''at least another generation of career growth.'' However, he points out that such career growth will have to take place by addressing ''areas that have not seen the extent of mathematization that has occurred in the physical sciences, and also to some extent, in military operations, and in the simpler and more tractable aspects of business such as finance and production.'' He points out that there are many areas of potential application of OR/MS methodologies in the social sciences and particularly in addressing social problems of consequence.

Some further discussion on the subject is offered by J. Scott Armstrong in his editorial comments preceding the article ''The Ombudsman: Academic Research in MS/OR: Science or Trivial Pursuit?'' by Halse and Lilien (1986, p. 41). Armstrong states that ''it is easy to do trivial work on important problems . . . but it is difficult to publish it. Far more profitable for the aspiring academic is to do rigorous work on trivial problems. This is easy to do and easy to publish. But how can universities encourage competent work on important problems? That is not easy to do nor to publish.'' Moreover, in ''Misapplications Reviews: An Introduction,'' Arnold Barnett (1982, p. 47) states that ''the widespread availability of sophisticated computer packages has put mathematical bazookas in the hands of some people who would be dangerous with an abacus. The result has been a distressing number of studies that contain everything but common sense, performed by individuals who do not know the underlying assumptions of the models they are using, let alone whether they are relevant to the problem at hand.'' This point of view is further elaborated on by Gary Lilien (1985, p. 12) in his editorial ''MS/OR on Thin Ice,'' ''The new technology (distributed computer processing, more powerful software, etc.) along with less disciplinary rigor in educational programs are in combination providing a rich environment for misapplications. Misuse of OR/MS tools produces erroneous results, resulting in a reduced credibility of the field . . . '' in the eyes of it's ultimate users and rightful clients—the decision makers in industry, government, and institutions.

The above quotes are but a sample of some significant soul searching that has taken place in the OR/MS literature during the decade of the 80s. This chapter attempts to place each of the above concerns into an epistemologic framework extracted from the literature of the history and philosophy of science. Several OR/MS subdisciplines are examined for purposes of illustrating the suggested framework.

EXTRACTS FROM THE LITERATURE OF HISTORY AND PHILOSOPHY OF SCIENCE

Thomas Kuhn (1962), an American philosopher of science, provided the inspiration for most contemporary criticisms of science. His thesis is based on two main concepts:

1. Normal Science

2. Paradigm Shifts

According to Kuhn, *normal science* presupposes an organized structure of assumptions required by the researchers as a group, to discuss their work rationally. However, they tend to somewhat nonrationally and nonempirically accept paradigms and trust them as guides even in the presence of anomalies. Under normal conditions (Kuhn 1962, pp. 35–42) the research scientist is *not* an innovator but a solver of puzzles, and the puzzles upon which he concentrates are just those which he believes can be both stated and solved.

Gleick (1987, p. 36) provides further elaboration: "In Kuhn's scheme *normal science* consists largely of mopping-up operations. Experimentalists carry out modified versions of experiments that have been carried out many times before. Theorists add a brick here, reshape a cornice there, in a wall of theory."

On the other hand, *extraordinary science* is, as Kuhn feels, a revolutionary period, which takes place rather seldom, and arises out of special circumstances. These typically result in shifts in paradigms.

A *paradigm*, according to Kuhn (1962), is basically the dominant theory or model, concerned with a particular field of interest. Normal science is governed by a specific paradigm, "although the paradigm may or may not fit experimental findings."

Knowledge growth during periods of normal science, he claims, is overwhelmingly "a process of accretion." He believes that development is based on the concept of normal science and paradigm shifts, which are basically the new paradigms or dominant theories that are accepted over the old ones. He takes the position that, at any one time, there is only one paradigm, or dominant theory. Kuhn believes that a researcher cannot work with two paradigms simultaneously. If one paradigm is accepted, the other is automatically rejected. According to an unbylined editorial in the *Economist* (1987, pp. 70–71):

Mr. Kuhn stressed the discontinuities in the history of science: the moments when new ideas replaced old ones. He pointed out that bad old theories were often not overthrown by an accumulation of contrary evidence, but rather by a new rival theory, which, for whatever reasons, scientists suddenly started to accept. Often, the victorious theory was expressed in a language which *discarded, rather than incorporated, the concepts of the old theory*. Relativity replaced Newtonian physics; evolution replaced special creation; plate tectonics replaced a geology in which continents did not drift; and so on. These revolutions, said Mr. Kuhn, were largely *shifts in fashion*.

Sir Karl Popper, another major figure in the field, began work in Vienna in the 1930s. He continued his work after moving to Britain. The basis of Popper's philosophy is *revolutionary science*. As Watkins (1965) points out, the motto of Popper's philosophy is "revolution in permanence." According to Popper, an essential criterion for growth of knowledge is revolution. This may occur in many ways, one being a researcher's self-confidence and critical thinking. Another is his ability to research topics that may or may not have an organized structure.

Popper focused on refutation instead of confirmation. He argued that the only real opportunity for the scientist was to falsify theories, not verify them. Scientists should propose testable theories and then try to knock them down. The best theory was the one that had passed the most stringent attempts at falsification. When a good scientist corroborates a general law, he does not thereby assert it to be true, or even probable. He merely asserts that it has passed severe tests, according to Popper.

With regard to the Popper falsification and refutation position, Lakatos (1970, p. 179) suggests that "criticism does not and must not kill as fast as Popper imagined. Purely negative, and destructive criticism, like demonstration or 're-futation' of an inconsistency doesn't eliminate a programme. Criticism of a programme is a long and often frustrating process, and must treat budding programmes leniently."

Kuhn and Popper have been known to disagree on some very basic issues. Their contributions to the concept of scientific development, however, have provided other philosophers and historians with the logic to develop models with a certain amount of validity. The Kuhnian framework is based on the concept of a single paradigm, normal science, and occasional paradigm shifts, whereas the Popperian framework deals with refutations, revolutions, and extraordinary science.

However, according to Hugh Miser, one of the early OR/MS practitioners, Jerome Ravetz (1971) and W. H. Newton-Smith (1981), both historians and philosophers of science, provide contributions that are more relevant to "what the working stiff in science (and in OR/MS) does from day to day, or even over a career." Ravetz "offers a very cogent description of the scientific process, both in some detail and as an overview" (personal correspondence, August 1989).

The Ravetz "overview," as well as his most relevant "detail," are very aptly summarized in Miser and Quade (1988, pp. 469–89). Ravetz (1971, p. 72) views science as a special sort of problem-solving activity.

We may think of a scientific problem as analogous to a textbook 'exercise,' with the following crucial differences: a major part of the work is the formulation of the question itself; the question changes as the work progresses; there is no simple rule for distinguishing a 'correct' answer from 'incorrect' ones; and there is no guarantee that the question, as originally set or later developed, can be answered at all.

Furthermore, Ravetz draws a distinction between scientific, technical and practical problems. The distinctions are summarized in Miser and Quade (1988, p. 486) as:

For scientific problems, the goal of the task is to solve the problem, and the function to be performed by the solution is to contribute new results to its field.

For technical problems, the function to be performed sets the problem. The task is accomplished—and the problem solved—if the solution enables the function to be performed.

For practical problems, the goal of the task is to serve some human purpose, and the problem is solved when a means for serving this purpose has been devised and shown to be effective.

A FRAMEWORK FOR AN EPISTEMOLOGIC VIEW OF OR/MS

Although there is hardly a consensus among contemporary philosophers of science, all of the above points of view are of extreme importance for obtaining an intuitive feel and/or understanding for the growth and development of science in general and OR/MS knowledge in particular.

For purposes of the discussion that follows, the above frameworks for knowledge growth are combined into a "learning curve" type format. Such a format has been amply demonstrated in the literature of technology forecasting (Bright 1972; Martino 1972a, 1972b) and in reviewing historical developments in various spheres of technology (Marchetti 1977, 1979, 1980, 1987). Moreover, it is analogous to W. Rostow's (1971) *Stages of Economic Growth* discussed in this context within Chapter 8.

Elaborating on Chapter 8, Figure 9.1 demonstrates the various stages of development in a field of knowledge. Note that most development is initially slow. During this period science first attempts to structure and/or describe the field. This is the pretakeoff and preparadigm stage. Having succeeded in the descriptive

Figure 9.1
The Knowledge Creation Learning Curve

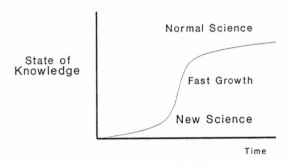

Figure 9.2
State of Development of Various OR/MS Subdisciplines

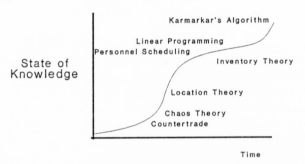

work, knowledge generation gains momentum as researchers refine the paradigm and abstract the knowledge base—the takeoff stage. This is followed by a period of diminishing returns in knowledge gains for the effort expanded. Finally a steady state, albeit with much activity, results in Kuhn's normal science or Popper's hypothesis advancement and refutation stage. As indicated in Chapter 8, this is similar to a chemical reaction that has reached steady state, at which time the forward reaction and the backward reaction attain equilibrium.

CURRENT STAGES OF DEVELOPMENT OF VARIOUS OR/MS SUBDISCIPLINES: A CROSS-SECTIONAL VIEW

Figure 9.2 illustrates the current stage of development for several selected OR/MS subdisciplines superimposed on the learning curve of Figure 9.1. Note the extension of the learning curve to accommodate Kuhn's concept of extraordinary science, the best recent OR/MS example of which is Karmarkar's algorithm (1986). Although it is not a new model of the phenomena of interest (e.g., linear programming), it does provide a new, novel, and powerful way of solving problems to which LP does apply.

OR/MS has developed significantly in some areas. It has, indeed, followed the path of scientific revolutions and change. The changes could be interpreted from the Kuhn, the Popper, and the Ravetz points of view. As stated earlier Karmarkar's (1986) algorithm represents a revolutionary contribution to LP methodology. However, one might ask whether the four-decade lull between the development of the Simplex Algorithm (Dantzig 1948) and Karmarkar's (1986) algorithms can be explained by the fact that at the time of its development, the Simplex Algorithm was accepted as the best solution procedure following futile research using other solution method paradigms. The answer might be found by contemplating Figures 9.1 and 9.2.

Except for Karmarkar's contribution, one has not seen many revolutionary changes in linear programming for some time. The Simplex Algorithm (Dantzig 1948) itself was a brilliant piece of work. Further research, however, has been relatively incremental and mostly directed to enhancing computational capability and/or efficiency. To be sure, the combination of computer hardware and software development along with the development of stable numerical methods has enabled practitioners to solve problems of over a million variables and ten thousand constraints (Dantzig 1965; Lasdon 1970).

In the more general field of mathematical programming, a number of special problem types have resulted in offshoots from linear programming. Among these are network theory, quadratic and general nonlinear programming, and integer programming. Network theory is most noteworthy because it blossomed both in terms of theoretical and computational developments (Jansen and Barnes 1980; Lawler 1976). However, much of the current literature in these subfields is also preoccupied with heuristics. Questions pertaining to the efficiency of an algorithm overshadow those addressing its validity and/or applicability. This may mean that a highly specialized version of a model can be solved, leading to what a researcher wants most, a publication. Mathematical programming appears to have reached the so-called normal science stage, where development is limited to the relatively minor ripples discussed in Chapter 2 (Reisman 1988a).

In the stochastic methodologies area, development has also been rather incremental over recent years. Some queuing models have been used in the real world. However, the general area has not experienced a revolutionary change for some time.

Many of the "applied" areas of OR/MS are now experiencing incremental growth. Among these are inventory theory, personnel scheduling, search theory, and so forth. These are realms of knowledge that were conceived in the field as practical problems in need of solution. However, they have passed the technical stage, and are now basically addressed by "input-type professionals" as scientific problems. Blackburn and Millen (1985, p. 443), reviewing the single-stage lot-sizing literature, state at the outset of their article that "the number of *new heuristics* proposed for the single-level lot-sizing problem continues to grow.

Some of these techniques represent incremental changes in existing algorithms. Surprisingly, upon closer inspection, others turn out to be equivalent to previously published methods.'' A recent paper on workforce scheduling research (Hung and Reisman 1988) begins, ''The literature has recorded many workforce scheduling models. Most are special cases of, or minor variations on the Burns and Carter (1985, p.1) landmark model.'' The above quotes clearly indicate a Kuhnian stage of normal science in the respective subdisciplines. Are researchers in these areas scared to diverge from established paradigms until a group of others do so? This sort of attitude, the ''mob rule'' (Lakatos and Musgrave 1968), is visible in many environments.

As a subdiscipline, which may have emanated from either a theoretical or applied setting, approaches the state of normal science, it is necessary to unambiguously monitor its progress. Taxonomic reviews of the literature along the lines suggested in Chapters 4 and 5 (Reisman 1988b, 1988–89) among others, allow for explicit and succinct statements of similarities and differences between the domains addressed in each paper.

Although such *meta-research*, or research on research, will delineate the state of the art and even pinpoint knowledge voids in any established OR/MS subdiscipline, it will not lead to the ''charting of new territories'' that OR/MS needs for its survival as a field. Blumstein (1987) is correct therefore in saying that what is really needed now is for OR/MS researchers ''to explore new areas of strategic decision making. By introducing into these areas, the OR/MS paradigm may well bring about the critical paradigm shift that Thomas Kuhn (1962, p. 928) used to characterize scientific revolutions. Such shifts are almost always generated by someone who comes to the discipline from elsewhere, and that is presumably because the newcomer brings to the field a more powerful paradigm, or because he is unencumbered by the traditional baggage that inhibits the card carrying members of the discipline.''

Recent examples of such exploratory work involves applications of OR/MS approaches and tools to structuring of countertrade, a modern variation on the ancient barter system (Reisman et al. 1987, 1988, 1989), innovation, entrepreneurship, intrapreneurship (COLIME 1989a, 1989b), and applications of expert systems and of decision support systems (Barriga et al. 1990). On the theoretical end, the new field of chaos (Gleick 1987) seems to have wide-ranging opportunities for a number of well-established OR/MS applications areas. Its importance, however, has not as yet been duly acknowledged by the management scientist.

STAGES OF DEVELOPMENT IN SEARCH THEORY: A LONGITUDINAL VIEW OF A SUBDISCIPLINE

The learning curve concept was used in Figure 9.2 to indicate the current stage of development of several OR/MS subdisciplines. Next, we take a longitudinal view focusing on search theory and trace its various stages of devel-

Figure 9.3
Search Theory: Stages of Development

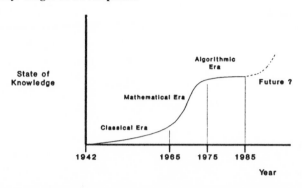

opment over time. Toward this end, we shall borrow heavily from Lawrence D. Stone's (1989) excellent discussion of the history and current status of search theory. He broadly classifies the development of this field into "four eras . . . based on the introduction and use of new approaches to solving search problems." They are

1. 1942–1965   Classical
2. 1965–1975   Mathematical
3. 1975–1985   Algorithmic
4. 1985–present   Dynamic

Figure 9.3 depicts these stages over time.

The year 1942 clearly marks the birth of search theory. Its birthplace is the Antisubmarine Warfare Operations Research Group of the U.S. Navy (Morse 1982).

At George Kimball's suggestion Koopman, Dobbie, and a few others were given the job of *pulling together the existing results on search into a coherent theory.*[1] Morse credits Koopman with providing the basic probabilistic foundation of the subject and finding the first results on optimal allocation of search effort, e.g., the optimal allocation of a fixed amount of search effort to detect a stationary target detection function. Koopman defined the elements of the basic problem of optimal search: a prior distribution on target location, a function relating search effort and detection probability, a constrained amount of search effort, and the optimization criterion of maximizing probability of detection subject to a constraint on effort.

"The resulting synthesis was published in *Search and Screening* (Koopman 1946). It defined many of the basic search concepts: sweep width, sweep rate, detection function, kinematic enhancement. It gave methods for designing barrier searchers (bow tie searchers) and (Anti-Submarine Warfare) ASW screens. It presented models for radar and visual search. This and its updated version (Koopman 1980) are still the classic references on basic search theory and are required reading for any operations analyst who wishes to tackle ASW search problems."

This era corresponds to the back-of-the-envelope stage of operations analysis. It provides maximum payoff per unit of effort required to master and use the concepts. The methods developed in *Search and Screening* allowed an analyst to educate his intuition about search problems and to plan good searches with paper, pencil, and, in those days, a slide rule. By understanding concepts such as sweep width and sweep rate one can design effective search systems. (Stone 1989, p. 501)

An excellent review of search theory developments during its "classical era" can be found in Dobbie (1968).

The "Mathematical Era [1965–1975] is characterized by an effort to understand the mathematical nature of search optimization problems, particularly search for stationary targets, and to develop tools for solving them."

A great deal of progress was made in solving stationary target problems during this period and most of it is summarized in Stone (1975). *This progress was the result of work by a large number of researchers in the United States and elsewhere.* A review of the references in Stone (1975) will give the reader an idea of the number and geographic distribution of contributors. With the exception of the problems of optimal search and stop, and of minimizing expected cost, stationary target problems reached a mature state at the end of this period. By mature I mean that solutions were found for most of the standard cases (e.g., regular detection function), and it has proven very difficult to obtain significant extensions of these results.

The results obtained during this period were often presented in a classical theorem-proof format with correspondingly careful attention paid to the mathematical assumptions, e.g., the correct measurability conditions. Analytic results and closed form expressions were stressed. An important part of the effort during this period was devoted to understanding the mathematical nature of the problems. This resulted in the discovery of very general necessary conditions for optimal search plans. (Stone 1989, p. 5a)

During this period, a serious attack was begun on the problem of optimal search for a moving target, although significant progress had to wait until the algorithmic era, 1975–1985.

This era was characterized by an intense effort to solve *moving target* problems and the increasing availability of cheap and powerful computers. *These characteristics shifted the emphasis in search theory from mathematical and analytic solutions to algorithmic ones.* This new emphasis produced *dramatic results* in terms of algorithms for finding optimal search plans for moving targets.

Most algorithms for computing optimal plans for moving targets apply only to one-sided search problems, i.e., problems in which the target does not react to the searchers. (Stone 1989, p. 502)

Stone provides an excellent review of progress made during the algorithmic/heuristic period of search theory. However, he points out that the results of this period assumed the plan would be followed until the target was detected. "The only feedback considered in these plans is whether the target has been detected or not." He describes the "dynamic era," starting with 1985, by pointing out that

In many search problems there is a requirement to have a dynamic search planning system that estimates the probability distribution on the target state based on all information available, detection, nondetection, subjective and objective. This updated estimate is maintained in real time and used as the basis for developing modified search plan rec-ommendations. The availability of cheap and powerful microcomputers with high reso-lution color graphics has recently made this dynamic approach feasible although many of the ideas on which it is based have been around for 15 years or more. (Stone 1989, p. 504)

In his concluding remarks Stone states that

The Navy has stopped supporting research in search theory. Future developments will have to be done on the fly as part of developing a system. This means that we are living off our past theoretical capital. At some point we will exhaust this.

This clearly implies that the field has reached Kuhn's normal science stage and that developments now are incremental (Reisman 1988a, p. 505) at best.

However, he goes on to say that

Parallel processing is a computer development that holds much promise for improving the speed and capability of search planning algorithms. Many of these algorithms have a great deal of natural parallelism.

Does that mean that an *external development* might launch search theory into a new takeoff stage? Time will tell.

GROWTH OF KNOWLEDGE VIS-À-VIS GROWTH OF LITERATURE: BOTH A LONGITUDINAL AND A CROSS-SECTIONAL VIEW

Figure 9.4 attempts to describe the nonlinear relationship between the growth in knowledge pertaining to a certain field and the number of articles published in its "scholarly" literature. Parenthetically, it should be said that this appears to apply to both theoretical and applications-oriented fields. In its infancy, as the field is structured, it is difficult to find journals that would recognize the "upstarts." "The problems that obsess these theorists are not recognized as legitimate lines of inquiry. Thesis proposals are turned down or articles are refused publication" (Gleick 1987, p. 37).

Early in his career, Richard Bellman ran into sufficient difficulty publishing his work in dynamic programming that he founded his own journal,[2] essentially in order to get a fair hearing. A recent saga in a new applications area was

Figure 9.4
Growth of Knowledge and of Publications in a Field

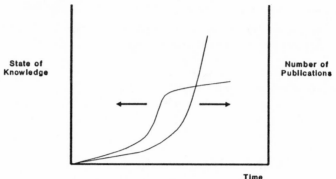

documented by this author (Reisman 1987c) and the rationale behind launching a new journal[3] was recently stated by its founding editor as

> The existence of a journal with a broad coverage will induce authors to write articles on many nontraditional topics. Articles on certain topics or articles using certain research paradigms are not being written simply because there is no such outlet. A paper will not be rejected just because it does not deal with one of the established topics or because it does not follow one of the traditional research paradigms or because it does not conform to the conventional wisdom.

As time goes on, and if the work proceeds undaunted, the rate of knowledge by far outpaces the number of publications. However, there comes a time in the life cycle of any discipline when a form of Parkinson's (1957) law takes over—the rate of publications output keeps rising exponentially while the growth in knowledge levels off.

J. Scott Armstrong (1986, p. 92) estimates that "the number of publications . . . in judgmental forecasting . . . has been growing at about 14 per cent per year over the past 30 years." Some of his comments in the same review article intimate that the growth of knowledge in that field has reached a *normal science* plateau and, at best remained there for some time.

Location theory provides yet another confirmation of exponential literature growth in a given field. A fairly exhaustive literature survey by Margaret L. Brandeau, involving 341 publications between the years 1929 and 1987, provided the data shown in Figure 9.5. These data include 103 entries in addition to those given in the excellent taxonomic review of location research by Brandeau and Chiu (1989). The equation $y = 0.6314 \times 1.1171t$, where t is the year (1929 corresponds to zero) and y is the number of publications, represents the best fit curve for these data. Location theory has not reached the stage of normal science. According to the authors, "Location theory is an active field of research with many new types of problems emerging in recent years. . . . Location models have been designed for an expanding range of applications including marketing and

Figure 9.5
Number of Publications in the Literature of Location Theory, 1961–1986

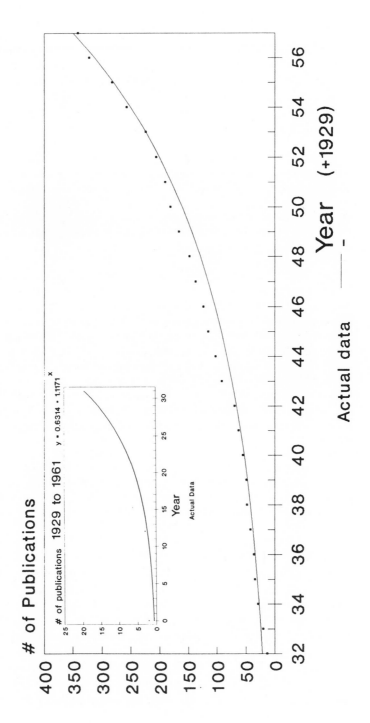

$$y = 0.6314 * (1.1171*x)$$

\# of Publications

Actual data ———

Year (+1929)

product design research'' (Gavish et al. 1983; Bachem and Simon 1981; Nelson 1986). Moreover, ''many location models have been integrated with other types of models, such as production models (Hurter and Martinich 1984), game theory models (Ghosh and Craig 1984; Hakimi 1983) and spatial interaction models (O'Kelly 1986). Finally, many recent models [such as Hodder (1984) and Jurion (1983)] have incorporated more realistic objective functions than the simple objectives used in earlier models.''

Returning to the Ravetz overview of science:

The extension of the boundaries of the known into the unknown does not take place like the spreading of a wet spot on a piece of blotting paper. Without strategy and tactics, a field of scientific inquiry has as little chance of success as an army in battle which is simply told to ''advance.'' The statement of a problem to be solved is analogous to an objective to be taken; and the selection of some problem for investigation, necessarily to the exclusion of others, must be governed by competent judgments based on sound principles. The judgments which determine such decisions are those of value, feasibility, and cost. (Ravetz 1971, p. 161)

To which Miser adds:

It is useful to distinguish three components in criteria of value: internal and external ones (both relating to the roles that can be played by finished work) and personal ones.

The internal components of value relate to how the solved problem will contribute to the field of which its objects of inquiry are a part: the extent to which knowledge will be advanced; whether or not light will be shed on an important area of concern; whether descendant problems will emerge that, if solved, will carry the field still further along; the extent to which the prospective finding will be interesting in its own right; and so on. Working scientists can easily lengthen this list—and must, *a fortiori*, agree that there is no single basis for judging internal components of value.

The external components of value relate to the contributions that the solved problem makes to problems or tasks outside its field. These contributions may be to other fields of science, to technology, to the solution of applied problems (such as those in a systems analysis study), to political or ideological problems, or even to philosophy. As in the case of the internal components of value, there can be no unitary basis for judging the external components. (Miser and Quade 1988, p. 479)

Hull, Tessner, and Diamond (1978, p. 718), in ''Planck's Principle: Do Younger Scientists Accept New Scientific Ideas with Greater Alacrity than Older Scientists?'' quote Plank as saying ''new scientific truth does not triumph by convincing its opponents and making them see the light, but rather because its opponents eventually die, and a new generation grows up that is familiar with it.'' They also say that T. H. Huxley ''was so convinced of the inability of older scientists to change their minds that he declared that men of science ought to be strangled on their 60th birthday.''

Acceptance of new ideas regarding the direction of the field in OR/MS appears to be affected by an *age inversion*. Early and midcareer men and women dominate and maintain the status quo based on inbreeding. The focus of publications, doctoral research, and teaching has increasingly turned to addressing what Ravetz called the scientific problems by and for Ackoff's input-oriented professionals. It is the OR/MS old timers that are calling for review, reevaluation, and for course correction. T. L. Magnanti (1986, p. 2) reflecting on the current status and on the future of OR/MS states that

> Many of us in the profession are now in a position similar to second generation immigrants in a new country. Although we retain some knowledge of our heritage, we experience it largely vicariously. Our capacity to reinforce our early triumphs may depend upon our ability to keep in touch with our roots while looking ahead with the openness characteristic of our forefathers.

Returning to Russ Ackoff's comments as stated at the outset of this chapter, tracing our roots leads indisputably to a market-driven, or at least an output-driven, orientation—that is, to solving the practical, or at least the technical, problems that abound. However, the mantle can be passed on to other generations without the degeneration of the field (the two meanings of devolution), if we just remain on guard against the "golden ruts" of normal science stages and do appreciate the exhilaration of bringing the OR/MS paradigms to bear on problems of social, economic, or political consequence. Changing the paradigms of OR/ MS itself, and once again structuring new arenas using existing OR/MS paradigms, will prove Russ Ackoff's predictions to be a bit harsh—an outcome that I am sure he would welcome. However, for those who dare to venture out and become missionaries in the Blumstein (1987) sense, we must again, as said by Lakatos (1970), learn to treat the "budding programmes leniently."

SUMMARY

During the 1980s the literature of OR/MS recorded a number of serious concerns regarding the current state of the profession and regarding its future. Moreover, these concerns were raised by some significant contributors to the profession's theoretical base, practice, education, and governance. This chapter attempts to embed these concerns in an epistemologic framework based on notions extracted from a more general literature, that of the history and philosophy of science. The viability of the proposed framework was illustrated *cross sectionally* (i.e., at this point in time) across a number of OR/MS subdisciplines and *longitudinally* (i.e., historically), reviewing the progress in terms of contributions to knowledge of a single subdiscipline and the growth of its literature.

NOTES

1. Italics are provided by this author for emphasis.
2. The *Journal of Mathematical Analysis and Applications*.

3. A letter from K. Singhal dated September 25, 1989, inviting this author to serve as Area Editor of *Production and Operations Management*.

REFERENCES

Ackoff, Russell. 1987. "OR: A Post Mortem." *Operations Research* 35(3): 471–74.

Ackoff, Russell, Shiv Gupta, and Sayer Minas. 1962. *Scientific Method*. New York: John Wiley and Sons.

The Economist, 1987. "The Philosophy of Science." April 25, pp. 70–71.

Armstrong, J. Scott. 1986. "Research on Forecasting: A Quarter-Century Review 1960–1984." *Interfaces* 16(1): 89–109.

Bachem, A., and H. Simon. 1981. "A Product Positioning Model with Costs and Prices." *European Journal of Operations Research* 7(3): 362–70.

Barnett, Arnold. 1982. "Misapplications Reviews, An Introduction." *Interfaces* 12(5): 47–49.

Barriga, Rosa M., E. P. Vanek, K. H. Mann, A. Reisman, and L. T. Kent. 1990. "Developing a Tutoring Module for Presentation of Computerized Patient Management Problems." *Socio-Economic Planning Sciences* 24(4): 273–83.

Blackburn, Jospeh D., and R. A. Millen. 1985. "A Methodology for Predicting Single-Stage Lot-Sizing Performance: Analysis and Experiments." *Journal of Operations Management* 5(4): 433–48.

Blumstein, Alfred. 1987. "The Current Missionary Role of OR/MS." *Operations Research* 35(5): 926–29.

Brandeau, M. L., and S. S. Chiu. 1989. "An Overview of Representative Problems in Location Research." *Management Science* 35(6): 645–74.

Bright, James R. 1972. *A Brief Introduction to Technology Forecasting: Concepts and Exercises*. Austin, Tex.: Permaquid Press.

Burns, R. N., and M. W. Carter. 1985. "Workforce Size and Single Shift Schedules with Variable Demands." *Management Science* 31(5): 599–607.

COLIME. 1989a. *Proceedings of TIMS Conference Sessions*. Vol I. Baltimore, Md.: College on Innovation and Entrepreneurship, The Institute of Management Sciences.

———. 1989b. *Proceedings of TIMS Conference Sessions*. Vol. II. College on Innovation and Entrepreneurship, The Institute of Management Sciences.

Dantzig, G. B. 1948. "Programming in a Linear Structure." In *Report of the Comptroller, U.S. Air Force*, Washington, D.C.

———. 1965. "Large Scale System Optimization: A Review." Operations Research Center, University of California at Berkeley, Report ORC 05–9.

Dobbie, J. M. 1968. "A Survey of Search Theory." *Operations Research* 16(3): 525–37.

Feyerabend, P. K. 1965. *Proceedings of the International Colloquium in the Philosophy of Science*, London.

Gavish, B., D. Horsky, and K. Srikanth. 1983. "An Approach to the Optimal Positioning of a New Product." *Management Science* 29(11): 1277–97.

Ghosh, A., and C. S. Craig. 1984. "A Location-Allocation Model for Facility Planning in a Competitive Environment." *Geographic Analysis* 16(1): 39–51.

Gleick, James. 1987. *Chaos: Making of a New Science*. New York: Viking.

Hakimi, S. L. 1983. "On Locating New Facilities in a Competitive Environment." *European Journal of Operations Research* 12(1): 29–35.

Halse, Ron, and Gary Lilien. 1986. "The Ombudsman: Academic Research in MS/OR: Science or Trivial Pursuit?" *Interfaces* 16(3): 41–48.

Hodder, J. E. 1984. "Financial Market Approaches to Facility Location." *Operations Research* 32(6): 1374–80.

Hull, David L., P. D. Tessner, and A. M. Diamond. 1978. "Plank's Principle: Do Younger Scientists Accept New Scientific Ideas with Greater Clarity than Older Scientists." *Science* 202 (Nov. 17): 717–22.

Hung, Rudy, and A. Reisman. 1988. "Workforce Scheduling: A Taxonomy of the Literature and Specification of Potential Research Topics." Technical Memorandum #649, Department of Operations Research, Case Western Reserve University, Cleveland, Ohio.

Hurter, A. P., Jr., and J. S. Martinich. 1984. "Network Production-Location Problems Under Price Uncertainty." *European Journal of Operations Research* 16(2): 183–97.

Jansen, P., and W. Barnes. 1980. *Network Flow Programming*. New York: Wiley and Sons.

Jurion, B. J. 1983. "A Theory of Public Services with Distance-Sensitive Utility." In *Locational Analysis of Public Facilites*, edited by J. -F. Thisse and H. G. Zoller. New York: North-Holland Publishing Co.

Karmarkar, Narendra. 1986. "Karmarkar's Algorithm." *AT&T Bell Laboratories Record*, New York. 64: 4–10.

Khachian. L. G. 1979. "A Polynomial Algorithm in Linear Programming." *Soviet Mathematics Doklady* 20(1):191–94.

Koopman, B. O. 1946. "Search and Screening." Operations Evaluation Group Report No. 56, Center for Naval Analyses, Alexandria, Va.

———. 1980. *Search and Screening: General Principles with Historical Applications*. New York: Pergamon Press.

Kuhn, Thomas. 1962. *Structure of Scientific Revolutions*. Chicago, Ill.: University of Chicago Press.

Kuttner, Robert. 1985. "The Poverty of Economics." *The Atlantic Monthly* pp. 74–84, February.

Lakatos, Imre. 1970. *Criticism and the Growth of Knowledge*. London: Cambridge University Press.

Lakatos, Imre, and Alan Musgrave. 1968. *Problems in the Philosophy of Science*. Amsterdam: North Holland.

Lasdon, Leon. 1970. *Optimization Theory for Large Systems*. New York: McMillan Publishing Co.

Laudan, Larry. 1984. *Science and Values*. Berkeley, Calif.: University of California Press.

Laudan, Larry, Rachel Laudan, and Arthur Donovan. 1988. *Scrutinizing Science, an Empirical Study*. Netherlands: Kluwer Academic Publishers.

Lawler, E. 1976. *Combinatorial Optimization: Networks and Matroids*. New York: Holt, Rinehart and Winston.

Leontief, Wassily. 1982. "Academic Economics." *Science* 217(4555): 104–7.

Lilien, Gary. 1985. "OR/MS on Thin Ice." *Interfaces* 15(4): 12–13.

Magnanti, T. L. 1986. "Editorial." *Operations Research* 34(1): 2–3.

Mandelbrot, Benoit. 1983. *The Fractal Geometry of Nature*. San Francisco: W. C. Freeman.

Marchetti, C. 1977. "Primary Energy Substitution Models: On the Interaction between Energy and Society." *Technological Forecasting and Social Change* 10(4): 345–56.

———. 1979. "Energy Systems—The Broader Context." *Technological Forecasting and Social Change* 14(3): 191–203.

———. 1980. "Society as a Learning System: Discovery, Invention, and Innovation Cycles Revisited." *Technological Forecasting and Social Change* 18(4): 267–82.

———. 1987. "Infrastructures for Movement." *Technological Forecasting and Social Change* 32(4): 373–93.

Martino, Joseph P. 1972a. *Technological Forecasting for Decision-Making*. New York: American Elsevier Publishing Co., Inc.

———. 1972b. *An Introduction to Technological Forecasting*. New York: Gordon and Breach, Science Publishers, Inc.

Miser, Hugh J., and E. S. Quade, eds. 1988. *Handbook of Systems Analysis: Craft Issues and Procedural Choices*. New York: Elsevier Science Publishing Co., Inc.

Morse, P. M. 1982. "In Memoriam: Bernard Osgood Koopman, 1900–1981." *Operations Research* 30(3): 417–27.

Nagel, Ernest. 1961. *Structure of Science*. New York: Harcourt, Brace and World.

Nelson, P. 1986. "New Product Pricing and Positioning in an Oligopolistic Market." Working Paper, Graduate School of Management, University of Rochester.

Newton-Smith, W. H. 1981. *The Rationality of Science*. London and New York: Routledge and Kegan Paul.

O'Kelly, M. E. 1986. "The Location of Interacting Hub Facilities." *Transportation Science* 20(2): 92–106.

Parkinson, C. N. 1957. *Parkinson's Law and Other Studies in Administration*. Boston, Mass.: Houghton-Mifflin.

Popper, Sir Karl. 1965. *Proceedings of the International Colloquium in the Philosophy of Science*, London.

Popper, Sir Karl. 1959. *The Logic of Scientific Discovery*. New York: Basic Books.

Ravetz, Jerome. 1971. *Scientific Knowledge and Its Social Problems*. Oxford, England: Oxford University Press.

Reisman, Arnold. 1987a. "Expansion of Knowledge via Consolidation of Knowledge." *ISMIS-87 Proceedings*, ONRL 6417 Oak Ridge National Laboratory, N.C. 159–72.

———. 1987b. "Some Thoughts for Model Builders in the Management and Social Sciences." *Interfaces* 17(5): 114–20.

———. 1987c. "Where Have We Lost Our Way." *OR/MS Today*, October, p. 7.

———. 1988a. "On Alternative Strategies for Doing Research in the Management and Social Sciences." *IEEE Transactions* 35(4): 215–21.

———. 1988b. "Finding Researchable Topics Via a Taxonomy of a Field of Knowledge." *Operations Research Letters* 7(6): 295–301.

———. 1988–89. "A Systems Approach to Identifying Knowledge Voids in Problem Solving Disciplines and Professions: A Focus on the Management Sciences." *Knowledge in Society: An International Journal of Knowledge Transfer* 1(4): 67–86.

Reisman, A., R. Aggarwal, and D. C. Fuh. 1989. "Seeking Out Profitable Countertrade Opportunities." *Industrial Marketing Management* 18(1): 1–7.

Reisman, A., D. C. Fuh, and G. Li. 1988. "Achieving an Advantage with Countertrade." *Industrial Marketing Management* 17(1): 55–63.

Reisman, A., G. Li, and D. C. Fuh. 1987. "A Decision Support System for Countertrade Negotiations." Paper presented at the Second Symposium on Cross-Cultural Consumer and Business Studies, Honolulu, Hawaii, December 14–18. Also in the conference *Proceedings*, pp. 41–45.

Ritchie, A. D. 1923. *Scientific Method*. New York: Harcourt, Brace, and World.

Rostow, W. W. 1971. *The Stages of Economic Growth: A Non-Communist Manifesto*. University Press at Cambridge.

Stone, Lawrence D. 1975. *Theory of Optimal Search*. New York: Academic Press.

———. 1989. "What's Happened in Search Theory Since the 1975 Lancaster Prize?" *Operations Research* 37(3): 501–6.

Watkins, J. W. N. 1965. *Proceedings of the International Colloquium in the Philosophy of Science*. London.

Part IV

Some Extended Examples

INTRODUCTION

One way to respond to Blumstein's (1987) challenge for doing "missionary work," for example, applying the management sciences in subject areas and/or economic sectors previously untouched by such approaches, is to create a structure that describes the field in a manner that is efficient in a communication sense and effective in that it describes the essentials at the proper level of specificity.

The chapters within the sections that follow show extended examples of such missionary structuring in several distinctly different arenas—each representing a significant sector of human activity.

The first set of examples (Section 1) attempts to provide some structure to what we know about a subject called transfer of technology. Technology transfer is viewed from the perspective of describing the transferor/transferee combinations (Chapter 10); from the perspective of the types of transactions involved (Chapter 11); and from the perspective of each of the rather disparate disciplines, such as management, engineering, economics, anthropology, and sociology, which have been concerned with the transfer of technology (Chapter 12).

The next example (Section 2) represents the world of the not-for-profits, sometimes referred to as the "third" economic sector (Chapter 13). It is estimated that this sector represents 10 percent of the country's gross national product (GNP) (Hodgkinson and Weitzman 1986). More importantly, it is the sector most responsible for making our society kinder, gentler, more informed, and for improving the status of our health. The world of the not-for-profits can be described by focusing on the types of agencies/institutions, on their managements, and/or on the managerial function.

The third set of examples (Section 3) represents countertrade—an outgrowth of the ancient barter system. This form of commerce represents 30 percent of world trade and the World Bank (1986) estimates that trade involving some form of reciprocity will reach a 50-percent level by the year 2000 (Chapter 14). However, countertrade is also well established in the not-for-profit sector (Chapter 15) where institutions/agencies use it as a form of extending resource bases.

Each of the above three sets of examples represents a field that is relatively virgin from a management science point of view—yet each is unquestionably significant from a human endeavor point of view. Because of the inherent complexity of each subject area, the examples suggest the need for more than just a single taxonomy.

The last examples (Section 4) address consolidation of knowledge in two mature management science methodology areas: discounted cash flow analysis and mathematical programming.

In discounted cash flow analysis (Chapter 16), it was deemed necessary to create a general model and a taxonomy to go along with it. This was first presented in Reisman and Buffa (1962).

Finally, Chapter 17 attempts to unify a large subset of mathematical optimization methodologies.

REFERENCES

Blumstein, A. 1987. "The Current Missionary Role of OR/MS." *Operations Research* 35(5): 926–29

Hodgkinson, V. A., and M. S. Weitzman. 1986. *Dimensions of the Independent Sector: Statistical Profile*. 2nd ed. Washington, D.C.

Reisman, A., and E. S. Buffa. 1962. "A General Model for Investment Policy." *Management Science* 8(3): 304–10.

World Bank. 1986. *Annual Report*. Washington, D.C.: The Bank.

Section 1

Technology Transfer

Interest in the notion of technology transfer has been gaining momentum during the last two decades. Technology transfer, however, has different meanings to different people. It may indeed have a variety of definitions to any one individual. Chapter 10 discusses an attempt to define the field in terms of its *players* and to delineate all its facets in a manner that is parsimonious yet discriminating. In other words, it is an attempt to create a *classification*, or *taxonomy*, of technology transfer in terms of who the providers and the recipients of such transfers are.

Chapter 11 suggests a taxonomy of the various types of technology transfer *transactions*. The characteristics used for classification include the time factor, payment requirements if any, the nature of technology transferred, and its modalities. Actual cases of recent technology transfer transactions are used to test the descriptive and discriminating abilities of the proposed taxonomy as well as its parsimony.

One reason that the technology transfer literature has grown exponentially during the last twenty-five years is that a number of disparate disciplines have shown concern for the subject. As in most emerging fields, but especially this one, its literature is disjoint. Although a number of taxonomies have been proposed, most are by and for a specific discipline, for example, economics or sociology. Chapter 12 offers a synthesis, an integrative review, of the various taxonomic efforts while taking into account each of the streams of technology transfer knowledge.

Technology Transfer:
A Taxonomic View

INTRODUCTION

During the last two decades, the literature and the media have recorded a great deal of interest in the notion of technology transfer. Organizational units dedicated to technology transfer have mushroomed in each sector of the American economy. Most of the fifty states (i.e., the *public sector*) now have such units. *For-profit* corporations and/or firms dedicated to brokering technology have been around for some time. Many of the *not-for-profit* sector private universities now have people devoted to technology transfer. In fact, there are some interesting coalitions involving all three sectors. For instance, Case Western Reserve University, a private (not-for-profit) academic institution, uses (public) state of Ohio money to support a new (for-profit) enterprise incubator.

Because the phrase *technology transfer* has several meanings, this chapter attempts a taxonomic structuring of the subject. However, prior to discussing a taxonomy, it is helpful to review some common definitions of the two words comprising the phrase.

In another context (Chapter 8), technology was defined by *Webster's Seventh Collegiate Dictionary* as "the totality of the means employed to provide objects necessary for human sustenance and comfort." As mentioned in Chapter 8, Joseph P. Martino (1983, p. 1), in discussing *technological forecasting*, accepts this definition with a proviso that the notion of objects "include not only goods but services." Thus, "technology [here] will mean the tools, techniques, and procedures used to accomplish some desired human purpose; that is, technology is not restricted to hardware only but may include know-how and software." Martino goes on to emphasize further that not all technology is science based. Much of it is still an art based on practical experience.

The *American Heritage Dictionary* (p. 1363) defines *transfer* as (1) To convey or shift from one person or place to another, (2) To make over the possession or legal title of one to another.

Combining these definitions, one can then safely consider technology transfer to mean *the conveyance or shift of the tools, techniques, procedures, and/or the legal titles thereto, used to accomplish some desired human purpose.*

Technology transfers as defined above can take place between and among

- Scientific Disciplines
- Professions
- Industries
- Economic Sectors
- Geographic Regions
- Societies/Countries

DISCIPLINE-TO-DISCIPLINE TRANSFERS

The history of science and technology has recorded many major breakthroughs resulting from transfers of technology between two or more scientific disciplines. To mention but a few, Mendel's (1865) transfer of probabilistic notions forever changed the science of genetics; mathematical modeling in the 1950s and beyond has forever changed the study of biologic phenomena (Mostow 1975); and the merger of statistical mechanics and thermodynamics (Brillouin 1962; Shannon and Weaver 1963) has influenced information theory and vice versa. Similarly, epidemiologic/mathematical methods have affected the discipline of information science and/or the profession called library science (Goffman 1980).

As indicated in Chapter 2 (Reisman 1988), technology transfer between disciplines and/or professions represents one of the major strategies for doing creative research. Moreover, it is also a major strategy in creatively and relatively easily solving real-world problems (Reisman et al. 1982).

DISCIPLINE-TO-PROFESSION TRANSFERS

Artificial intelligence and expert systems are beginning to alter the way physicians learn and, in fact, do medical diagnosis (Barriga et al. 1990). Algorithmic structuring has greatly influenced the teaching and the practice of medical decision making (Clancey et al. 1984; Page and Fielding 1980; Congress of the U.S. 1979).

PROFESSION-TO-PROFESSION TRANSFERS

Engineering/simulation has greatly influenced pilot training for flight within and beyond the earth's atmosphere and the teaching of anesthesiology (Abrahamson 1967). Electric-circuit techniques have induced changes in the architectural design of heating, ventilating, and air conditioning (Buchberg et al. 1964), and also in the analysis of hydraulic transients in the design of systems used for generating electric power from both thermal (Taylor et al. 1961) and hydraulic sources of energy (Taylor et al. 1959). In fact, the last two are examples where early computer science was also invoked.

INDUSTRY-TO-INDUSTRY TRANSFERS

The computer industry, for example, has affected, and in fact wiped out, many professions. It has greatly affected both the theoretic base and the practice of management science. It has revolutionized the management of all economic sectors across many national boundaries. American industry is making a slow but very discernible progress in manufacturing, which is changing from labor-intensive and/or "hard-wired" automation to "flexible manufacturing" (Ayres 1988). Here, computers essentially control flexibly automated production cells. The fully automated production line, where management "turns the air conditioning system down" and "shuts the lights off," is more than science fiction.

The way this very book was typed in its various drafts and the way it will ultimately be published is greatly different from what it would have been like a decade ago—yet another example of industry-to-industry technology transfer.

In the context of this chapter, *industry* comprises all establishments, firms, companies, or institutions having a common output, be that a product or a service. Thus all universities, public and private, are considered the higher-education industry.

SECTOR-TO-SECTOR TRANSFERS

There is a private for-profit armaments industry and a government defense establishment. Weapons-systems research and development as well as manufacturing done in both sectors. Moreover, many not-for-profit universities do research under contract with agencies of the Department of Defense (DOD).

Weapons-systems technology is forever being transferred between the private-sector manufacturers and DOD "clients." DOD laboratories are engaged in basic research and development, the results of which are transferred to DOD contractors. In another example of intersector transfer, we can point to the National Aeronautics and Space Administration (NASA), which both serves and uses the DOD and other public and private vendors. Moreover, it has spun off much technology into the consumer market.

For the purpose of this taxonomy, the entire economy is subdivided into three sectors: for-profit, public or government, and not-for-profit. Thus universities fall into either the public or the not-for-profit domain. On the other hand, weapon-systems or armaments industry establishments can be found in any one of the three sectors. For example, the Harry Diamond Laboratory is owned and operated by the U.S. government, whereas the Jet Propulsion Laboratory was for many years owned and operated by the California Institute of Technology, a private, not-for profit institution.

REGION-TO-REGION TRANSFERS

During the decades of the 1960s and the 1970s we have seen much technology transfer from the "rust bowl" to the "sun belt," within the continental United States. On a global scale, much technology has been transferred from the West to the East. Japan, Taiwan, South Korea, and Singapore are among the more successful economies that have been thriving on U.S. and Western-European-developed technology.

COUNTRY-TO-COUNTRY TRANSFERS

The media, including many professional and trade publications, almost daily discuss technology transfers between countries. Institutions in Israel are seeking supercomputers from the United States, while the Russian Republic is looking for personal computer technology. Moreover, we find that postindustrial societies, such as the United States and Western European countries, are beneficiaries of technologies created in newer and less developed nations. The Israeli-developed and marketed system for computer-aided color composition (Scitex) has affected the printing trades in the publishing and textile industries worldwide. The U.S. Army and Navy have a number of Israeli-developed and private-sector built drones (pilotless aircraft). These were used effectively by the multinational forces during the Gulf War.

FURTHER ELABORATION ON PROFESSIONS

To complicate things a bit further, any one profession, such as engineering or medicine, may not be homogeneous in relation to technology transfer types.

Chapter 9 included a discussion of Russ Ackoff's (1987) three categories of professionals, that is, those who are *market-oriented, output-oriented*, and *input-oriented*.

Clearly, the three kinds of professionals differ in the types of technology they transfer *in* and the types they transfer *out*. Such transfers, moreover, do not follow any unidirected graph. In fact, the three types can well substitute for the more aggregated category called "professions" discussed throughout this chapter as shown in Figures 10.1, 10.2, 10.3, and 10.4.

THE TAXONOMY

The six entities—disciplines, professions, industries, sectors, regions, and countries—can be thought of as either origins or destinations (nodes) in a network representing potential technology transfers. Alternatively, as shown in Figure 10.1, they can comprise a six-dimensional matrix.

One could then find examples to fill most, if not all, of the cells of such a matrix. As indicated earlier, this matrix need not be directional in the sense that

Figure 10.1
Matrix of Pairwise Technology Transfers

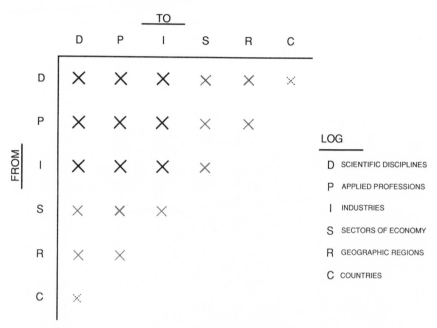

Figure 10.2
A Hierarchical View of Technology Transfers

TECHNOLOGY DOMICILES		
Primary	Secondary	Tertiary
DISCIPLINES PROFESSIONS INDUSTRIES	SECTORS REGIONS	COUNTRIES

Figure 10.3
The Universe of Technology Transfers: A Taxonomic View

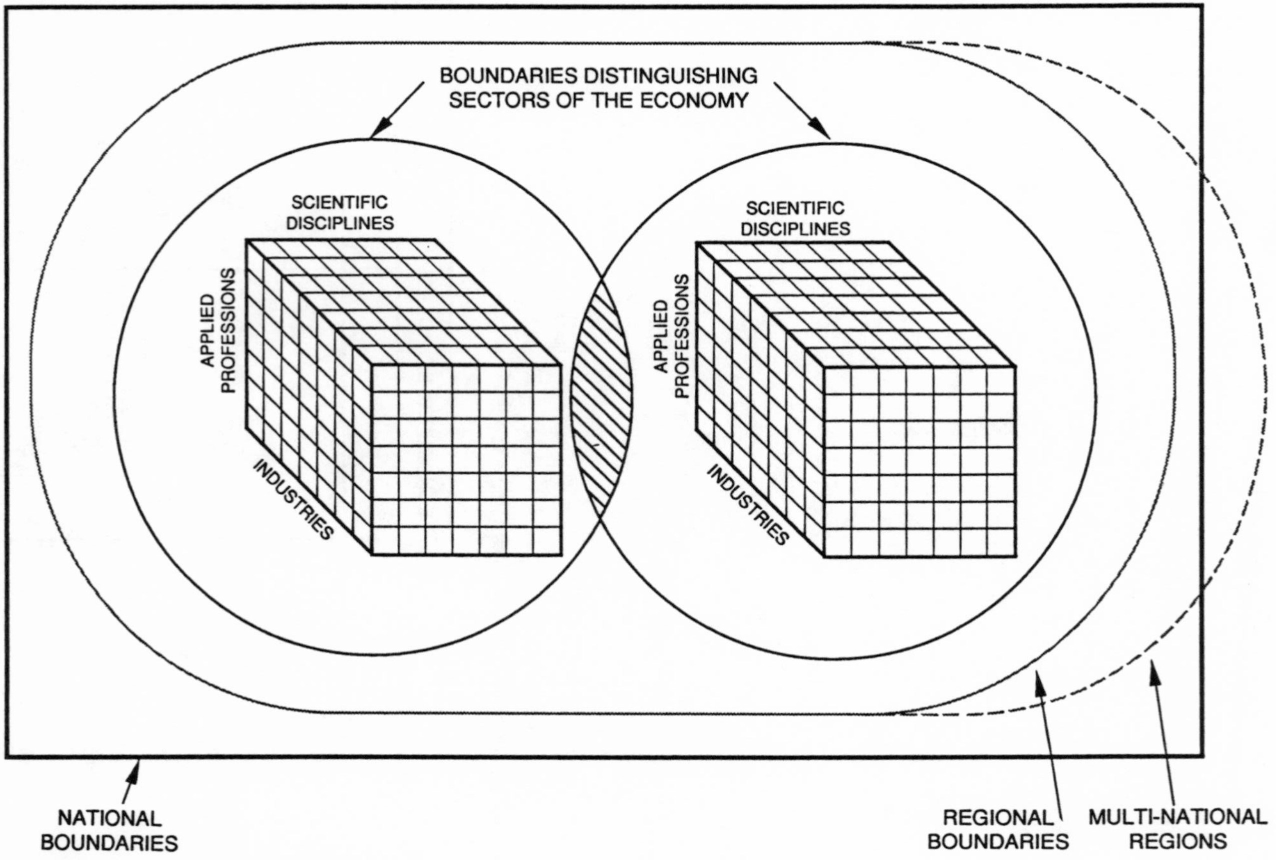

Figure 10.4
Delineation of Generically Different Types of Technology Transfers

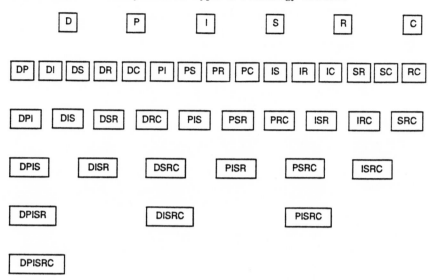

all transfers follow the usual and customary path from a scientific discipline to a profession to an industry and then ultimately across national lines to less-developed nations. The media have expended much effort telling us that Americans are living longer and that their health care costs per capita have been rising for many years at a rate twice that of general inflation. There are many reasons for both of the above phenomena, one of which is the transfer of technology. For example, the high-tech industries are creating new generations of more powerful and more costly imaging equipment, which in turn affects the way physicians practice medicine. Here is an industry affecting a profession. And that same industry is using many scientists of various disciplines and a number of different professionals to design, build, test, and market their equipment.

The transfer of technology may take place between any pair, any triplet, or any quadruplet of cells in the matrix discussed earlier. That is, university-based scientists from one country may influence government professionals and/or industrial professionals in another country. For example, *professors* Einstein and Fermi crossed both national and sector boundaries to influence *professional politicians* concerned with government policy in connection with the atomic bomb and subsequently atomic power.

These latter examples suggest the need to recognize that some of the nodes in the above mentioned network or descriptors in Figure 10.1 are different from the others. Thus, the disciplines, professions, or the industries are, for lack of a better word, the primary *domiciles* for any given technology. Transfers involving these nodes are depicted by the bold Xs in Figure 10.1.

Sectors, regions, and countries, on the other hand, represent secondary technology domicile descriptors. Hence the lesser boldness of the Xs in Figure 10.1 when involving these nodes. In fact, if regions are presumed to be geographic subsets of any one country, then one could argue that the country descriptor stands apart from the other two. Hence it is a third level, or a meta-descriptor, as shown in Figure 10.2, and is represented by the lightest of Xs in Figure 10.1. Putting it another way, sectors, regions, or countries typically do not create, own, or ultimately use any technologies; people and organizations/institutions do. These are all embedded in the sectors of the economy of a given region. The regions, as stated earlier, are a geographic portion of a country or transcend several countries. This latter form of delineating technology transfers is depicted in Figure 10.3.

Incidentally, the crossover area between sectors shown in Figure 10.3 allows for the possibility of institutions in one sector having operating divisions in another. A for-profit enterprise, such as a bookstore owned by a nonproprietary university, is a fairly typical example. The new enterprise incubator operated by a private university with public funds is another.

Thus, a given technology can fall into the province of one or a few professions and be otherwise universal if such *professionals* are found in many *industry groupings* that, in turn, can be located in all three *sectors* within all *regions* in all *countries*. The use of X-rays for medical diagnostics is, by now, quite universal. Its practitioners are physicians, dentists, podiatrists, and veterinarians having institutional affiliations in proprietary, in public, or community (not-for-profit) hospitals and clinics; in (for-profit) pharmaceutical companies; or in government- or university-based laboratories, worldwide. On the other hand, the more advanced generations of imaging technology may be found only in some of the more advanced countries and, in some cases, only in the major metropolitan areas.

Yet another way of classifying technology transfers is shown in Figure 10.4. The transfers designated by a single letter (top row) involve but one boundary crossing, the rest being the same. Specifically, the box containing D alone means that a transfer took place between two disciplines, and did *not* affect any professions. Moreover, this transaction took place within the same industry, the same sector, and the same region of the same country. The box containing only P delineates interprofessional transfers that do *not* involve any disciplines and take place within a given industry, sector, region and country. There are six such generically different transfers.

The next row in Figure 10.4 shows fifteen generically different transfers involving all combinations of letter descriptors taken two at a time. Thus the first box (DP) delineates a transfer involving a discipline and a profession, but remaining within the *same* industry, sector, region, and country. Clearly, the most general case of technology transfer is represented by the box depicted by DPISRC.

Although Figure 10.4 shows forty-one distinctly different transfer types, it is not sufficiently discriminating in the sense that it does not indicate the direction of the transfer. It presumes that transfer D to P or DP is identical to a transfer from P to D or PD and so forth. In order to explicitly delineate the directionality of a transfer as well, one would have to go beyond showing just the *combinations* of the letter symbols taken one, two, three, four, five, and six at a time as we have done. One would need to also show each of the respective permutations. This would increase the number of generically different possibilities to a total of 1,320.

At this time, it does not appear that such a complication of the taxonomy is justified. However, what must be explicitly recognized is the fact that not all transfers are binary in the sense that there is but one "from" and one "to" node. If it is necessary to depict transfers involving multiple nodes (i.e., two or more disciplines, professions, industries, sectors, regions, and/or countries) one can simply subscript the respective descriptor with the appropriate number. Specifically, DP_2 means that a single discipline provided technology to two different professions. A development in solid-state physics may, for example, affect both electrical and computer engineering. However, in light of the directional discussion above, this could also mean that two different professions affected a single discipline. An example of such a case might involve electrical and computer engineering efforts resulting in a new instrument affecting experiments in biology. Unfortunately it could also mean that a single profession transferred technology to both another profession and a discipline.

CONCLUDING REMARKS

Mapping the universe of technology transfers would not be complete without at least mentioning the dichotomy between transfers that are legal, ethical, and moral and those that fall short of any of the above. This opens up the entire area of patent and copyright laws, international and industrial intelligence and counterintelligence, and the various caveats and admonitions addressing issues of ethics, as well as the various technologies to *prevent* unauthorized transfers.

NOTE

This chapter is based on a paper of the same name that appeared in the *Journal of Technology Transfer*, 14(3&4): 31–36, 1989.

REFERENCES

Abrahamson, S. 1967. "A Computer Based Patient Simulator for Anesthesiologists." In *Engineering: A Look Inward and a Reach Outward, Proceedings of a Speaker Series*, edited by A. Reisman. College of Applied Science & Engineering, University of Wisconsin-Milwaukee, Summer.

Ackoff, R. 1987. "OR: A Post Mortem." *Operations Research* 35(3): 471–74.

American Heritage Dictionary of the English Language. 1981. Wm. Morris, editor-in-chief Boston: Houghton Mifflin Co.

Ayres, R. U. 1988. "Future Trends in Factory Automation." *Manufacturing Review* 1(2): 93–103.

Barriga, R. M., E. P. Vanek, K. H. Mann, and A. Reisman. 1990. "Developing a Tutoring Module for Presentation of Computerized Patient Management Problems." *Socio-Economic Planning Sciences* 24(4): 273–83.

Brillouin, L. 1962. *Science and Information Theory.* New York: Academic Press Inc.

Buchberg, H., B. Bussell, and A. Reisman. 1964. "On the Determinations of Optimal Thermal Enclosures." *International Journal of Biometeorology* 8(2): 103–11.

Clancey, W. J., E. H. Shortliffe, and B. G. Buchanan. 1984. "Intelligent Computer-aided Instruction for Medical Diagnosis." In *Readings in Medical Artificial Intelligence: The First Decade,* edited by E. H. Shortliffe and W. J. Clancey. Reading, Mass.: Addison-Wesley Publishing Co.

Congress of the United States, Office of Technology Assessment. 1979. "Computer Technology in Medical Education and Assessment: Background Report." Washington, D.C.

Goffman, W. 1980. *Scientific Information Systems and the Principle of Selectivity.* New York: Praeger Publishers.

Martino, Joseph P. 1983. *Technological Forecasting for Decision Making.* 2nd ed. New York: North-Holland Publishers.

Mendel, G. 1865. "Experiments in Plant-Hybridization (translation)." In *Classic Papers in Genetics,* edited by J. A. Peters. Englewood Cliffs, N.J.: Prentice-Hall.

Mostow, G. D., ed. 1975. *Mathematical Models for Cell Rearrangement.* New Haven and London: Yale University Press.

Page, G. G., and D. W. Fielding. 1980. "Performance on PMPs and Performance in Practice: Are They Related?" *Journal of Medical Education* 5(6): 529–37.

Reisman, A. 1988. "On Alternative Strategies for Doing Research in the Management and Social Sciences." *IEEE Transaction on Engineering Management* 35(4): 215–20.

Reisman, A., S. Kotha, L. Gonzaga, B. Kidd, and T. Murray. 1982. "IE's Find Ways to Improve Throughput, Worker Morale on a Firm's Wrap-Line." *Industrial Engineering* 14(9): 70–80.

Shannon, C. E., and W. Weaver. 1963. *The Mathematical Theory of Communication.* Urbana, Ill.: University of Illinois Press.

Taylor, E. H., A. Reisman, E. C. Deland, and H. H. Baudistel. 1961. "Analog Computer Solution of a Complex Transient-Hydraulic Problem in the Power Industry." *Transactions of the American Society of Mechanical Engineers, Journal of Basic Engineering* 83(Series D, No. 3): 433–44.

Taylor, E. H., A. Reisman, and J. W. Ward. 1959. "Unsteady Flow in Conduits with Simple Surge Tanks." *Proceedings of the American Society of Civil Engineers,* 85(HY2): 1–11.

Technology Transfer Transactions: A Taxonomic Perspective

INTRODUCTION

Knowledge concerning the transfer of technology is growing rapidly. As is often the case in an emerging area of discipline, its descriptive as well as normative theories and any available data are at best fragmented and disjointed (Reddy and Zhao 1990). As of the time of this writing it is difficult to pinpoint a general model or structure for the field. People thus far have merely strung information and insight on an invisible thread and hoped that the thread would continue to hold (Robinson 1988). This is especially so because the subject of technology transfer (TT), as discussed in greater detail in Chapter 12, has been of concern to several of the basic social science disciplines, (e.g., economics, sociology, anthropology, etc.) and to several major professions (such as engineering, management, law, etc.). Moreover, as implied in Chapter 10, it is of concern to policy makers in the public, private, and the not-for-profit sectors. Moreover, it is of concern to decision makers at the company or institution, the community, the region, and the nation-state levels. Lastly, it is of concern to each of the multinational (regional) economic communities. Some, such as the European Economic Community (EEC), are established and thriving. Some, like the Caribbean Community CARICOM, are emerging while others like the former Communist Economic block COMECON have fallen apart.

This chapter is the second in a series attempting to pull together our knowledge of TT. Chapter 10 presented a number of taxonomic approaches classifying the "from's" and the "to's," that is, the sources and the end-destinations of the various kinds of TTs (Reisman 1990). The third attempts to classify the perceived role of TT, its taxonomic characteristic and perspectives as viewed by each of the major social science disciplines concerned with the subject (Zhao and Reisman 1990). Herein we suggest a taxonomy of the various types of TT transactions along the lines delineated in Reisman (1987).

On the one hand, this taxonomy is much narrower than all others in the TT literature. It focuses on the types of transactions involved in the broad field of TT. On the other hand, it attempts to be much broader in scope and has a wider variety of potential uses/objectives than any of the other existing taxonomies. Primarily, it is designed to serve as an aid for describing the breadth of practice. It is intended for corporate executives to formulate and implement technology-driven strategies and for educators to present the subject matter in a comprehensive yet comprehendible manner. The novice can thus grasp more easily the wide spectrum of transactions possible in TT. At the risk of belaboring a cliché, this facilitates seeing the "big-picture," the "forest," while knowing the exact size, shape, color, texture, and so forth of any specific tree.

Moreover, the taxonomy can facilitate marketing of TT management curricula, courses, or workshops through its efficient description of the diversity of transactions types and the key issues that need to be addressed in each. It can be used by current corporate or institutional managers and/or trustees to develop strategies for institutional growth/expansion, mergers, acquisitions, and/or divestitures. It can be used as a vehicle for collecting data to describe the profile or mix of TT practices in and/or by any one enterprise, community, state, or region for purposes of

- Stating job creation and/or employment levels
- Stating wealth generation
- Stating dollar expenditures
- Justifying fund raising
- Setting priorities for
  —Public funds allocation
  —Philanthropic giving
  —Philanthropic fund raising
- Identifying voids in services provided

If such data are compiled in a uniform manner across companies/institutions in a given industry, community, and/or region, researchers, planners, policy analysts, and policy makers would have a better "grounding" for their efforts.

Lastly, vendors can use the taxonomy and the data discussed above for developing marketing strategies.

Technology is defined as "the tools, techniques, and procedures used to accomplish some desired human purpose" (Martino 1983, p. 1). Moreover, technology is assumed "to involve know-how and software as well as hardware." Technology transfer is defined as the conveyance or shift of the tools, techniques, procedures, and/or the legal titles thereto, used to accomplish some desired human purpose. That generic definition of technology transfer will serve as a basis for this chapter as well. Note, however, that in this chapter we are not concerned with what is sometimes referred to as pure science and the transfer of knowledge that is generated thereby. We shall focus on applied science, which is assumed to include research, development, and/or engineering, manufacturing, management, and service.

As indicated earlier, the notions of technology and of technology transfer were recently reviewed from the vantage point of each of several social sciences. Specifically, Zhao and Reisman (1990) reviewed both concepts from the view of the literatures of economics, sociology, anthropology, and that of management. This chapter leans more heavily on the definition used within the literature of management. However, because the word transaction popularly implies considerations of money and/or cost, this chapter shall provide and use a more general definition of the word. Specifically, *Webster's New International Dictionary, Unabridged Second Edition*, defines the word transaction as "an action or activity involving two parties or two things mutually affecting or reciprocally influencing one another." For the purposes of the discussion that follows this definition will be modified as follows. A transaction is an action or activity involving two or more parties or two or more things mutually or unidirectionally affecting or influencing one or the other.

In the technology transfer literature, transaction is generally defined as a process in which at least two parties are interacting with the objective of consummating some exchange of tangible or intangible properties and/or of services. Because of its importance, the transaction element has occupied the bulk of the TT researcher's time (Reddy and Zhao 1990).

Having defined TT and TT transactions, we now need to identify the characteristics or dimensions that can be used to describe and to classify TT transactions. Among these might be the time duration that is involved. Thus, a single transaction may be consummated at once, such as one-time purchases of technology (Lenac and Helena 1984). Alternatively, it may be a long-term relationship between the various parties. The latter might be found in cases involving joint ventures.

This dimension is important for technology transfer transactions because it usually implies something about the nature of the technology transferred, the transactional relationship between the responsibility of each party, the strategy and capability of transferor and transferee, the influence of the third parties, and so forth.

Second, we have to consider whether or not there are any financial ramifications to the transaction. That is, a number of transactions take place at zero cost to either the transferor or the transferee (Arrow 1969; Johnson 1970). Such is the case in professional exchanges at conventions, conferences, conversations, correspondence, or through journal articles. There may, however, be financial ramifications (Rosenberg and Frischtak 1985). Such is the case in sales of hardware and/or intellectual property on a one-time basis or as part of a long-time relationship as in a joint venture. Moreover, financial considerations should not, or need not, be limited to monetary formats. These could include, in whole or in part, in-kind transfers of goods and/or services. That is, the transaction involves a form of commerce known as barter or more broadly as countertrade (Reisman et al. 1988, 1989). The various formats of countertrade practice are classified in Chapter 14.

Since technology transfer may or may not involve financial ramifications, many researchers question the appropriateness of the term "transfer." For example, Vaitsos (1975) laments the inappropriateness from a commercial perspective. He argues that transfer connotes the free, noncommercial movement of something from one location or possessor to another. In the business world, however, TT usually implies a "sale" of some technology. For this reason the term "commercialization of technology" has been argued to be generally more appropriate (e.g., Farrell 1979).

The significance of this dimension lies in its relevance to the issues in the technology transfer research and practice such as pricing of technology transfer, concentration of technology, technology transfer cost of resource requirements, determinants of transfer costs, technology transfer payment, conflict and code of conduct in international technology transfer, and the effectiveness of the transfer.

It is necessary to distinguish between transfers of proprietary technology from that which falls in the public domain (transfers of nonproprietary technology). Thus, the nature of the technology transfer dimension distinguishes between the two types.

Lastly, an important characteristic describing a TT transaction is the modality involved. This could be separated into two primary categories. One of these is an external transfer that is from one entity (organization) to another (Robinson 1988). The other could be internal transfer (Kroner 1980). Internal transfers are typically among different units of an organization. In the former category we could have the transaction take place in the form of a joint venture; in the form of licensing or cross-licensing; and in the form of cooperation agreements, sales, publications, conferences, visitors, and/or work study. In the case of internal transfers, different units of a particular organization may form an internal joint venture (Shortell and Zajac 1988), license one another, cross-license one another, or simply exchange information.

The modality of technology transfer as a subject has generated considerable interest. Issues related to this dimension include choice of modality, determinants of transfer mode, effectiveness of transfer, transfer costs, pricing of technology, multinational companies, firms in developing countries, and so on.

VALIDATION OF THE TAXONOMY

In this section we will state a number of TT examples and classify each on the basis of the above mentioned dimensions. The vehicle for doing this is shown in Figure 11.1. This figure encapsulates all of the possible combinations of dimensions in the form of a matrix where the cells that are meaningful are

Figure 11.1
Taxonomy of Technology Transfer Transactions

		Modalities										
		External Transfer (E)						Internal Transfer (I)				
		Info Exch. i	Sales s	Co-op Agrt. c	A.L. Licens. a	Franch. f	Joint Venture j	Info. Exch. i	Co-op Agrt. c	A.L. Licens. a	Internal Joint-V. j	W.O. Subsid. w
Time Frame	t	1.1	2.1	–	4.1	–	–	7.1	8.1	9.1	–	–
	T	1.2	–	3.2	4.2	5.2	6.2	7.2	8.2	9.2	10.2	11.2
Payment Requirement	p	1.3	–	3.3	–	–	6.3	7.3	8.3	9.3	10.3	11.3
	P	–	2.4	3.4	4.4	5.4	6.4	–	8.4	9.4	10.4	11.4
Nature of T.T.	n	1.5	2.5	3.5	–	5.5	6.5	7.5	8.5	9.5	10.5	11.5
	N	–	2.6	3.6	4.6	5.6	6.6	–	8.6	9.6	10.6	11.6

N - Proprietary
n - Nonproprietary
P - Payment
p - No Payment
T - Long Term
t - Short Term

i - Information Exchange
s - Sales
c - Cooperative Agreement
a - Arm's Length Joint Venture
f - Franchising
j - Joint Venture
w - Wholly Owned Subsidiary

numbered. The cell numbers that, in turn, are relevant to classifying each example appear in parentheses following the example's description.

External Transfers

1. Information Exchange

   Programs: Sabbaticals, Scholarship Programs such as the Fulbright awards, work-study arrangements, internship, etc. (1.2, 1.3, 1.5)[1]

Conferences and Symposia: The IEEE International Engineering Management Conferences (1.1, 1.3, 1.5)

Technical Correspondence: Memoranda, reports (1.1, 1.3, 1.5)

Free Technical Services: Consultation (1.1, 1.3, 1.5), training (1.2, 1.3, 1.5)

Professional Journal Publications: *Management Science, The Journal of Engineering and Technology Management*, etc. (1.1, 1.3, 1.5)

2. Sales

Sales of Equipment and/or Intellectual Properties: A single piece of equipment or an entire system such as a factory, turn-key projects, etc., a formula, new designs, drawings, blueprints, procedures, market surveys, demographic statistics (2.1, 2.4, 2.5 or 2.6)

Sales of Services: Consulting assistance, user manuals, equipment maintenance, etc. (2.1, 2.4, 2.5 or 2.6)

3. Cooperative Agreement

Co-production: The GE (U.S.)–SNECMA, (French) collaboration in the aerospace industry (3.2, 3.3, 3.6) (Robinson 1988)

Co-research

Co-design

4. Arm's Length Licensing

Licensing: Conveyance of manuals, blueprints, design drawings or data (4.3, 4.4, 4.6); provision of technical and managerial assistance (4.2, 4.4, 4.6)

Cross Licensing: (same as above)

5. Franchising

McDonald's hamburgers in U.S.S.R., P.R.C., etc.; Holiday Inn Hotels in United States (5.2, 5.4, 5.5)

6. Joint Venture

Equity Joint Venture: Maruyasu Industries (Japan)–Curtis Products (U.S.) joint venture in the automobile industry (6.2, 6.3, 6.6) (Tyebjee 1988)

Contractual Joint Venture: AMC (U.S.)–Beijing (China) automotive industry joint venture (6.2, 6.4, 6.6) (Mann 1989)

Internal Transfers

7. Internal Information Exchange

Meetings: Technical meetings, managerial meetings (7.1, 7.3, 7.5)

Correspondence: Memoranda, reports (7.1, 7.3, 7.5)

Publications: Newsletters (7.1, 7.3, 7.5)

8. Cooperative Agreement

(Similar situations as in 3)

9. Arm's Length Licensing

(Similar situations as in 4)

10. Internal Joint Venture

   Equity joint ventures between divisions (10.2, 10.3, 10.6)

11. Wholly Owned Subsidiary

   IBM's R&D units in Japan (11.2, 11.3, 11.6) (Robinson 1988)

The examples listed under each modality are clearly not exhaustive.

CONCLUDING REMARKS

Clearly, the dimensions we have identified may not ultimately be the exhaustive set describing TT transactions. However, as a first cut it is a fairly complete set of transaction/descriptors as shown through a set of real examples classified using a taxonomy based on the above dimensions.

NOTES

This chapter is based on the paper "A Taxonomy of Technology Transfer Transaction Types," by Arnold Reisman and Liming Zhao, *Journal of Technology Transfer*, Vol. 16, no. 2, Spring 1991.

1. The numbers in the parentheses refer to the cells in Figure 11.1 where the situations or examples fit.

REFERENCES

Arrow, K. 1969. "Classificatory Notes on the Production and Transmission of Technological Knowledge." *American Economic Review, Papers and Proceedings*.

Farrell, T. M. A. 1979. "A Tale of Two Issues: Nationalization, The Transfer of Technology and the Petroleum Multinationals in Trinidad Tobago." *Social and Economic Studies*, March: 234–81.

Johnson, H. G. 1970. "The Efficiency and Welfare Implications of the International Corporation." In *International Corporation*, edited by C. Kindle-Berger, 35–36. Cambridge, Mass.: MIT Press.

Kroner, M. 1980. "U.S. International Transactions in Royalties and Fees: 1967–1978." *Survey of Current Business*, January: 29–35.

Mann, J. 1989. *Beijing Jeep*. New York: Simon and Schuster.

Reddy, N. M., and L. Zhao. 1990. "International Technology Transfer: A Review." *Research Policy* 19: 285–307.

Reisman, A. 1971. *Managerial and Engineering Economics*. Boston, Mass.: Allyn and Bacon Publishing Company of Boston.

——— 1987. "Expansion of Knowledge Via Consolidation of Knowledge." Proceedings ISMIS-87, Second International Symposium on Methodologies for Intelligent Systems, ORNL–6417, Oak Ridge National Laboratory.

——— 1989. "Technology Transfer: A Taxonomic View" *Journal of Technology Transfer* 14(3&4, Summer-Fall): 31–36.

Reisman, A., R. Aggarwal, and D. C. Fuh. 1989. "Seeking Out Profitable Countertrade Opportunities." *Industrial Marketing Management* 18: 65–72.

Reisman, A., D. C. Fuh, and G. Li. 1988. "Achieving an Advantage With Countertrade." *Industrial Marketing Management* 17:55–63.

Robinson, R. 1988. *The International Transfer of Technology: Theory, Issues and Practices*. Cambridge, Mass.: Ballinger Publishing Co.

Rosenberg, N., and C. Frischtak. 1985. "Preface." In *International Technology Transfer*: Concepts, Measures, and Comparisons, edited by N. Rosenberg and C. Frischtak, VII-XVII. New York: Praeger Publishing Co.

Shortell, S. M., and E. J. Zajac. 1988. "Internal Corporate Joint Ventures: Development Processes and Performance Outcomes." *Strategic Management Journal*. 9: 527–42.

Tyebjee, T. T. 1988. "A Typology of Joint Venture: Japanese Strategies in the United States." *California Management Review*, Fall: 75–86.

Vaitsos, C. V. 1975. "The Process of Commercialization of Technology in the Andean Pact." In *International Firms and Modern Imperialism*, edited by H. Radice. Penguin Press, Harmondsworth.

Zhao, L., and A. Reisman. 1991. "Toward Meta Research on Technology Transfer." Forthcoming In *IEEE Transactions on Engineering Management*.

Toward Meta-Research on Technology Transfer

INTRODUCTION

Technology transfer (TT) has been used by many a firm to enhance its competitive advantage (Baughn and Osborne 1989). As indicated in Chapter 10 it has also been used as a strategy for enhancing the competitive position of an entire industry, a region, and indeed, of an entire nation (Reisman 1989). It has been the means toward economic progress, social development, quality of life and culture, and even of value systems (Reddy and Zhao 1990). It is therefore no wonder that studies of technology transfer have attracted increasing interest in the media and in the academic literature during the last three decades. In their respective literatures, various aspects of TT have been addressed by economists, sociologists, anthropologists, engineers, and both the behavioral and the quantitative management theorists. However, the very definition of TT differs among the various approaches and certainly across the many disciplines addressing this subject. Moreover, its scope has rarely been delineated or systematically analyzed. As discussed later in this chapter, the existing literature has recorded a variety of taxonomies. Yet, currently TT can be understood only in a limited way from a strict disciplinary framework such as those prevailing in each of the social sciences. Because of the multidisciplinary nature of TT, a meta (cross disciplinary) approach is needed to study the subject of TT. Recently one of the authors of a paper, on which this chapter is based, collaborated in an extensive review of TT literature (Reddy and Zhao 1990) as viewed from different perspectives by some disciplines. Chapter 10 suggests a generic taxonomy framework for TT (Reisman 1990), and Chapter 11 provides a taxonomy of the various types of transactions encountered in TT. This chapter offers a synthesis of TT taxonomies transcending all of the disciplinary approaches by including each into its design.

This synthesis framework, incorporating interdisciplinary dimensions, at-

tempts to be much broader in scope and has a wider variety of potential uses/
objectives than any currently known taxonomy of TT. Primarily, it is designed
to serve as a framework for describing and analyzing this field of knowledge so
as to further our understanding of TT at both the conceptual and the operational
levels. It is intended for the researcher who chooses to study TT in an interdisciplinary manner. It is intended to facilitate the educator who wishes to present
the subject matter in a comprehensive yet comprehendible manner. In general,
it allows us to identify the wide spectra of TT practices and of TT-related theory
and findings. As do most taxonomic contributions, it facilitates seeing the "big
picture," the "forest," while knowing the exact size, shape, color, and texture
of any specific tree.

It can aid corporate managers and/or directors in developing TT strategies for
growth/expansion, mergers, aquistitions, and/or divestitures. Practitioners can
use this taxonomy to pinpoint the market niche, the structural, operational, and
the like characteristic profile of his or her interest in TT and to do so in the
context of the field at large. It can be used by policy makers to formulate
meaningful TT and/or TT policies. The taxonomy can facilitate marketing of
TT curricula through its efficient description of the field's diversity, richness,
importance, and relevance, and the functions therein that need to be understood
and managed. It can be used as an organizing framework in collecting and/or
collating TT related data at the company/institution, region, economic sector,
and/or national levels for purposes of

- Doing meta-research in the subject of TT
  —Adoption of an integrative approach
  —Adoption of an interdisciplinary approach
  —Development of new concepts
- Describing the extent of the practice
  —By design
  —By diffusion
- Pinpointing voids/weaknesses in transfer
  —Mechanisms
  —Institutions
  —Policies
- Pinpointing "ports of opportunity"
  —To communities/states/regions/countries
  —To companies
  —To research institutions
  —To professions
  —To scientific disciplines
  —To individual researchers

DISCUSSION

Discussion of technology transfer is hampered by the difficulties posed in defining the concept of technology. TT studies define the term technology differently, depending on the disciplinary perspective of the author. This creates confusion (Afriqie 1988). The way technology is viewed influences the definition and hence any taxonomy of TT in general.

Technology is an inescapable feature of social existence. However, social science, to date, seems to lack an appropriate social sciences framework for dealing with technology (Long 1979).

The next section reviews, albeit succinctly, the role, definition, and any existing taxonomies of technology as viewed by each of the major disciplines and professions concerned with TT.

ROLE, DEFINITIONS, AND TAXONOMIES OF TECHNOLOGY: DISCIPLINARY PERSPECTIVES

Economics Discipline

Role of Technology. The importance of technology at macroeconomic and microeconomic levels is well established. Economists view technology as a major input requirement for economic development. Adam Smith was one of the first to examine manufacturing technology systematically in 1776. In the early works of Marx (1874) and Schumpeter (1928), technology was seen to be at the center of growth. Powerful evidence or confirmation of the impact of technical change on the economy is provided by Abramovitz (1956) and Solow (1957). The rich literature on technological change (Hahn and Matthews 1969; Mansfield 1968; Denison 1974; Rosenberg 1986; among others) has attempted to address technology's role in productivity change and economic development.

In their conceptual studies of TT, many economists treat technology as exogenous (e.g., Rodriguez 1975; Chipman 1982; McCulloch and Yellen 1982; Koizumi and Kopecky 1977; Findlay 1978; and Krugman 1979) in their models. Other theorists, however, view technology as endogenous (see, e.g., Dudley 1974; Feenstra and Judd 1982; Pugel 1982; Findlay 1978). Different treatments of technology result in different economic models and hence different conclusions.

Definition of Technology. To economists, a technology consists of a body of generic knowledge, in the form of generalizations about how things work, key variables influencing performance, the nature of currently binding constraints and approaches to pushing these back, widely applicable problem-solving heuristics, and the like. Dosi (1988) calls these packages of generic knowledge "technological paradigms."

The *received theory* school of thought conceives of technology as information necessary to design and produce a given good by any number of alternative methods. This concept of technology as information holds that technology is generally applicable and easy to reproduce and reuse (Arrow 1962) and that firms can produce and use innovations mainly by dipping freely into a general stock or pool of technological knowledge (Arrow 1969; Johnson 1970). However, a majority of economists do not treat technology as a free good in their research (e.g., Mansfield 1975; Teece 1977).

Taxonomy of Technology. Useful taxonomies are provided in Mansfield (1975), who uses the "embodied" versus "disembodied" classification (in some studies the bundled versus unbundled classification is used instead). Madeuf (1984) elaborates this classification as capital embodied, human embodied, and disembodied technology. In the economic literature, technology is also characterized as product versus process technology. Hall and Johnson (1970) distinguish not only among "product-embodied," "process-embodied," and "person-embodied" technology but also among "general technology" (information common to an industry or trade), "system-specific technology" (information concerning the manufacture of a certain item or product that any manufacturer of the item or product would obtain), and "firm-specific" technology (information that is specific to a particular firm's experience and activities, but that cannot be attributed to any specific item the firm produces). The literature of economics has a traditional tendency to classify technology in dichotomous terms such as appropriate versus inappropriate (from the transferee's and host country's perspective) (Brown 1977; Dasgupta 1979), labor-intensive versus capital-intensive (from the nature of technology perspective) (Lall and Streeten 1977; Vaitsos 1976), and small-scale versus large-scale (from the economic scale perspective).

Sociology Discipline

Definition of Technology. Many sociologists tend to make distinctions between innovation and technology. They define an innovation as an idea, practice, or object that is perceived as new by an individual or other unit of adoption (Rogers 1983). Technology is defined as design for instrumental action that reduces the uncertainty in the cause-effect relationships involved in achieving a desired outcome (Rogers 1983). Since most new ideas are technological innovations, sociologists often use innovation and technology as synonyms (Rogers 1983).

Role of Technology. According to sociologists, an innovation presents an individual or an organization with a new alternative or alternatives, with new means of solving problems. Although sociologists agree that innovations or new technologies play an important role in social living, they argue that all innovations are not necessarily desirable, and that some innovation may be desirable for one adopter in one situation but undesirable for another protential adopter in a different situation.

Taxonomy of Technology. Sociologists argue that any transfer of technology is likely to hasten the development of a modern consciousness. Modernization refers to the transfer of attitudes on both a national and individual level (Lerner 1958; Riesman 1952; Rogers 1969). Furthermore, the transfer of technology and the transfer of modern consciousness usually proceed simultaneously, and often unintentionally. Sociologists emphasize the social aspects of technology transfer. Against this background, Chatterjee and Ireys (1981) introduce the concept of *social technology* as opposed to the technology developed from the natural and other nonsocial sciences. Social technologies are means of manipulating the social environment; whereas natural and biomedical technologies are means to manipulate the natural or other nonsocial environment.

Anthropology Discipline

Role of Technology. Anthropologists' work focuses on culture (Foster 1962). Naturally, they perceive the role of technology in the context of cultural evolution (Merrill 1972). Technology is viewed as one of the prime movers for the cultural evolution (Service 1971) or as a factor that, along with others, affects the alternatives available in a society (Merrill 1972). Technology is inert and passive. By itself it does nothing. Only when people use a technology in some way does it have an impact on human life. Therefore, they argue that we cannot say anything about the actual effects connected with a particular technology until we understand why and what people do with it.

Definition of Technology. According to anthropologists, technologies are means for doing things (Merrill 1972). In the anthropological sense, technology is a cultural system concerned with the relationship between humans and their natural environment (Terpstra and David 1985). Unlike economists, anthropologists perceive technology as more specific, concrete, and practical. Therefore, anthropologists do not study technology in general; they study specific, individual technologies.

Anthropologists are generally not concerned with the economic cost of technology. They view technologies as existing and available.

Taxonomy of Technology. Derived from the anthropologist's definition of technology, an anthropological taxonomy of technology is rather functional. Terms like medical, educational, food, community development, and agricultural technology are widely used in their studies.

Management Discipline

Role of Technology. In management research, technology has been suggested as a strategic asset (Drucker 1985; Froham 1985; O'Connell and Zimmerman 1979). Management theorists (Porter 1985; Pappas 1984; Ketteringham and White 1984; Harris, Shaw, and Sommers 1984) treat technology as one of the paramount forces in competitive strategy. Technology can actually alter the structure of an industry (Willard and Cooper 1985) and is important because it affects the industry's competitive advantage (Porter 1985, p. 105).

Definition of Technology. Management theorists conceive of technology as a firm-specific information concerning the characteristics and performance properties of the production process and of the product design. The production process or operations technology is embodied in the equipment or the means to produce a specific good. The product design or product technology, on the other hand, is that which is manifested in the finished product. Technology, hence, is mainly differentiated knowledge about specific applications, tacit and often uncodified, and largely cumulative within firms (Pavitt 1985). Because of this, technology is included among the firm's "intangibles" (Caves 1982) or "firm-specific" assets (Dunning 1981). These are assets that form the basis of a firm's competitiveness, to be generally released only under special conditions.

Taxonomy of Technology. In the management field, TT researchers frequently use those taxonomies of technology given by the economists. In addition, Robock (1980) and Chudson (1971) separate technology as product designs, production techniques, and managerial functions. Madeuf (1984) draws a distinction between technology "alienated" by property rights (patents) or secrecy and know-how that could not be transferred without an effective participation of the firm holding it. The National Science Foundation (1971) decomposes technology as "research," "development," and "engineering." From the operational perspective, in many studies, technology is decomposed into research and development (R&D), engineering, and manufacturing. Robinson (1988) makes a further decomposition of technology: user technology (skill to use product), product adaptive technology (skill to adapt), manufacturing technology (skill to replicate), design modification (skill to modify product and/or process), and design technology (skill to design new products and/or processes). Management researchers have included management expertise into the domain of technology transfer. Therefore, the term *management technology*, the technology of getting results through organization, has been used in the literature (Deihl 1987; Glinow and Teagarden 1988; Merrifield 1988). A summary of the above mentioned taxonomies is shown in Table 12.1.

ROLE, DEFINITIONS, AND TAXONOMIES OF TECHNOLOGY TRANSFER: DISCIPLINARY PERSPECTIVE

The phrase *technology transfer* was originally introduced by economists. It has been extensively used in the literatures because of its great relevance to many social science disciplines. Using the meta- approach, this section reviews and examines the various taxonomies of TT.

Economics Discipline

Role of Technology Transfer. Economists have long recognized that the transfer of technology is at the heart of the process of economic growth, and that the

Table 12.1
Technology: A Synthesis of Taxonomies

Discipline	Perceived Role of T	Taxonomic Distinctions	Perspective taken within Discipline	Author(s)
Economics	Major input requirement for economic growth	Embodied T Disembodied T (Bundled T Unbundled T)	Public good vs. Private good	Mansfield [1975]
		Capital embodied T Human embodied T Disembodied T	Operational definition	Madeuf [1984]
		Product embodied T Process embodied T Person embodied T	Operational	Hall & Johnson [1970]
		General T System specific T Firm specific T	Ownership	Hall & Johnson [1970]
		Appropriate T Inappropriate T	Transferee/ Host country	Brown [1977] Dasgupta [1979]
		Labor-intensive T Capital-intensive T	Characteristic of T	Lall & Streeten [1977]
		Small-scale T Large-scale T	Economic scale	Vaitsos [1976]
Sociology	Problem solving	Technological innovation Non-Technological innovation	Nature of innovation	Rogers [1983]
		T derived from the natural and other non-social sciences Social T	Nature of TT	Chatterjee & Ireys [1981]
Anthro- pology	One of the prime movers for cultural evolution	Medical innovation Educational innovation Food innovation Agricultural innovation Community development etc.	Functional	Foster [1962]

Table 12.1 (continued)

Discipline	Perceived Role of T	Taxonomic Distinctions	Perspective taken within Discipline	Author(s)
Management	Strategic asset	In addition to economic taxonomies:		
		Product designs Production techniques Managerial functions	Nature of T	Robock [1980] Chudson [1971]
		Alienated T Non-alienated T	Property right	Madeuf [1984]
		Management T Technological T	Nature of T	Deihl [1987] Glinow & Teagarden [1988]
		Research T Development T Engineering T	Level of T	Merrifield [1988]
		R & D Engineering Manufacturing	Operational definition	NSF [1971]
		User T Product adaptive T Manufacturing T Design modification Design T		Robinson [1988]

progress of different regions, in both developed and developing countries, depends on the extent and efficiency of such transfer (Mansfield et al. 1983). In other words, the economic treatment of TT keeps in mind the economic goals.

Definition of Technology Transfer. The term *transfer* has been analyzed by Vaitsos (1975), who laments its inappropriateness because transfer connotes the free, noncommercial movement of something from one location or possessor to another. In fact, however, with technology, what is usually involved is a "sale" of such technology. For this reason the term *commercialization of technology* has been argued as generally more appropriate (Farrell 1979, p. 53).

Brooks' (1966) generalized concept of technology transfer is useful to understanding the economist's perspective:

Technology transfer is the process by which science and technology are diffused throughout human activity. Wherever systematic rational knowledge developed by one group or institution is embodied in a way of doing things by other institutions or groups, we have technology transfer. This can be either transfer from more basic scientific knowledge into technology or adaptation of an existing technology to a new use. Technology transfer differs from ordinary scientific information transfer in the fact that to be really transferred, it must be embodied in an actual operation of some kind.

Taxonomy of Technology Transfer. On the basis of the above generalized concept of TT, Brooks (1966) makes a distinction between two types of TT: vertical TT (the process from new scientific knowledge through first industrial adoption of technology to the consumption) and horizontal TT (adaptation of a technology from one application to another). Useful taxonomies are also provided in Teece (1977) who distinguishes between the transfer of physical items and the transfer of information.

From the macroeconomic perspective, the literature stresses taxonomies such as region-to-region transfer and technology transfer between different industries and economic sectors.

From the nation-state perspective, economists classified TTs as domestic and as international in nature (technology transfers that cross national borders). Within the international TT literature, there are politico-economic terms like West-East TT, North-South TT, transfer from developed countries to developing countries, and so forth.

Anthropology Discipline

Role of Technology Transfer. Anthropologists view TT from a broader perspective and within the context of cultural evolution. They look on technological development as change in the patterns of culture and society. The successful technology transfer simply constitutes a special case in the whole broad process of cultural and social change (Foster 1962). On the other hand, anthropologists think the proper adoption/diffusion of new technologies has an impact on the advancement, or the development, of more complex societies.

Unlike economists, anthropologists are more concerned with the relationship between developing technology and culture, the psychological character of the people who are changing, and the difficulties of the institutions responsible for the change. Compared to other disciplines, anthropology has been more concerned with the transfer of technological innovations from one society to another (as compared to the diffusion of a new idea within a society or system).

Definition of Technology Transfer. From an anthropologist's point of view, TT takes its place in the context of cultural evolution. Anthropologists argue that a technology is adopted when people or groups find it desirable and possible to change what they are doing in ways that involve particular uses of that technology. Such people and groups are the active, initiating elements of the change in technical practices (Merrill 1972). Anthropologists are more interested in studying the agents and objects of changes and its spin-off effects.

Taxonomy of Technology Transfer. Anthropological literature lacks the term technology transfer. Nevertheless, the issues involved in the concept have been studied in more general terms such as transfer of technological innovation or technical aid programs or projects. Terms used in anthropological studies include cross-culture transfer (from the cultural perspective); group, community, and village programs (from the institutional perspective); and rural, urban, and regional programs (from the geographical perspective).

Sociology Discipline

Role of Technology Transfer. Sociologists are concerned more with the effect that the process of technology transfer has on social living than the economic goals of technology transfer. They view the role of technology transfer as a critical vehicle to aid in developing the capacity for individuals and societies to cope with modernization and the constant change that accompanies it (Chatterjee and Ireys 1979).

Definition of Technology Transfer. Similar to anthropological literature, sociological literature also lacks the term *transfer of technology*. The issues involved in TT have been treated by sociologists through the study of diffusion of innovation. The term *diffusion* is used to include both the planned and the spontaneous spread of innovation.

Sociologists argue that the probabilities of a new alternative being superior to previous practice are not exactly known by the individual problem solvers. Thus, they are motivated to seek further information about the innovation in order to cope with the uncertainty that it creates. So the diffusion of innovation is defined as a social process by which an innovation is communicated through certain channels over time among the members of a social system (Rogers 1983).

Taxonomy of Technology Transfer. Sociologists think that it is important to distinguish stages of the process of innovation diffusion. For instance, Rogers (1983) distinguishes among knowledge, persuasion, decision, implementation, and confirmation stages. Other useful taxonomies used in the sociological literature include diffusion of innovation and adoption of innovation, diffusion of natural and biomedical technologies versus diffusion of social technology (Chatterjee and Ireys 1979), and centralized versus decentralized diffusion (Rogers 1983).

Management Discipline

Role of Technology Transfer. In the management literature, TT is viewed as a vehicle to either gain or sustain a firm's competitive advantages or to bring financial and other benefits to the collaborating firms.

Definition of Technology Transfer. In business activities, TT is viewed in more specific terms and is usually conceived as the transfer of specialized know-how, which may be either patented or nonpatented, from one enterprise to another. As Baranson (1976) defines it, transmission of such knowledge enables the recipient enterprise to manufacture a particular product or to provide a specific service. Other researchers (Teece 1976) define TT as the transfer of know-how. As distinct from the sale of the machinery and equipment that embodies technology, they argue that the transfer of technology, in most cases, calls for a sustained relationship between two enterprises over a period of time, so that the receiving enterprise can reproduce the product with the desired level of quality standards and cost efficiency. This relationship model of technology transfer is consistent with the work of Contractor (1980) and Robinson (1988). Chesnais (1986) argues that the transfer of technology implies the transfer to the recipient not only of the technical knowledge needed to produce the product but also of the capacity to master, develop, and later produce autonomously the technology underlying such products.

Taxonomy of Technology Transfer. Management theorists also think that it is important to distinguish among the phases of TT. Hayami and Ruttan (1971) distinguish among three phases of horizontal TT, that is, focusing on transfers of materials (sale of new products or materials without any adaptation), design transfer (transfer of a capability to manufacture the product, or to use the process independently), and capacity transfer (transfer of R&D capability).

Researchers in the management field use all TT taxonomies suggested by the economists and add some of their own in their studies. Baranson and Roark (1985) draw distinction between TTs that impart operational, duplicative, and innovative capabilities. Lake (1979) identifies three levels of TT: the market level, the production level, and the research and development level.

From the ownership perspective, interfirm transfer versus intrafirm transfer; internal transfer versus "arm's-length," market-mediated transfer (Teece 1976); and TT to a wholly owned subsidiary, to a joint venture, or to an independent company (through arm's-length licensing) are extensively used to distinguish different ways to transfer technology.

The term *transfer of management technology* has also been widely used in the literature (Glinow and Teagarden 1988; Merrifield 1988). In the management field, international technology transfer refers to the transfer of the capability to manufacture a product or process from firms in one country to firms in another (Baranson 1976; Chesnais 1986).

A META-TAXONOMY FOR TECHNOLOGY TRANSFER

The various taxonomies of technology transfer reviewed in this chapter are encapsulated in Table 12.2. Tables 12.1 and 12.2, respectively, address the existing taxonomies of technology and of technology transfer. They provide a succinct, parsimonious review of the key issues of concern in the literatures of economics, sociology, anthropology, and management/engineering. Citations of landmark articles identify the position taken by the author(s) on each of the taxonomic dimensions, for each discipline/profession.

These tables summarize for the reader the essence and the breadth of the various points of view. Clearly, for a more in-depth understanding the reader is encouraged to read the works cited and, in turn, any citations contained within those works. The strategy in choosing what to read and in what order to read it can be facilitated by these tables as well.

Specifically, one can focus first on some specific roles that technology is perceived to play. Thus, sociology may not be the literature of obvious choice to an engineer concerned with problem solving. Similarly, anthropology may not be the literature of choice to an engineering policy maker or staff analyst interested in biomedical innovation. Alternatively, an economist concerned with technology or TT policy setting may more easily recognize the need to consider the management/engineering literature on the subject and be given a starting point for such explorations by Tables 12.1 and 12.2, respectively.

"Literature reviews are playing an increasingly important role in social scientists' definition of knowledge" (Cooper 1988, p. 104). Integrative reviews are clearly the most useful reviews because they show the similarities and the differences between the individual contributions. More importantly, they classify, or pigeonhole, each contribution in the overall context of the field. Lastly, as discussed in Chapter 2, they can be used to identify voids in a field's knowledge base (Reisman 1988, 1989). A good taxonomic scheme, once again, is indispensable to an effective review of a literature and especially to the efficiency of its presentation.

SUMMARY

TT involves more than just technological or engineering dimensions. With improved understanding of the multidimensional facets and the multidisciplinary views of TT, engineering and technology managers and/or policy makers can better formulate strategy so as to transfer technology more effectively. Although TT, as a subject of study, has accumulated a vast body of research, our knowledge about TT is still fragmented, unsystematic, and single-perspective oriented. A

Table 12.2
Technology Transfer: A Synthesis of Taxonomies

Discipline	Perceived Role of TT	Taxonomic distinctions	Perspective taken within Discipline	Author(s)
Economics	Economic growth	Vertical TT Horizontal TT	Flow of technology	Brooks [1966]
		Physical item TT Information TT	Content of technology	Teece [1977]
		Industry-industry TT Sector-sector TT Region-region TT	Macro-economic	Extensively used
		Domestic TT International TT	Nation-state	Extensively used
		West-East TT North-South TT DC-LDC TT	Politico-economic	Extensively used
Anthropology	Cultural change	Cross-cultural TT	Cultural	Foster [1962]
	Advancement of society	Group program Community program Village program	Institutional	Foster [1962]
		Rural program Urban program Regional program	Geographic	Foster [1962]
Sociology	Improvement of social living	Diffusion of innovation Adoption of innovation		Rogers [1983]
		Diffusion of social technology Diffusion of non-social technology	Nature of technology	Chatterjee & Ireys [1979]

Table 12.2 (continued)

Discipline	Perceived Role of TT	Taxonomic Distinctions	Perspective taken within Discipline	Author(s)
		Centralized diffusion Decentralized diffusion	Institutional	Rogers [1983]
Management	Strengthens firm's competitive-ness; Firm gains financial and other benefits	In addition to economic taxonomies: Material TT Design TT Capacity TT	Phase of TT	Hayami & Ruttan [1985]
		TT imparts operational capability TT imparts duplicative capability TT imparts innovative capability	Nature of TT	Baranson & Roark [1985]
		Market level TT Production level TT R&D level TT	Nature of TT	Lake [1979]
		Inter-firm TT Intra-firm TT	Ownership	Extensively used
		Internal TT Arms-length TT	Control	Extensively used
		TT to wholly-owned subsidiary TT to joint venture TT to independent company	Modality of TT	Extensively used

call for consolidation, synthesis, and systematic analysis of the TT literatures has been sounded by Reddy and Zhao (1990). However, in order to better understand the broad nature of TT, we need to first solve its definitional problems and to resolve confusions about TT. The meta-taxonomy proposed in this chapter is a step toward that end.

The meta-taxonomic framework, consisting of five elements—the discipline, perceived role, and definition of TT; taxonomic distinctions; and the perspective taken—is a useful and an appropriate way to delineate and synthesize the TT taxonomies in the existing, although disjoint, literatures. A reexamination of existing TT taxonomies with some meta-taxonomic framework facilitates our understanding of TT taxonomies, and in turn, of the whole notion of TT.

NOTE

This chapter is based on the paper "Toward Meta Research on Technology Transfer," by Liming Zhao and Arnold Reisman, which is forthcoming in *IEEE Transactions on Engineering Management*, 39 (1) 1992.

REFERENCES

Abramovitz, M. 1956. "Resource and Output Trends in the United States Since 1870." *American Economic Review Papers and Proceedings* 46(2)(May): 5–24.

Afriqie, K. 1988. "A Technology-Transfer Methodology for Developing Joint Production Strategies in Varying Technological Systems." In *Cooperative Strategies in International Business*, edited by F. J. Contractor and P. Lorange, 81–128. Lexington, Mass.: Lexington Books.

Arrow, K. 1962. "Economic Welfare and the Allocation of Resources for Invention." In *The Rate and Direction of Inventive Activity*, edited by R. Nelson, 609–25. Princeton, N.J.: Princeton University Press.

———. 1969. "Classificatory Notes on the Production and Transmission of Technological Knowledge." *American Economic Review, Papers and Proceedings* 59(2): 29–35.

Baranson, J. 1976. *International Transfer of Industrial Technology by U.S. Firms and Their Implications for the U.S. Economy*. Washington, D.C.: United States Department of Labor.

Baranson, J., and R. Roark. 1985. "Trends in North-South Transfer of High Technology." In *International Technology Transfer: Concepts, Measures and Comparisons*, edited by N. Rosenberg and C. Frichtak, 24–42. New York: Praeger Publishing Co.

Baughn, C. C., and R. N. Osborne, 1989. "Strategies for Successful Technological Development." *Technology Transfer* 14(3&4): 5–13.

Brooks, H. 1966. "National Science Policy and Technology Transfer." *Proceedings of a Conference on Technology Transfer and Innovation*, Washington D.C. National Science Foundation Publication No. NSF 67(5): 53–64.

Brown, R. H. 1977. "Appropriate Technology and the Grass Roots: Toward a Development Strategy from the Bottom Up." *The Developing Economies*, September, pp. 253–79.

Caves, R. 1982. *Multinational Enterprise and Economic Analysis*. Cambridge, Mass.: Cambridge University Press.

Chatterjee, P., and H. Ireys. 1979. "Technology Transfer: Views From Some Social Science Disciplines." *Social Development Issues* 3(3): 54–75.

———. 1981. "Technology Transfer: Implications for Social Work Practice and Social Work Education." *International Social Work* 24(1): 14–23.

Chesnais, F. 1986. "Science, Technology and Competitiveness." *STI Review* no. 1, (Autumn): 85–129.

Chipman, J. S. 1982. "Capital Movement as a Substitute for Technology Transfer: A Comment." *Journal of International Economics* 12(1/2): 107–9.

Chudson, W. A. 1971. "The International Transfer of Commercial Technology to Developing Countries." UNITAR Research Report, No. 13, New York.

Contractor, F. J. 1980. "The Composition of Licensing Fees and Arrangements as a Function of Economic Development of Technology Recipient Nations." *Journal of International Business Studies* 11(3): 47–62.

Cooper, C. M. 1988. "Organizing Knowledge Syntheses: A Taxonomy of Literature Reviews." *Knowledge in Society* 1(4): 104–26.

Dasgupta, P. 1979. "On Appropriate Technology." In *Appropriate Technologies for Third World Development*, edited by A. Robinson, 13–25. New York: St. Martin's Press.

Deihl, L. W. 1987. "The Transferability of Management Technology to Third World Countries." *Akron Business and Economic Review* 18(3): 70–81.

Denison, E. 1974. *Accounting for United States Economic Growth, 1929–1969*. Washington, D.C.: Brookings Institute.

Dosi, G. 1988. "The Nature of the Innovative Process." In *Technical Change and Economic Theory*, edited by G. Dosi, C. Freeman, R. Nelson, G. Silverberg, and L. Soete. London: Printer Publishers, Ltd.

Drucker, P. F. 1985. "The Discipline of Innovation." *Harvard Business Review* 63(May-June): 67–72.

Dudley, L. 1974. "Learning and the Interregional Transfer of Technology." *Southern Economic Journal* (40): 563–70.

Dunning, J. H. 1981. *International Production and the Multinational Enterprise*. New York: George Allen and Unwin Publishers.

Farrell, T. 1979. "A Tale of Two Issues: Nationalization, the Transfer of Technology and the Petroleum Multinational in Trinidad-Tobago." *Social and Economic Studies* 28(March): 234–81.

Feenstra, R. C., and K. L. Judd. 1982. "Tariffs, Technology Transfer and Welfare." *Journal of Political Economy* 90:1142–65.

Findlay, R. 1978. "Relative Backwardness, Direct Foreign Investment and the Transfer of Technology: A Simple Dynamic Model." *Quarterly Journal of Economics* 92(1): 1–16.

Foster, G. 1962. *Traditional Cultures and the Impact of Technological Change*. New York: Harper Publishing Co.

Frohman, A. L. 1985. "Putting Technology into Strategic Planning." *California Management Review* 27(Winter): 49–59.

Glinow, A. V., and M. Teagarden. 1988. "The Transfer of Human Resource Management Technology in Sino–U.S. Cooperative Ventures: Problems and Solutions." *Human Resource Management* 27(2): 201–29.

Hahn, F. H., and R. C. G. Matthews. 1969. *The Theory of Economic Growth: A Survey.* New York: Macmillan, St. Martin's Press.

Hall, G. R., and R. E. Johnson. 1970. "Transfer of US Aerospace Technology to Japan." In *The Technology Factor in International Trade*, edited by R. Vernon, 305–58. New York: National Bureau of Economic Research, Columbia University Press.

Harris, J. M., R. M. Shaw, and W. P. Sommers. 1984. "The Strategic Management of Technology." In *Competitive Strategic Management*, edited by R. B. Lamb. Englewood Cliffs, N.J.: Prentice-Hall.

Hayami, Y., and V. Ruttan. 1971. *Agricultural Development and International Perspective.* Baltimore, Md.: Johns Hopkins.

Johnson, H. G. 1970. "The Efficiency and Welfare Implications of the International Corporation." In *International Corporations*, edited by C. Kindleger, 35–56. Cambridge, Mass.: MIT Press.

Ketteringham, J., and J. White. 1984. "Making Technology Work for Business." In *Competitive Strategic Management*, edited by R. B. Lamb. Englewood Cliffs, N.J.: Prentice-Hall.

Koizumi, T., and K. J. Kopecky. 1977. "Economic Growth, Capital Movements and the International Transfer of Technical Knowledge." *Journal of International Economics* 7(1): 1–20.

Krugman, P. 1979. "A Model of Innovation, Technology Transfer and the World Distribution of Income." *Journal of Political Economy* 87(2): 253–66.

Lake, A. W. 1979. "Technology Creation and Technology Transfer by Multinational Firms." *Research in International Business and Finance* 1: 137–77.

Lall, S., and P. P. Streeten. 1977. *Foreign Investment, Transnationals and Developing Countries.* London: MacMillan.

Lerner, D. 1958. *The Passing of Traditional Society: Modernizing the Middle East.* New York: Free Press, p. 89.

Long, F. 1979. "The Role of Social Scientific Inquiry in Technology Transfer." *American Journal of Economics and Sociology* 38(3): 261–74.

Madeuf, B. 1984. "International Technology Transfers and International Technology Payments: Definitions, Measurement and Firms' Behavior." *Research Policy* 13(3): 125–40.

Mansfield, E. 1968. *The Economics of Technological Change.* New York: Norton Publishing Co.

———. 1975. "International Technology Transfer: Forms, Resource Requirements and Policies." *American Economic Review* 65(2): 372–76.

Mansfield, E., A. Romeo, M. Schwartz, D. Teece, S. Wagner, and P. Brath. 1983. "New Findings in Technology Transfer, Productivity and Development." *Research Management* 26(2): 11–20.

Marx, K. 1874. *Capital.* Vol. 1. London: Lawrence & Wishart.

McCulloch, R., and J. L. Yellen. 1982. "Technology Transfer and the National Interest." *International Economic Review* 23(2): 421–28.

Mendeleyev, D. I. 1889. "The Periodic Law of the Chemical Elements (Faraday Lecture)." *Journal of the Chemical Society* 55: 634–56. (Reprinted in *Faraday Lectures*, Chemical Society 1928, *Lectures Delivered Before the Chemical Society.* London: Chemical Society, 1869–1928.)

Merrifield, D. B. 1988. "Industrial Survival via Management Technology." *Journal of Business Venturing* 3(3): 171–85.

Merrill, R. 1972. "The Role of Technology in Cultural Evolution." *Social Biology* 19(3): 246.

National Science Foundation. 1971. *Research and Development in Industry*, 73–305. Washington, D. C.: National Science Foundation.

O'Connell, J. J., and J. W. Zimmerman. 1979. "Scanning the Environment." *California Management Review* 22(Winter): 15–33.

Pappas, C. 1984. "Strategic Management of Technology." *The Journal of Product Innovation Management* 1(1): 30–35.

Pavitt, K. 1985. "Technology Transfer Among the Industrially Advanced Countries: An Overview." In *International Technology Transfer: Concepts, Measures and Comparisons*, edited by N. Rosenberg and C. Frischtak, 3–23. New York: Praeger Publishing Co.

Porter, M. E. 1985. "Technology and Competitive Advantage." In *Competitive Advantage: Creating and Sustaining Superior Performance*, edited by M. E. Porter, 104–200. New York: The Free Press.

Pugel, T. A. 1982. "Endogenous Technological Change and International Technology Transfer in a Ricardian Trade Model." *Journal of International Economics* 13(3/4): 321–35.

Reddy, M., and L. Zhao. 1990. "International Technology Transfer: A Review." *Research Policy* 19(4): 285–307.

Reisman, A. 1988. "Finding Researchable Topics Via a Taxonomy of a Field of Knowledge." *Operations Research Letters* 7(6): 295–301.

———. 1989. "A Systems Approach To Identifying Knowledge Voids in Problem Solving Disciplines and Professions: A Focus on the Management Sciences." *Knowledge in Society* 1(4): 67–86.

———. 1990. "Technology Transfer: A Taxonomic View." *Journal of Technology Transfer* 14(3&4): 31–36.

Riesman, D. 1952. *Faces in the Crowd: Individual Studies in Character and Politics*. New Haven, Conn.: Yale University Press.

Robinson, R. D. 1988. *The International Transfer of Technology: Theory, Issues and Practice*. Cambridge, Mass.: Ballinger Publishing Co.

Robock, S. H. 1980. *The International Technology Transfer Process*. Washington, D.C.: National Academy of Sciences.

Rodriguez, C. A. 1975. "Trade in Technical Knowledge and the National Advantage." *Journal of Political Economy* 83(1): 121–35.

Rogers, E. 1969. *Modernization Among Peasants*. New York: Holt, Rinehart, Winston Publishing Co., p. 14.

———. 1983. *Diffusion of Innovations*. New York: The Free Press.

Rosenberg, N. 1986. "The Impact of Technological Innovation: An Historical View." In *The Positive Sum Strategy*, edited by R. Landau and N. Rosenberg, 17–32. Washington, D.C.: National Academy Press.

Schumpeter, J. 1928. "The Instability of Capitalism." *Economic Journal* 38(September): 361–86.

Service, E. R. 1971. *Cultural Evolutionism: Theory in Practice*. New York: Holt, Rinehart, and Winston.

Solow, R. 1957. "Technical Change and the Aggregate Production Function." *Review of Economics and Statistics* 39(1): 312–20.

Teece, D. 1976. *The Multinational Corporation and the Resource Cost of International Technology Transfer*. Cambridge, Mass.: Ballinger Publishing Co.

————. 1977. "Technology Transfer by Multinational Firms: The Resource Cost of Transferring Technological Know-How." *The Economic Journal* 87(346): 242–61.

Terpstra, V., and K. David. 1985. *The Cultural Environment of International Business*. Cincinnati, Ohio: South-Western Pub. Co.

Vaitsos, C. V. 1975. "The Process of Commercialization of Technology in the Andean Pact." In *International Firms and Modern Imperialism*, edited by H. Radice. New York: Penguin Press.

————. 1976. "Employment Problems and Transnational Enterprises in Developing Countries: Distortions and Inequality." Geneva: ILO World Employment Programme Working Paper No. 11 (mimeo).

Willard, G. E., and A. C. Cooper. 1985. "Survivors of Industry Shake-outs: The Case of the U.S. Color Television Set in Industry." *Strategic Management Journal* 6(4): 299–318.

Section 2 _____

Not-for-Profit Sector

The U.S. economy is often considered as composed of three sectors. These are respectively the for-profit sector, the public sector, and the not-for-profit (private) sector. Much has been written about each of these sectors. However, a comprehensive approach to the management of the third, the not-for-profit sector, is just beginning to emerge. Chapter 13 attempts to classify this sector on the basis of the types of institutions and the types of managerial functions one can find therein. Moreover, the taxonomy offered in this chapter tends to subsume all previous attempts at classifying this sector.

Toward a Generic Taxonomy of the Not-for-Profits, Not-for-Profit Managers, and Not-for-Profit Managerial Functions

The most incomprehensible thing about the world is that it is comprehensible.

A. Einstein

INTRODUCTION

The world of not-for-profits encompasses organizations as varied in size, functionally diverse, and geographically dispersed as the American Red Cross to the tiniest of neighborhood associations. This rather mixed bag of institutions comprises the third largest economic sector, variously estimated to represent about 10 percent of this country's gross national product, (GNP) (without considering the health care sector, which, by itself, comprises 12 percent of the GNP) (Hodgkinson and Weitzman 1986). According to O'Neill and Young (1988) the sector employs as many civilians as the federal government and the fifty states combined. Moreover, the Reagan administration, as a matter of ideology, contributed to privatization of a number of services previously provided by government (Blumstein 1988). This trend is not likely to be reversed in the near future.

In light of the above and the fact that management education directed at the not-for-profits is in its infancy, although gaining momentum (O'Neill and Young 1988), there is a need for understanding what not-for-profit managers do in the myriad of institution types comprising this sector. As stated in Reisman (1987a, 1987b, 1988b), if such knowledge is systematized, unified, and efficiently classified it is so much more useful for purposes of teaching, learning, researching, recalling, and the like.

In the Foreword and the first chapter of *Educating Managers of Nonprofit Organizations*, O'Neill and Young (1988) synthesize a number of essays commissioned for presentation and discussion at a recent conference on the subject. The synthesis and the essays attempt to classify managers, their functions, and their institutions in the rather complex world of nonprofits.

Moreover, literature has recorded a number of taxonomies for the nonprofits. Although they can all be used in a variety of ways, each of the developers had a clear and specific use/objective in mind. Thus, Simon (1988) clarifies the tax implications of structuring nonprofits in different ways; the National Center for Charitable Statistics (NCCS) (1987) taxonomy is designed to assist government to refine the way it collects and reports data on the nonprofit sector; and Hansmann's (1980) four way classification is used to base his theory of why nonprofit organizations exist for certain purposes.

The taxonomy of this chapter attempts to be much broader in scope and has a wider variety of potential uses/objectives. Primarily it is designed to serve as an aid for describing the sector in a manner that is both efficient and effective. It is intended to enable the educator to present the subject matter in a comprehensive yet comprehendible manner. The novice can thus more easily grasp the wide spectra of institutions comprising this sector by understanding the fact that there exists a full spectrum of organization types, on each of a large number of dimensions or characteristics. Even a seasoned worker can use this taxonomy to pinpoint the market niche, structural, operational, or other characteristic profile of his or her institution and do so in the context of the sector at large. This facilitates seeing the "big-picture," the "forest," while knowing the exact size, shape, color, texture, and so forth of any specific tree.

The taxonomy can facilitate marketing of management curricula through its efficient description of the diversity of institutions, and in each, the function that needs to be managed. It can be used by current institutional managers and/or trustees to develop strategies for institutional growth/expansion, mergers, acquisitions and/or divestitures. Putting it another way, the taxonomy can be used for institutional trouble shooting. By comparing the actual organization to some ideal organization, based either on an imagined view of the agency or the typical pattern by successful models, the organization can discover which of its areas call for modifications. It can be used as a vehicle for collecting data to describe the profile or mix of institutions in any one community, state, or region for purposes of

- Stating employment levels
- Stating volunteer time patterns
- Stating dollar expenditures
- Justifying fund raising
- Setting priorities for
  —Public funds allocation
  —Philanthropic giving
  —Philanthropic fund raising
- Identifying voids in services provided

If such data are compiled in a uniform manner across communities, researchers, planners, policy analysts, and policy makers would have a better "grounding" for their efforts.

Vendors can use the taxonomy and the data, discussed above, for developing marketing strategies.

In summation, "there is a need for a general taxonomy, within which the variety of organizations can be appropriately identified so that analysis and research, and understanding of management implications, can progress" (Stein 1980, p. 13).

LITERATURE REVIEW

There is a significant literature that distinguishes the not-for-profit sector from both the for-profit and the public sectors (see, e.g., O'Neill and Young 1988; Ben-Ner 1986; Hansmann 1980; Weisbrod 1975). This chapter, however, focuses strictly on creating a taxonomy that can be used to distinguish *between* not-for-profits in the most discriminating yet parsimonious manner possible.

The literature has also recorded a number of attempts to classify nonprofits. Each of these was intended to serve a specific purpose. In this section, we review some of these efforts and place them in the context of the more global mission of this attempt at creating a classification.

No classification of nonprofits is complete without addressing the tax status of an institution. Toward this end, we invoke J. G. Simon's (1988) four-ring concept.

The nonprofit sector is subject to special treatment under federal individual and corporate income taxes, estate and gift taxes, and certain excise taxes. There are, in fact, four separate treatments, one for each of four principal categories into which the federal tax laws divide the nonprofit sector. In [Figure 13.1] each category is represented by a ring embracing a set of organizations that are subject to a substantially similar tax regime, distinct from the regimes applicable to the adjoining rings. The rings are so arranged that together they make up a group of concentric circles, which, as one moves outward from Ring IV, contain increasingly larger portions of the nonprofit world.

Thus, the full circle, encompassing Rings I through IV, includes all entities that are exempt from federal income tax (the tax otherwise imposed on corporations, unincorporated associations, or trusts) under the principal exemption statute, §501 of the Internal Revenue Code. Almost all these groups share the condition of being organized on a not-for-profit basis, which means not that the entity is forbidden to generate a profit but that any such profits may not be distributed to owners or other private persons. Membership corporations that finance farm crop operations and are exempt under §501(c)(16) are permitted to issue capital stock and distribute dividends to participating members, subject to certain constraints. Hansmann (1980) refers to this rule as the "nondistribution constraint." This constraint is imposed on these institutions by the legal instrument under which they are organized under state law—the "charter" or "articles" in the case of a nonprofit corporation or an unincorporated association, or the "deed of trust" or other

Figure 13.1
A Schematic Model of Nonprofit Tax Categories

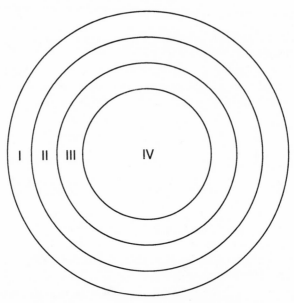

trust instrument in the case of a charitable trust (Fremont-Smith 1965). (Which of these legal forms of organization a nonprofit group adopts is almost wholly irrelevant for determining that group's federal tax treatment.) (Simon 1988, p. 68)

Simon then goes on to discuss the difference between the charitables, Rings II to IV, and noncharitables, Ring I. The former typically fall into IRS §501(c)(3) category and the other into §§501(c)(4)-(21). He then discusses the differences in the "charitable world," Rings II–IV. "Private foundations" fall into Rings III and IV and those not deemed to be charitable foundations fall into Ring II. Next he discusses separation of "public charities" in Ring II, "operating foundations" in Ring II, and "nonoperating foundations" (the grant making ones) in Ring IV.

Needless to say this classification serves a specific purpose (i.e., issues of taxation) and is highly subject to interpretation of the legislation, rulings, and precedents. As important as it is for assigning tax status it is not discriminating along the many dimensions suggested in this chapter and can hardly be judged to be parsimonious.

Hansmann (1980, and O'Neill and Young 1988) provides a four-way categorization of nonprofit firms (see Figure 13.2). He first distinguishes firms according to their *source of income* and second in the way they are *controlled*. Both classifications have but two categories. The former includes "donative" nonprofits, firms whose income derives *primarily* or *exclusively* from donations

Figure 13.2
A Four-Way Categorization of Nonprofit Firms

	Mutual	Entrepreneurial
Donative	Common Cause National Audobon Society Political Clubs	CARE March of Dimes Art Museums
Commercial	American Automobile Association Consumers Union * Country Clubs	National Geographic Society ** Educational Testing Service Hospitals Nursing Homes

Source: Adapted from Hansmann 1980.
   * Publishers of CONSUMER REPORT
  ** Publishers of NATIONAL GEOGRAPHIC

(Hansmann 1980, p. 835). "Commercial" nonprofits, on the other hand, are those deriving their income *primarily* or *exclusively* from the sales of goods or services. The bipolar nature of this part of the Hansmann taxonomy renders it less discriminating than Figure 13.3, which explicitly recognizes the continuum of institution types along this particular dimension. The *ultimate control* of a nonprofit, Hansmann's (1980) other classifying dimension, is also bipolar.

Firms in which ultimate control (the power to elect the board of directors) is in the hands of the organization's patrons Hansmann calls "mutual" nonprofits. Other nonprofits—including, in particular, those in which the board of directors is self-perpetuating—he calls "entrepreneurial" nonprofits (Hansmann 1980, p. 841)

In a forthright manner, Hansmann (1980) does recognize the lack of sensitivity of his scheme in classifying those nonprofits that do not fall at the extreme ends of these dimensions.

The boundaries between the four categories are, of course, blurred. Many private universities, for example, depend heavily on both tuition and donations for their income and thus are to some extent both donative and commercial. Also, university boards of trustees commonly comprise some individuals who are elected by the alumni (who are past customers and present donors) and some who are self-perpetuating, with the result that the universities cannot be cate-

Figure 13.3
Taxonomy of Nonprofits According to Funding Sources

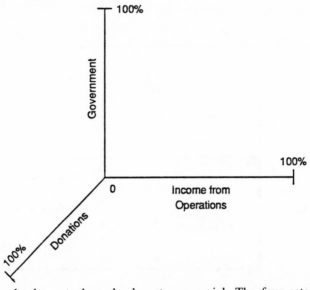

gorized as clearly mutual or clearly entrepreneurial. The four categories are, then, simply polar or ideal types, offered for the sake of clarifying discussion. (Hansmann 1980, p. 841–842).

These problems are addressed in Figure 13.3, 13.4 and later in the chapter in Figure 13.10.

Atkinson (1989) expands the above taxonomy by introducing "a third factor, the Locus of Benefits that Nonprofits Provide" to Hansmann's *means of finance* and *locus of control*. This results in a "ten-part division of the nonprofit world," as shown later in Figure 13.15.

Another taxonomy is offered[1] by the NCCS (1987, p. 1).

The purpose of the National Taxonomy of Exempt Entities [NTEE] is to provide a system for classifying nongovernmental, nonbusiness tax-exempt organizations with a focus on philanthropic [IRS Section 501(c)(3)] organizations to accurately describe and define the voluntary nonprofit sector in the United States.

The taxonomy uses an alpha-numeric system involving a four-digit code. (p. 3)

The system is designed as a 3-part 4-digit code representing a Major Group Code, a Major Activity or Program Focus Code, and a Beneficiary Code as explained below:

1. **Major Group Code [X-XX-X]**—This first-digit code is used to describe or identify as accurately as possible all entities by primary purpose, broad field of service (e.g., Food, Shelter, Jobs) or type of organization. It is an attempt to answer the following types of questions: What is the basic purpose of this agency? What is its general area of service? What type of organization is it?

Figure 13.4
Taxonomy of Nonprofits According to Organizational Issues

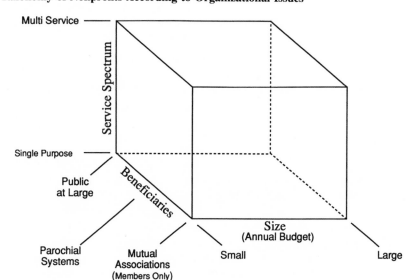

2. **Major Activity or Program Focus Code** [X-**XX**-X]—The next two digits [X-**XX**-X] are used to specify the particular focus of activity or program conducted by the agency within the Major Group identified. For example, if an agency is classified in the Major Group Code "J" for Employment/Jobs then we ask, what is the major program activity of this "Employment/Jobs" agency? We look under Major Group Code "J" for the two-digit code (01 through 99) which best describes the program focus of this "Employment/Jobs" agency. Suppose the answer is "Employment Training," then we assign code 22. Thus, the code J-22 will describe an agency whose purpose is to help people get jobs and whose major program activity (specific type of help provided) is "training."

    Major Activity or Program Focus Codes 01 through 20 [X-**XX**-X]—Codes 01 through 20 are designed as fixed or reserved codes as they describe functions or activities potentially common among all Major Group Codes. For example, Code **09** is reserved throughout the system to denote "Research" as the major activity or program focus of the agency being classified regardless of the Major Group code assigned. Thus, Code **J-09** denotes "Employment/Jobs" related Research and Code **V-09** denotes "Voluntarism, Philanthropy, Charity" related Research; Code **09** for "Research" being common to both Major Group classifications.

    Major Activity or Program Focus Code 21–99 [X- **XX**-X]—Codes **21** through **99** have significance unique to each Major Group classification. Thus, Code **A-21** denotes "Architecture/ Design," whereas, Code **B-21** denotes "Nursery School/Early School Admissions."

    Major Activity or Program Focus Code 99 [X- **XX**-X]—This 99 code is used as a catch-all code under each Major Group Code and should be used only as a code of last resort. For example, in the case of the above "Employment/Jobs" agency, if we are not able to identify the major activity or program focus of this agency but we learn that it is an "employment" agency then we assign code J-99.

3. **Beneficiary Code** [X-XX-**X**]—The fourth digit of the coding scheme is known as the Beneficiary

Code. This code is designed to identify the **primary** (and not necessarily exclusive) intended beneficiary/client/recipient group of the entity. Tax-empt organizations are often created to help a particular segment of the population (e.g., children, women, aging, minorities). This type of information is of practical value to many user groups and is not currently available on a large scale. (For further information, please see under Beneficiary Code descriptions.)

This is an excellent cataloging system and it can be used in lieu of the approach described by Figure 13.5 of this chapter. The system however, falls short of addressing the other dimensions for classifying institutions, such as size, form of governance, and the like.

CLASSIFICATION OF AGENCIES/INSTITUTIONS

This section suggests classifications of nonprofits, each based on one of many distinctly different yet relevant dimensions for doing so. The order of their presentation here however, has no implied significance.

Sources of Income

Figure 13.3 suggests the three-dimensional continuum of an agency's sources of funds. These sources include philanthropy (donations), government (public funds), and what we shall call income from operations (fees for service and income from auxiliary enterprises). This three-dimensional space can be used to vividly describe any organization based on its income mix. At one extreme there are the government agencies, which provide services at no cost to the beneficiary and have no income other than that from the public trough. At another extreme we find private sector agencies with no public funds providing no-cost services to their constituents. Lastly, there are not-for-profits fully funded from fees for services rendered and/or products sold. Most institutions, however, exist on some mix of funding sources. Clearly, these would fall within the space bounded by the above extremes on Figure 13.3, and are more fully discussed within a taxonomic framework in Reisman and Wayman (1990). Parenthetically it can be said that *nonprofit* organizations (e.g., religious institutions) often provide no-cost services and use no public funds. For-profits are usually funded by investors' equity, borrowing, and income from operations.

Organizational Issues

Figure 13.4 suggests a classification based on organizational issues, such as size, measured by annual budget; the number of distinguishable services provided;[2] and the limitations, if any, on the beneficiaries of its services.

Market Structure

Figure 13.6 suggests a classification based on the structure of the "market" in which the institution operates. The three-dimensional spectrum includes at its

Figure 13.5
Classification of NFP According to Services Performed and Clients Served:
Incidence Diagram

AGENCY SERVICES	Client Age Group					
	1. Pre School	2. Elem. School	3. High School	4. College Age	5. Adult	6. Aged
1. Individual Counselling (Vocational- Educational)						
2. Group Counseling (Vocational- Educational)						
3. Individual Counseling (Psycho-social)						
4. Group Counseling (Psycho-social)						
5. Family Counseling (Psycho-social)						
6. Family Life Education						
7. Intake & Referral						
8. Formal Education (Primary Religious Focus)						
9. Religious Day School Education						
10. Registered Activities (Primary Focus)						
11. Registered Activities						
12. Unregistered Activities (Primary Religious Focus)						
13. Unregistered Activities						
14. Social Action/Advocacy						
15. Adoptive Service						
16. Foster Care						
17. Group Foster Care						
18. Institutional Health & Living						
19. Temporary Shelter						
20. Homebound Services						
21. Day Care						
22. Day Camp						
23. Residential Camp						
24. Resettlement						
25. Job Placement						
26. Religious Activities						
27. Institutional Health Services (Short-Term)						
28. Institutional Health Services (Long-Term)						
29. Noninstitutional Health Services						
30. Sheltered Workshop						
31. Archival/Information Services						
32. Trade and Benevolent Associations						
33. Third Party Financing						

Figure 13.6
Taxonomy of Nonprofits According to Their Market Structure

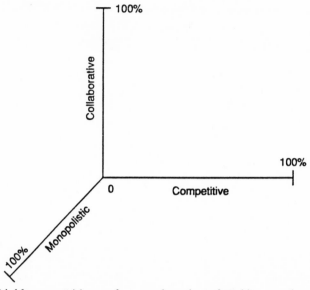

extremes highly *competitive* markets, such as those faced by most hospitals these days in major metropolitan areas, as opposed to the one regional hospital serving essentially a rural population. The latter clearly enjoys a monopolistic position in its market. Regional blood banks are further examples of institutions that have a monopoly even though they may operate in major metropolitan areas.

The third extreme representing a collaborative market place is represented by the various federations of community agencies such as the United Ways, Jewish Community Federations, Catholic Charities, and the like. In applying most of the figures to specific organizations/agencies the dimensions on all axes of the figure must total 100 percent. Thus, using Figure 13.6 as an example, if an organization is 35 percent monopolistic (*A*), 40 percent competitive (*B*), and 25 percent collaborative (*C*), lines would be drawn on the axes corresponding to those percentages. The extreme corner of the resulting three-dimensional box specifies the degree of influence of all three factors on the organization.

Staff Mix

Figure 13.7 suggests a classification based on the mix of staff (e.g., paid versus volunteer staff ratio). Staff mix can be measured by gross numbers, Full Time Equivalents (FTE), percentage of salary, or percentage of budget, and so on, whichever measure is most meaningful and useful to the agency at that time. In the paid category, it further subdivides professional versus nonprofessional categories. As examples, we can cite a psycho-social counselling community agency that would typically have a high percentage, if not 100 percent, of paid

Figure 13.7
Classification of Nonprofits According to Their Human Resources Base

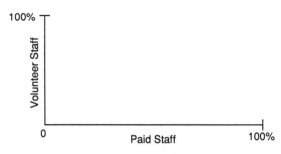

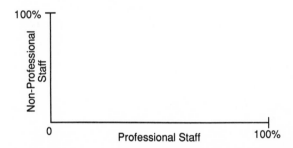

staff and among those a high percentage of professionals as opposed to clerical and/or housekeeping staff. On the other hand, the Girl Scouts of America are predominantly staffed by volunteers with approximately a 1 percent paid staff.

Another way of approaching this classification is shown in Figure 13.8. Here the staff mix is delineated on a three-dimensional spectrum with volunteers representing one axis and the administrative/clerical/janitorial and the professionals showing up on the other two.

Success Criteria

Figure 13.9 provides yet another basis for classification of not-for-profits. The three-dimensional spectrum in this case addresses the criteria by which the institution measures its success. At one extreme of the scale we have those institutions that create their own definition of success based on considerations of the services provided (e.g., quality, quantity, cost effectiveness, etc.). Thus, a community hospital with a balanced budget might focus on its "census" (e.g., bed utilization), a museum on the number of visitations and the like.

At another extreme we have political action groups that focus on the number of votes obtained on a given campaign issue. Lastly, we have an extreme concerned with profitability and/or market share. In the absolute sense, profitability

Figure 13.8
Classification According to Staff Mix

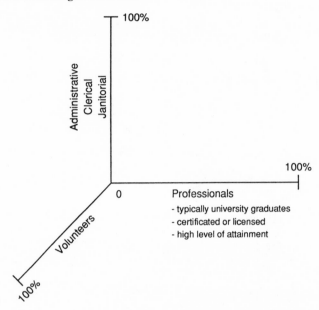

Figure 13.9
Taxonomy of Nonprofits According to Criteria Used to Measure Success

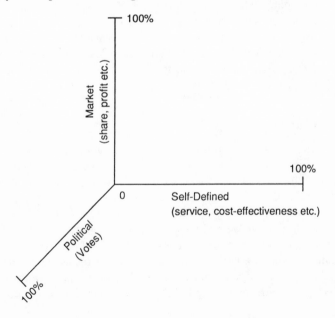

Figure 13.10
Classification of Nonprofits According to Their Governance and Accountability

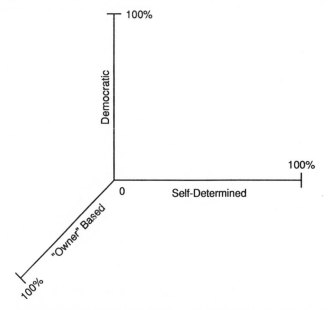

in the not-for-profit might be considered an anachronism. However, many non-profits now have wholly owned enterprises such as gift shops and/or cafeterias, the profits of which contribute to the overall agency budgets. Market share is totally consistent with the notion of nonprofits. Religious institutions vie for parishioners in a community as do private schools for enrollees.

Governance and Accountability

Figure 13.10 classifies nonprofits along a three-dimensional continuum dealing with governance and/or accountability. At the extreme called "owner" based we have both governance and accountability directed by an outside agent. This may be the funding source. Such is the case in many corporate foundations or an external hierarchy such as the case in some churches.

At the other extreme there is the highly democratic governance where the eligible public elects and evaluates the institution's administration. Local school or library boards fit in this category. Lastly, the self-determined extreme includes many religious institutions (e.g., temples, etc.).

Allocation of Resources

The next two classifications, shown in Figure 13.11, are based on the allocation of resources within the organization and are each expressed on a two-dimensional continuum.

Figure 13.11
Taxonomy of Nonprofits According to Resource Allocation

Constrained   Discretionary

Constraints on Expenditures

Distributional   Efficiency or
                                                               Cost Effectiveness

Resource Allocation Criteria

The first addresses the level of constraints on expenditures. Thus at one extreme are the highly constrained agencies that can use their resources only in meeting some mandated need or goal, as is the case with a private foundation that can dole out money in only limited quantities to well-described recipients for highly specified use. Most private community foundations have much latitude or discretion in how they distribute their funds. Moreover, public and/or private foundations can be highly constrained. Benefactors can be very specific as to which programs they will or will not support, and an attempt to expand or alter the types of recipients can curtail or increase the amount of money available for distribution. Legal action against the executive director and/or board are also possible repercussions.

The second continuum deals with criteria used for allocating institutional resources. At one extreme is the distribution-oriented agency that attempts to cover all those entitled to receive their entitlements, such as a soup kitchen or a blood bank. At the other extreme are the agencies and institutions that allocate resources so as to maximize the cost effectiveness or the efficiency in attaining stated goals.

Organizational Structure

The next classification, Figure 13.12A, is based on the organizational structure of the institution. At one extreme we find the federated structure, which is best

Figure 13.12A
Taxonomy of Nonprofits According to Their Organizational Structure*

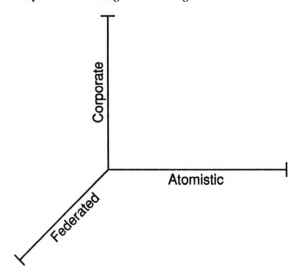

*The above taxonomy requires a judgement expressed on a scale from say 0 to 1. It is not meaningful
to use percentages.

Figure 13.12B
Subtaxonomy of Federated Nonprofits*

*The above taxonomy requires a judgment expressed on a scale from say 0 to 1. It is not meaningful
to use percentages.

exemplified by the United Ways; the Jewish Community Federations, such as
the one in Cleveland, and Catholic Charities. These are voluntary coalitions of
independent agencies sharing some common ideology and/or resource base.
Atomistic organizations may work with other organizations in some areas but
are, by and large, individualistic and self-sustaining, relying on their own efforts
to raise operating funds and determine policy.

As much as the Jewish Community Federation of Cleveland represents a
federated structure when dealing with the twenty or more independent community
agencies such as Cleveland's Jewish Community Center or Mount Sinai Hospital,
it is very much *corporate* in its internal organization. At the third extreme, most
neighborhood associations could well be classified as being *atomistic* in structure.

As indicated in Figure 13.12B the federated structures can in turn be *loose* at
one extreme or *tight* on the other. An example of a loose federation can be found
in Cleveland's University Circle Inc. (UCI), a federation of over thirty diverse

Figure 13.13
Service-Client "Packages" Offered at the Cleveland Bellefaire Agency

SERVICES OFFERED	CLIENTS SERVED	
	Elementary School	High School Age
Individual Counselling (Psycho-social)	X	
Group Counselling (Psycho-social)		X
Intake and Referral	X	X
Formal Education (Primary Jewish Focus)	X	
Registered Activities	X	X
Institutional Health and Living	X	X

independent institutions located in close geographic proximity. These include major museums, hospitals, a university, an orchestra, and several institutes as well as an English nanny school, among others. UCI provides planning, security, and parking services for member institutions. An example of a more *tight* federation is the Jewish Community Federation of Cleveland. It provides a number of centralized services to each of some thirty diverse agencies. However, the *tightness* issue arises from the fact that the federation runs the annual fund raising campaign in the community and allocates the money to member agencies based on priorities and decision rules arrived at by lay leaders of the community who comprise the federation's planning and budgeting committee.

Number of Distinguishable Services

Another classification format is based on the mix of distinguishable services provided and the mix of clients served (see Figure 13.5). For an example of this we draw on the findings of a study involving agencies of the Jewish Community Federation of Cleveland (Reisman et al. 1969; Mantel et al. 1969, 1975; Service et al. 1972). To the list of thirty services identified in that study, however, we added archival/information services; trade and benevolent associations, which include labor unions, and third party financing institutions (e.g., foundations). However, the classification of clients by age appears robust enough to remain intact. The results are shown in Figure 13.13. For example, the Cleveland Bellefaire Agency provides residential treatment for emotionally disturbed children. It is vividly and unambiguously described in Figure 13.13 using the taxonomy of Figure 13.5. As mentioned earlier, the National Taxonomy of Exempt Entities (NTEE) could well substitute for Figure 13.13.

Clearly, there are other dimensions for classifying members of the nonprofit world of institutions. The IRS status of a *charitable* (deductible contribution) versus an *advocacy* (nondeductible contribution) represents a relatively clear-cut dichotomy. However, the typically used classification by field of service (e.g., health care, education, benevolent association, etc.) is neither sufficiently discriminating nor parsimonious, especially when dealing with multiservice agencies such as those catering to the geriatric population. These are more the rule than the exception.

Figures 13.5 and 13.13 allow for a very specific description of the services and programs offered by the organization.

CLASSIFICATION OF MANAGERS

For many years, nonprofit organizations were considered to have inferior status. Knoke and Prensky (1984) wrote that since voluntary organizations are limited in the incentives they can offer potential leaders, they tend to attract people seeking ideological benefits. "For the most part, these people are zealots, and they derive a great deal of satisfaction from their jobs. Associations are the only type of organization in which amateur leaders predominate, although some analysts indicate an accelerating trend toward professionalism, at least among national headquarters staffs" (p. 9). They charge that a limited career ladder causes "frequent turnover in leadership positions, with attendant loss of continuity. Fortunately, the leadership of such associations does not require great technical mastery (engineering, accounting, law, or administration) but mainly public relations skills and political contacts" (p. 10). This viewpoint has undergone considerable alteration, and most people realize that a tax-exempt organization needs many of the same skills and tools for its management as do those in the for-profit sector.

This classification of nonprofit managers will be at first based on the extent to which they fulfill *business* versus *program* type functions. Figure 13.14(a) is a "coarse sieve" classification to serve the above needs. Figure 13.14(b) takes a more deaggregated view for the program oriented managerial functions. Specifically, it assigns the relative proportions of time devoted by a program manager to directing or coordinating activities dealing with clients, staff, volunteers, and supporters or sponsors. The percentages in Figure 13.14(b) add up to 100 percent, which in turn may represent only some fraction of a manager's time if he or she also doubles as a business manager.

More specifically, Figure 13.14 vividly shows where managers spend their time. A comparison between the responses of those in the nonprofit sector and their for-profit counterparts might prove particularly revealing, especially in the areas involving volunteers and fund raising.

Figure 13.14
Classification of Not-for-Profit Managers According to Who and What They Manage

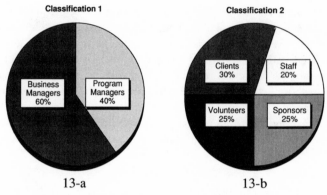

13-a   13-b

CLASSIFICATION OF MANAGERIAL FUNCTIONS

Similarly, the business manager's functions can be broken down to reflect the nature of people managed, for example, the extent (percentage of time) devoted to managing professionals (art historians, social workers, nurses, physicians, accountants, lawyers, etc.) vis-à-vis administrative, clerical, and/or janitorial staff, on the one hand, and volunteers on the other, as shown in Figure 13.8. Surely, one can supplement this classification with identification of the functional area being managed (e.g., finances, information systems, human resources, etc.) and/or by the programs/projects being directed. Whereas the number of functional (business) areas is finite and parallels the usual business school disciplines, the number of program/project possibilities is infinite. Figure 13.3 is indicative of such possibilities. Combining one service area with one client group at a time in Figure 13.5 yields 33 × 6 = 198 potential programs. Once we start considering multiservice programs serving multiage group clients, as we did in Figure 13.13, we quickly confront very large numbers of combinations.

DISCUSSION

There are differences between public and private organizations, just as there are between manufacturing and service-providing companies. These differences and similarities can be vividly illustrated by their placement on specific taxonomy figures. Not all the dimensions are unique to the nonprofit sector. Nonprofit organizations share many of the same characteristics of for-profit and public sector agencies. However, many characteristics are unique, for example, the use of volunteers and the dependence on donations for income. Many agencies spend a lot of time recruiting and training volunteers. Using Figures 13.7 and 13.8 may indicate the types (e.g., fund raising, service, leadership) and dimensions of the role those volunteers actually play.

It was very difficult to fit the two public sector organizations that were part of the study onto some of the axes. Basically, they felt 100 percent on only one dimension (e.g., Figures 13.3, 13.6, 13.9, 13.10, 13.11, and 13.12 [see examples]). A comparison could be made with for-profit organizations that would likely reveal similar single-dimension determinants.

The number of characteristics is wide, but narrowing them would not alter the actual diversity within agencies. The more knowledge one has of an organization, the better one can understand and manage that organization. The taxonomy offers an organization the ability to take a "Picasso" view of itself, providing a three-dimensional look at several factors on a two-dimensional plane.

Most organizations do fit somewhere on most, if not all, the taxonomies. The order, therefore, is of no importance. It can be compared with information on a driver's license or tests for a complete medical examination. The order of recording height, weight, eye color, EKG readings, pap test results, or blood pressure is not as important as the fact that all are finished before the record is complete.

Which of the characteristics are used in any application of this taxonomy depends on its purpose, the intended use of the information, or the insight to be gained. Developing a strategic plan for a merger by an agency would require much more information than determining efficient allocation of staff time and services within a particular agency. Identifying complimentary, competing, or identical funding sources, market structure, or criteria used to measure success can be used to predict the ease or difficulty of a merger. For example, would a funder supporting two similar agencies continue to give the same amount of money to them if they merged, would it reduce the amount based on lowered expenses, or raise it because of more efficient operation?

In a recent test (Reisman and Wayman 1990) of the classification scheme proposed, many respondents in a diverse sample group viewed the taxonomy as a starting point and found it helpful to know what nonprofits are doing in general terms and to compare them. One respondent found the visual approach easier to understand, analyze, and compare than the typical verbal descriptions. With their help, he was able to discern areas of conflict within his organization and, by showing the image of operations to members of the staff, increase communication and understanding throughout the organization. By comparing the taxonomies of various types of organizations, the scholar can quickly see the similarities and differences among the three major sectors and within the nonprofit sector itself. Researchers, especially industrial psychologists and organizational behaviorists, can analyze taxonomies of similar organizations to discern patterns, which can be used to examine, diagnose, and predict well-functioning and malfunctioning organizations.

Governments rely on nonprofits to perform many of the functions they are not able to handle directly. With the taxonomy, policy makers can see the types of services and clients served by those nonprofits to determine which are not being provided or served. By knowing what is available, government can also analyze the taxonomies to determine the best way to expand services: government sponsored, government financed but operated by nonprofits or for-profits, or strictly nonprofit/for-profit. The federal government, especially, can examine sources of funding to better understand how changes in tax laws might affect nonprofits and how realistic it is for government reduction of services and funding to be picked up by the nonprofit or public sectors.

The taxonomy does not prejudge how "success" should be measured, for example, by number of clients, votes, efficiency, and the like. Each organization is encouraged to make that decision for itself, and then apply those criteria to the taxonomy.

To make the taxonomy useful to an organization, it must put the pieces together in the manner that best serves its needs and purposes at that specific time. Some pieces may not be needed in some situations. Some may be more important than others. There is no way to provide specific rules to follow without losing the important flexibility that this plan offers.

The following are compilations, by type of organization, of most of the figures.

Figure 13.1 is J. G. Simon's (1988) four-ring concept. It applies only to nonprofit organizations with 501(c)(3–21) status, thereby visually displaying a major difference between the nonprofit sector and the public and private sectors. Most charitable organizations appear in Ring II. Ring I is for noncharitables, such as mutual associations, Ring III for operating foundations, and Ring IV for nonoperating foundations.

Government agencies are excluded on Figure 13.2, also. Firms in the private sector would appear in the lower half, with the great majority being in the entrepreneurial/commercial quadrant. Among the nonprofits, that category applies mainly to private colleges and universities and hospitals. The mutual/donative quadrant includes religious organizations, neighborhood associations, and federations, with cultural organizations being an entrepreneurial mix, with stronger donative characteristics.

Figure 13.3 divides funding sources into donations, government, and operations. Most public sector agencies receive their funding directly from the government (e.g., public schools, courts, transit systems, the military, etc.). Some money may come through donations (library book fund) or operations (bake sale, admission to special programs), but the amount is minimal in comparison.

Most for-profit organizations, on the other hand, receive their revenue from investors (partners, stockholders) borrowing, and operations. They might benefit from a special taxonomy containing those dimensions. They may also receive government money in payment for products supplied (military hardware) or services rendered (for-profit hospitals). Most do not receive donations.

Nonprofits typically rely very heavily on donations (religious and health organizations). Some, such as hospitals, receive large proportions of their income from operations, directly through private or government insurance reimbursements but mostly through third parties. Both public and private universities and neighborhood associations may receive government funding. Most receive income from a variety of sources. In the arts area, for example, newer organizations may rely more on donations and government funding while they build their reputation and endowment funds so they can later switch to operations for income. A study by Smith and Rosenbaum (1981) provided sources of receipts by nonprofits, by industry, on a national level for 1989 that were quite close to the figures supplied by our sample.

Agencies in the public sector would serve the public at large. Budget sizes would vary, although most would be larger than some private and nonprofit organizations. They would range from single purpose (state liquor stores) to multiservice (a local city hall).

Private sector organizations, seeking the largest possible market for their products, would primarily serve the public at large with product or service cost being the determining factor. Budgets can range from very small (a cottage industry) to extremely large (General Motors). Most would be near the lower end of the service spectrum, manufacturing, selling, or repairing a limited number of products or services.

Nonprofits, as shown in our sample, also tended to serve the public at large, with religious organizations being a notable exception. Others serving a narrower group would include unions or country clubs. Budgets were quite diverse, ranging from $40,000 for a small religious organization to several billion dollars for a national, specialized health agency. There was also wide diversity along the service spectrum. There was some clustering, for example, in the education industry, but the variations point out the uniqueness of the individual agencies.

Figure 13.6 divides the market structure into monopolistic, collaborative, and competitive segments. Most public sector agencies are monopolistic (e.g., courts, the military, government, welfare). Some are competitive, to greater or lesser degrees (e.g., the postal service, trash collection) and some award monopolies to private, profit making firms (e.g., cable television and road construction). Collaboration is usually financial rather than physical, although the donation of meeting space in a community building for a community organization is an example of the latter as are public schools working together or with other organizations.

For-profits are usually designed to be competitive. Some may start off monopolistic, but, if successful, find competitors relatively soon. Because of government regulations against collusion, collaboration may be difficult and dangerous, although it does happen.

Nonprofits provide a wide mix of structures, sometimes for the same organization. Zoos and Arts organizations, such as museums, theater, musical and dance organizations might be monopolistic in one area, but face a lot of competition from entertainment in general, each other, television, movies, and/or sports events. Religious organizations, nonpublic schools, and health and/or related agencies tend to exhibit more collaboration than for-profit organizations. Successful nonprofits, such as hospitals, nursing homes, or day care centers, often begin facing competition from new for-profits.

Just as the public and private sectors receive very few cash donations, they also receive few services from volunteer staff (exceptions are hospitals, nursing homes, and education organizations). Nonprofits, especially health services and religious organizations, may have large numbers of volunteers serving on a regular basis. In many cases, the organization could not exist without their services. Figuring on a full-time equivalent or percentage of budget basis, however, the paid staff actually does the bulk of the work (over 90 percent for most organizations).

The public and private sectors would have a high ratio of nonprofessional staff to professional staff. Attorneys and doctors, for example, will have at least a receptionist, secretary, bookkeeper, and/or nurse. In the private sector, many companies have no professional staff members (e.g., small wholesale/retail stores). The nonprofit sector has a lot of professionals, be they social workers, clergy, professors, or nurses. The ratio fluctuates, depending on the type and size of agency.

Figure 13.8 is an extension of Figure 13.7, adding volunteers as a separate axis of staff mix.

Figure 13.9, comparing market, political, and self-defined measures, displays the largest differences between the nonprofit, public, and for-profit sectors. The motivating factor in the public sector is often political. Although other factors, such as cost-effectiveness and service, are often vital, the bottom line is getting enough votes to implement any given policy or elect any given individual.

The bottom line for almost the entire for-profit sector is market: Does the organization receive enough income based on sales, services, or programs to enable it to continue in business?

Nonprofits are frequently able to define their own criteria. The only art museum, ballet company, or specialized health or social service agency in town must find ways to grow without relying on votes or market share.

Figure 13.10 classifies organizations according to their governance and accountability. Public sector agencies tend to be democratic or, in the absence of close public or governmental scrutiny, self-determined. Companies in the private sector are frequently owner based. Nonprofits show great diversity with an emphasis on self-determination for most health and educational agencies.

The constraints and allocation criteria of organizations is shown on the two-dimensional Figure 13.11. There is a very wide range in both areas for nonprofits, leaning toward discretionary for constraints and toward the extremes of distributional and efficiency or cost-effectiveness for allocation criteria. Being driven by market factors, most companies in the private sector have few constraints and seek efficiency or cost-effectiveness to influence allocations. Public sector agencies, supported by tax money, are usually constrained by regulations regarding where that money may be spent. Many services are distributional (e.g., police, fire, sanitation, parks) but can also be restrained by hiring contractors and buying supplies based on public bidding.

There are also differences between the three sectors based on their organizational structure. Most public and private sector organizations have a corporate structure. Most nonprofits also are corporate, but to a lesser extent because of the influence of affiliations (both program and financial). Both small neighborhood nonprofits and small private businesses can have a high degree of atomistic structure (see Figure 13.12).

Figure 13.14(a) shows variations in all sectors. Managers of cultural institutions spent more time on business than on programs, while those in the smaller educational institutions spent more time on programs than on business. The public sector would also be mixed while the private sector would be weighted toward business.

The volunteer influence shows up again in Figure 13.14(b). Except for the volunteer director, nonprofit managers spent up to 60 percent of their time, with most between 20 and 30 percent, working with volunteers and up to 45 percent of their time with sponsors. Most companies in the private sector have no volunteers and there are a few in the public sector. The sponsors in the private sector either own and operate their own companies or are stockholders whose main direct contact is at the annual meeting. Clients and sponsors are often the same for the public sector and many elected and appointed/hired government employees spend a lot of time dealing with taxpayers. In the private sector, many managers deal entirely with staff, such as in large retail establishments. In large manufacturing concerns, client contact may be limited to one or two people.

Figure 13.15 carries Figure 13.2 into more detail. Private sector companies would appear primarily in the type 6 category: commercial entrepreneurials, not for benefit of (FBO) patrons. Government organizations would be type 5: donative mutuals, FBO donors.

CONCLUDING REMARKS

This taxonomy allows more specificity on more dimensions. For example, Mintzberg (1983) stated,

The elements of structure should be selected to achieve an internal consistency or harmony, as well as a basic consistency with the organization's situation, its size, its age, the kind of environment in which it functions, the technical systems it uses, and so on. (p.3)

In examining organizational structure, he found that organizations are comprised of five basic parts: strategic apex, middle line, operating core, support staff, and technostructure. In addition, organizations could be categorized under five basic configurations: simple structure, machine bureaucracy, professional bureaucracy, divisionalized form, and adhocracy. An organization's placement into a category could be determined by the way the five basic parts interacted, for example, the prime coordinating mechanism, the key part of the organization, the main design parameters, and situational factors. Included in these are size,

Figure 13.15
Taxonomy of Nonprofit Organizations*

		LOCUS OF CONTROL			
		ENTREPRENEURIAL (Controllers ≠ Financers)			MUTUAL (Controllers = Financers)
		Controllers ≠ Financers or Beneficiaries	Controllers = Beneficiaries		
LOCUS OF BENEFIT		Beneficiaries ≠ Financers	Beneficiaries = Financers	Beneficiaries = Controllers	Beneficiaries ≠ Financers	Beneficiaries = Financers
M O D E O F F I N A N C E	**D O N A T I V E**	Type 1 Donative Entrepreneurials Not FBO (for benefit of) Donors	Type 2 Donative Entrepreneurials FBO Donors	Type 3 Donative Entrepreneurials Controlled by Beneficiaries	Type 4 Donative Mutuals Not FBO Donors	Type 5 Donative Mutuals FBO Donors
	C O M M E R C I A L	Type 6 Commercial Entrepreneurials Not FBO Patrons	Type 7 Commercial Entrepreneurials FBO Patrons	Type 8 Commercial Entrepreneurials Controlled by Beneficiaries	Type 9 Commercial Mutuals Not FBO Patrons	Type 10 Commercial Mutuals FBO Patrons

*Adapted from R. Atkinson, 1989, "Altruism in Nonprofit Organizations," PONPO Working Paper No. 145, Yale University.

the decision-making process, standarization and formalization of processes, skill and professional levels, and centralization.

Mintzberg believes that "the design of an effective organizational structure, in fact, even the diagnosis of problems in many ineffective ones, seems to involve the consideration of only a few basic configurations" (p. 2). A useful example would be reducing turnover due to a mismatched top management style and the needs of the organization, based on its key coordinating mechanism and key part.

Because of their small size, many nonprofit organizations would be classified as professional bureaucracies or adhocracies. Others, such as hospitals, universities, or major national associations and their local affiliates would be divisionalized. Being able to identify an organization as a configuration, or a combination of more than one configuration, provides a useful tool to an administrator as he or she works to maintain or improve his or her organization. However, there are many more factors involved that would differentiate between organizations that share a configuration. This is where the proposed taxonomy would be helpful.

There are major differences between for-profits and nonprofits, even though they may share a configuration. Because so much time and energy is spent on it, fund raising and the amount and type of volunteer involvement are two examples. Within the nonprofit would, there are wide variations among organizations. Greater or lesser degrees of leeway in areas such as allocations, reaction to the environment, success criteria, and market structure all shape how organizations function. By using this taxonomy, it is possible to go beyond the basic black and white organizational outline and fill in the shades that produce a multidimensional picture of the organization, thereby exposing more surface for study and understanding.

This taxonomy, based as it is on all of the previously cited taxonomic efforts, subsumes each and therefore shows each as a special case. In turn it is hoped that future taxonomers will use this effort as a stepping stone for broader and/ or deeper (more discriminating) approaches. As discussed in Chapters 2, 4, and 5, a taxonomy's breadth can be expanded in at least two ways: enlarging the definition of the field classified (e.g., enlarging the part of the universe included within the taxonomy) and enlarging the number of dimensions considered relevant for classification purposes. A good example of the latter approach is embodied in Atkinson's (1989) expansion of Hansmann's (1980) contribution. By introducing a third factor, *locus of benefits*, he transformed a four-way pigeonholing into a ten-way classification. As can be seen by comparing Figure 13.2 with Figure 13.15, the latter provides much more deaggregation and therefore descriptive power. As a general rule, it can be said that the more independent, yet relevant, characteristics incorporated in a taxonomy the more discriminating is its power. On the other hand, the methodology becomes less manageable and less parsimonious with inclusion of more characteristics. An attempt has been made to empirically validate the discriminating power, manageability, and the parsimony of the proposed taxonomy. A full discussion of this validation is given in Reisman and Wayman (1990).

It has been said before but it is worth repeating. The history of science and technology is replete with examples of taxonomic work that rendered a great diversity of known facts more manageable to assimilate, to comprehend, to teach, and to do further research on. The Periodic Table of Chemical Elements is the best known of such developments (Mendeleyev 1889). As we embark into development of curricula to teach future managers *expressly* for the not-for-profit sector we need a *compact* yet *effective* statement regarding what this sector is comprised of. It is equally important to have a compact, effective, yet *generic* statement of managerial functions within this sector. Consequently, this chapter represents an attempt to classify not-for-profits, their managers, and the functions of such managers. It is intended to initiate a discussion of the subject that hopefully will lead to a better and, most importantly, a clearer understanding of not-for-profit management.

Developing a comprehensive taxonomy of organizations is far from simple, particularly if it is to achieve consensus. It is, however, a necessary context within which the growing nonprofit sector in the economy can be better understood. (Stein 1980, p. 12).

NOTES

This chapter is based on a paper of the same name by Arnold Reisman and Judith B. Wayman, Technical Memorandum #647, Department of Operations Research, Case Western Reserve University, Cleveland, Ohio. This work is partially supported by a grant from the Mandel Center for Nonprofit Organizations, Case Western Reserve University, Cleveland, Ohio. The authors are greatly indebted to Dennis Young, Director of the Mandel Center for a number of substantive and editorial suggestions contained in the paper.

1. In the form of a flyer.
2. Delineated in Figure 13.5 and discussed in a subsequent section of this chapter.

REFERENCES

Atkinson, R. 1989. "Altruism in Nonprofit Organizations." PONPO Working Paper No. 145, Yale University.

Ben-Ner, Avner. 1986. "Non-Profit Organizations: Why Do They Exist in Market Economies?" In *The Economics of Nonprofit Institutions: Studies in Structure and Policy*, edited by Susan Rose-Ackerman, 94–113. New York: Oxford University Press.

Blumstein, A. 1988. "President's Symposium: The Current Missionary Role of OR/MS." *Operations Research* 35(6): 926–29.

Fremont-Smith, M. R. 1965. *Foundations and Government*. New York: Russell Sage Foundation.

Hansmann, H. 1980. "The Role of Nonprofit Enterprise." *Yale Law Journal* 89: 835–901.

Hodgkinson, V. A, and M. S. Weitzman. 1986. *Dimensions of the Independent Sector: Statistical Profile*. 2nd ed. Washington, D. C.: Independent Sector.

Holtmann, A. G. 1983. "A Theory of Non-Profit Firms." *Econometrica* 50(2): 439–49.

Knoke, D., and D. Prensky. 1984. "What Relevance do Organization Theories Have for Voluntary Associations?" *Social Science Quarterly* 65(1): 3–20.

Mantel, S. J., A. L. Service, and A. Reisman. 1975. "A Social Service Measurement Model." *Operations Research* 23(2): 218–39.

Mantel, S. J., A. L. Service, and R. Ronis. 1969. "Measurement of Output in a Jewish Communal System." *Journal of Jewish Communal Service* 46(1): 84–92.

Mendeleyev, D. I. 1889. "The Periodic Law of the Chemical Elements (Faraday Lecture)." *Journal of the Chemical Society* 55: 634–56. Reprinted in *Faraday Lectures*, Chemical Society 1928, *Lectures Delivered before the Chemical Society*. London: Chemical Society, 1869–1928.

Mintzberg, H. 1983. *Structure in Fives: Designing Effective Organizations*. Englewood Cliffs, N.J.: Prentice-Hall.

National Center for Charitable Statistics (NCCS). 1987. "National Taxonomy of Exempt Entities." Washington, D.C.: Independent Sector.

O'Neill, M., and D. Young. 1988. *Educating Managers of Non Profit Organizations.* New York: Praeger Publishers.

Reisman, A. 1987a. "Some Thoughts for Model Builders in the Management and Social Sciences." *Interfaces* 17(5): 114–20.

———. 1987b. "Expansion of Knowledge Via Consolidation of Knowledge." Paper presented at the Second International Symposium on Methodologies for Intelligent Systems. Published in the *ISMIS-87 Proceedings*, Oak Ridge National Laboratory, ORNL-6417, 159–72.

———. 1988a. "Entrepreneurship, Intrapreneurship, Grantsmanship and Philanthropy or Parlaying Your Wits Into More Services Rendered and Cash in the Bank Account." Technical Memorandum #648, Department of Operations Research, Case Western Reserve University, Cleveland, Ohio.

———. 1988b. "A Systems Approach to Identifying Knowledge Voids in Any Problem Solving Discipline or Profession." *Knowledge in Society: An International Journal of Knowledge Transfer* 1(4): 67–86.

Reisman, A., N. Eisenberg, and A. Beckman. 1969. "Systems Analysis and Description of a Jewish Communal System." *Journal of Jewish Communal Service* 46(1): 78–84.

Reisman, A., and J. B. Wayman. 1990. "An Empirical Validation of a Generic Taxonomy for Not-For-Profits." Technical Memorandum #686, Department of Operations Research, Case Western Reserve University, Cleveland, Ohio.

Service, A. L., S. J. Mantel, and A. Reisman. 1972. "Systems Analysis and Social Welfare Planning: A Case Study." In *Systems Approach and The City*, edited by M. Mesarovic and A. Reisman, 343–73. Amsterdam, Holland: North-Holland Publishing Co.

Simon, J. G. 1988. "The Tax Treatment of Nonprofit Organizations: A Review of Federal and State Policies." In *Nonprofit Sector: A Research Handbook*, edited by W. W. Powell, 67–98. New Haven: Yale University Press.

Smith, B., and N. Rosenbaum. 1981. "The Fiscal Capacity of the Voluntary Sector." In *The Nonprofit Economy*, by B. A. Weisbrod, 197. Cambridge, Mass.: Harvard University Press. 1988.

Stein, Herman D. 1980. "The Concept of the Human Service Organization: A Critique." *Administration in Social Work* 4(2): 1–13.

Weisbrod, B. 1975. "Toward a Theory of the Voluntary Non-Profit Sector in a Three-Sector Economy." In *Altruism, Morality and Economic Theory*, edited by E. S. Phelps, 171–97. New York: Russell Sage Foundation.

Section 3

Countertrade

There is some question as to what is the oldest profession; however, there is no question whatsoever as to what is the oldest form of commercial transaction. It is, of course, barter. This form of commerce has survived the millenia of time and the diversity of cultures/societies that were/are in existence at any given point in time. Moreover, it has evolved to a fine art in commercial practices that *do* include ''sales'' of high technology in the postindustrial societies. Chapter 14 reviews the practices in the for-profit sector, while Chapter 15 addresses such practices in the not-for-profit sector. Both of these chapters use the taxonomic approach to structuring and presenting much of what we know about the subject of countertrade.

Chapter 14

Growth and Types
of Countertrade

INTRODUCTION

Barter is the oldest form of doing business and has been practiced since prehistory. Recently discovered evidence suggests that this form of commerce was used by cave dwellers around 8300 B.C. (Mellaart 1967). It has been practiced over the centuries in agrarian, developing, and industrialized societies. The sports section of tomorrow's newspaper may well carry a story on a trade among clubs of professional athletes. World trade continues to grow faster than world production in spite of mounting protectionism. One reason may be the increased role being played by barter and countertrade, forms of trade especially designed to overcome various economic, technical, marketing, and political barriers. It is somewhat of a puzzle that these ancient forms of trade, predating the use of money, continue to be popular and continue to grow in importance. This chapter reviews the recent growth and types of countertrade.

Modern countertrade covers various forms of trading arrangements, each with some reciprocity component, where part or all of the payment for the purchased goods or services may be in the form of other goods or services. It is a grown-up's version of little boys trading in baseball cards and marbles (for similar reasons, i.e., lack of cash and trade of "priceless" items). Barter is a highly inflexible form of trade and suffers from serious inconveniences; it requires a coincidence of needs in terms of products and timing and a lack of an acceptable measure of value for the goods to be traded. However, because of its ability to overcome market imperfections and provide opportunities for extraordinary profits, countertrade is increasingly being used as an important part of business strategy, especially by companies that operate internationally.

GROWTH OF COUNTERTRADE

No reliable figures as to countertrade's overall volume are available since there is much secrecy in this business. Estimates are unreliable, especially since only one in twenty attempted deals actually materializes. The U.S. Department of Commerce estimates that countertrade currently involves between 20 and 30 percent of all world trade and may grow to involve 50 percent of world trade by the year 2000 (Cooper 1984). According to a 1984 survey by the National Foreign Trade Council Foundation, 8 percent of all U.S. export transactions involved countertrade and the comparable figure for the aerospace industry was 47 percent. According to a 1985 survey by the U.S. International Trade Commission, exports of defense-related products for the period 1980–1984 totaled $22 billion with offsets amounting to $12 billion, or 55 percent of the total. In any case, as these estimates indicate, countertrade has grown to be an important and significant part of doing business across borders.

In some areas of the world, such as the formerly COMECON (Eastern European) countries and the less developed countries (LDCs), countertrade represents a higher percentage of total trade. Although it represents a lower percentage for trade among developed countries, it nevertheless is significant. Countertrade began by being important in trade with COMECON countries. Later, it gained importance in trade with the developing and newly industrialized countries, such as Brazil, Mexico, China, Indonesia, Iran, and Nigeria. Recently it has become important in large trade deals among developed countries such as Sweden, Switzerland, Austria, Canada, Japan, and Italy. It has been estimated that over a hundred countries now require some form of countertrade, while only fifteen countries did so in 1972. Although U.S. companies are still becoming aware of it, European and Japanese companies have had longer experience with countertrade.

Many countertrade deals run into the hundreds of millions of dollars (some are even in the billion-dollar range). Both India and China, for example, have prepared billion-dollar government purchasing lists, each to be paid for on some reciprocal or countertrade basis.

In recognition of the growing importance of barter and countertrade, in 1983, the Trade Policy Staff Committee of the U.S. Department of Commerce established a formal set of guidelines regarding countertrade and barter transactions by U.S. firms. Generally, the guidelines state that, while the U.S. government opposes countertrade and barter, it will not oppose U.S. companies' participation in those activities unless national security is involved. The U.S. government also agreed to provide continuing advisory and market intelligence services.

TYPES OF COUNTERTRADE

Examples of modern countertrade include a wide range of transactions, from simple to increasingly complex deals. The simplest examples involve various forms of barter. They include, for example, the sale of recordings of the Swedish group ABBA in the formerly COMECON countries in exchange for commodities such as fresh fruits, chemicals, and even machine tools, which were then sold for hard currencies in Western Europe. As another example, the British subsidiary of PepsiCo sends Pepsi concentrate to Soviet bottling plants and in payment receives bottles of Stolichnaya Vodka, which are then marketed in the West.

Chrysler sold two hundred pickup trucks to Jamaica in 1982 in a more complicated five-party barter deal involving aluminum ore. Flush from this success, it has since engaged in other barter deals involving simultaneous trading of Peruvian copper ore; Sudanese cotton; and Liberian rubber, coffee, and cocoa. Douglas Aircraft Company sold Yugoslavia seven DC-9 airplanes. It was paid partly in cash but also agreed to sell $9 million worth of Yugoslav goods in Western markets, including $40,000 worth of hams for its cafeterias.

In another type of countertrade allowing trade over a longer time period, East Germany and Brazil agreed to barter machine tools for coffee so that at the end of their two-year bilateral trade agreement, the value of machine tools bought by Brazilian companies must equal the value of coffee bought by the East Germans. However, Brazil ended up buying machine tools valued at about 30 percent more than the coffee bought by the East Germans. The East Germans then sold their coffee contract obligation (at a discount) to a Western private company for hard currency. This company arranged a three-way transaction in which Israel "sold" potash to Poland, which in turn "sold" sugar to Brazil, which "sold" coffee to Israel. All three "sales" were arranged and agreed to simultaneously and the values of the three commodities "sold" were exactly equal.

Another type of long-term countertrade deal is the example of Technip of France building a chemical plant in the People's Republic of China and planning to recover the cost of its equipment and services by selling part of the plant's output in Western countries. Similarly, General Tire furnished equipment and technology for a Rumanian truck tire plant in exchange for radial truck tires from that plant (marketed in the West under the "Victoria" brand).

As these examples of increasingly complex countertrade deals indicate, countertrade covers a wide range of transactions. The following discussion is an attempt to bring some order to this chaos by classifying these various countertrade transactions.

Terminology used in countertrade is unfortunately characterized by a lack of standardization with a number of expressions often used to mean the same thing, and sometimes the same expression is used with several different meanings. Examples of some terms used are barter; countertrade; counterpurchase; countersale; clearing agreements; switch trading; bilateral trading; offset trading; reciprocal trading; parallel trading; linked trading; triangular trading; compensation agreements or arrangements; buy-sell, pay-back, back-to-back transactions; and other terms too numerous to list here. All of these represent trading arrangements that use a mixture of money and goods and services to obtain goods and services from another party.

However, the various forms of countertrade can be classified into four major categories: barter, clearing arrangements, switch trading, and compensation arrangements. Each of these four categories is explained in greater detail below.

1. *Barter* is a one-time exchange of goods with no direct use of money. There can be many variations of this basic exchange:

   a. Parallel barter, counterpurchase, or buy-back takes place when goods are exchanged for equal amounts of money.

   b. Offset is parallel barter with a promise to assist in the sale of goods replacing one of the contractual obligations to purchase goods.

   c. Reverse reciprocity is parallel barter for scarce goods such as oil for nuclear power plants.

   d. Multilateral barter is a chain of barter transactions contracted simultaneously among more than two parties.

   e. Parallel barter with cooperation is a set of two offsetting, cash sale arrangements or a set of two offsetting, parallel barter arrangements between three organizations.

   f. Barter with cooperation and bank credit allows for a timing difference between the two parts of a parallel barter.

Examples of barter include transactions such as Occidental Petroleum's exchange of its phosphate rack for molten sulphur of equal value each year from Poland, and Volkswagen's sale of ten thousand automobiles (Rabbits) to East Germany for other East German goods.

2. *Clearing Arrangements* are bilateral trade agreements between two countries who agree to exchange specified amounts of goods and services over a specified time period. Each country extends to the other a line of credit in terms of an artificial clearing currency that can usually be used only to purchase the goods offered under the agreement. The balance of trade in these goods may "swing" only up to a certain maximum amount in either countries' favor (say, 30 percent of the total). Trading under these arrangements generally stops until the unfavorable balance of trade, the swing, is eliminated or reduced from its maximum amount.

Examples of clearing arrangements: It is estimated recently that eighty-three countries had at least one clearing arrangement and a number of these countries had numerous clearing arrangements. For example, the U.S.S.R. had thirty, Mexico nineteen, Brazil seventeen, and even France had twelve. Specific examples of clearing arrangements include Moroccan oranges for Soviet capital equipment; Hungarian electrical equipment for Egyptian cotton; a Soviet clearing arrangement with India that allows Britain's Rank Xerox to export copiers from India to the U.S.S.R.

3. *Switch Trading* occurs when the responsibility for completing a bilateral clearing arrangement is shifted to a third party by a switch-trading broker. Switch-trading brokers operate in a secondary market to sell unused credits in bilateral clearing arrangements to third parties. Switch trading can be a tricky business especially since there often are legal restrictions on the sale in third countries of goods covered by such bilateral clearing arrangements. Sometimes these legal restrictions are actually enforced and other times they are there only for appearance. There is also often a great deal of artificiality in the prices of products covered by such switch credits and broker discounts vary from 5 to 6 percent for some commodities to as much as 40 percent for some high-technology products. Switch trading can often be combined with various financing arrangements to structure complex countertrade deals.

Examples of switch trading include U.S. Tire making equipment for an East European formerly (COMECON) country's clearing credits exchanged for Turkish lira credits in a bilateral agreement with the formerly COMECON country. The Turkish lira were used to buy chrome from Turkish sources, which was then sold for hard currency. As another example, Greece sold $1 million of Rumanian credits for $700,000 of hard currency. These credits were used by an African country to purchase Rumanian canned goods. Iranian credits for Polish shoes worth $200,000 were sold to a switch broker for $160,000 who, in turn, sold them to a buyer in East Africa for $165,000.

4. *Compensation Agreements* are the countertrade equivalent to foreign equity investments in countries where such investments are either not welcome or are ideologically not permissible (for example, when it was not possible to own a means of production as in a formerly communist country). Typically, a Western corporation will supply equipment and technology for a plant and agree to take full or partial payment, spread over a number of years, in the form of the goods produced by that plant.

Examples of compensation arrangements: A Yugoslav licensee of Fiat supplies automobiles back to Fiat for resale. Monarch Wine Company equipment and technology are provided to China in exchange for beer and vodka from the plant and distribution rights to China's Tsingtao brand beer. Pierre Cardin technical advice is provided to China in exchange for its silks and cashmeres. An East German auto transmission plant costing $370 million was built by the French company Citroen, and is being paid for with auto transmissions exported from that plant back to Citroen. Levi jeans are produced in Hungary with Levi paid with part of the output. General Motors technology was provided to a van plant in Poland in exchange for part of the plant's output in the form of auto parts.

According to a 1984 survey, clearing arrangements accounted for 55 percent of all U.S. countertrade transactions, compensation for 33 percent, switch trading for 8 percent, and barter for 4 percent. This survey also found that the proportion of countertrade varied between industries with 47 percent of aerospace exports involved in countertrade to 20 percent in electronics and defense and 15 percent in minerals and chemicals.

CLASSIFICATION OF COUNTERTRADE

As the above discussion indicates, countertrade involves a number of factors not present in money-based transactions. Countertrade transactions may involve trade over an extended period of time, trade among a number of parties, and varying degrees of financing and technology transfer. Thus, the various forms of countertrade can be classified based on four major factors: (1) contract time duration, (2) requirements of financing if any, (3) the number of parties involved, and (4) the extent of technology transfer.

1. Classification by the time factor
   a. Short-term, one-time transactions (denoted by t)
   b. Long-term, multiple transactions (denoted by T)

2. Classification by financing requirement
   a. No financing is needed (denoted by f)
   b. Some form of financing (or cash payment) is required (denoted by F)

3. Classification by the number of parties involved
   a. Only two parties are involved (denoted by n)
   b. More than two parties are involved (denoted by N)

4. Classification of technology transfer
   a. No technology transfer is involved in the transaction (denoted by k)
   b. Technology transfer is involved in the transaction (denoted by K)

We can seen from the above classification that the most complicated (or general) case of countertrade is described by T, F, N, and K. At the other extreme, the simplest case is described by t, f, n, and k. Figure 14.1 graphically represents all the major subgroups of countertrade formats based on the above classification scheme.

Most of the popular forms of countertrade described in an earlier section can be classified using this taxonomy, as the following examples show.

Barter: A barter is a short-term transaction between two parties calling for the direct exchange of goods and/or services. In terms of the above taxonomy, it corresponds to *tfnk*.

Compensation: This consists of two separate and parallel exchanges, in one contract a trader agrees to build a plant or provide equipment or technology with a down payment, usually made by the opposite party on delivery. In the second contract, the trader agrees to buy a portion of the plant's products.

Referring to the earlier taxonomy, compensation may take on the *tfnK*, *TfnK*, and *TFnK* formats. Processing arrangements are typically of the *TFnK* or the *TfnK* variety, and the joint ventures are represented most often by *TFnK*.

Figure 14.1
Taxonomy of Countertrade

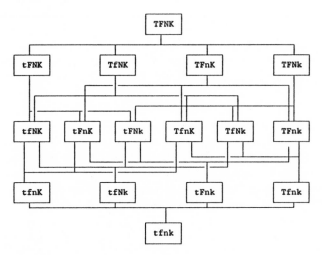

t - One time transaction
T - Long term, multiple transaction

f - No financing is required
F - Some form of financing is needed

n - Only two parties are involved
N - More than two parties are involved

k - No technology transfer is involved in the transaction
K - Technology transfer is involved in the transaction

Counterpurchase: Two separate contracts are involved: one in which a trader "sells" products for cash and/or credit, and one in which the supplier agrees to "purchase" and market products from the opposite party (*tFnk*).

Offset: Two separate exchanges operating similarly to a counterpurchase, with the distinction that the reciprocally acquired goods/services can be used by the trader in his or her business (*tFnk*).

Switch: Switch is an arrangement in which the party to a bilateral agreement transfers some or all of its goods to a third party or nation (*tfNk, TFNk*).

Swap: This is an arrangement wherein goods destined to different locations are redirected in the most economical way. In other words, they find their way to markets physically closer to the point of origin (*tfNk, TFNK*).

Clearing: This is a bilateral agreement between two countries to exchange a specified amount of each other's products over a period of time (*Tfnk*).

Cooperation Agreement: Three separate exchanges among a party in a developing country and two Western suppliers with one specializing as a seller and the other as a buyer; these three-party arrangements may be handled through a triangle barter deal or counterpurchase (*tfNk, TfNK*).

Blocked Currency: This is a method of getting products out of a country to compensate for the currency restrictions and the difficulties of repatriating holdings (*Tfnk*, TFnk).

Joint Venture: A Western nation provides capital and technology and a less developed country (LDC) offers materials and labor to set up a plant in the LDC. Both parties share the output produced. Joint venture has two different versions— equity and contractual joint ventures. In an equity joint venture, whatever the form of investment, the equity ratio must be calculated in money terms; the risks and profits are shared according to this ratio. In a contractual joint venture, on the other hand, investment may be made in different forms and the equity ratio is not necessarily in money terms, but is stipulated in the contract. Moreover, in an equity joint venture the foreign partner's (Western countries) investment can be recovered only from that partner's share of profits. In contractual joint ventures, the foreign partner's investment can be recovered in a variety of ways. Joint ventures are represented most often by *TFnK*.

ADVANTAGES OF COUNTERTRADE

Every country has its specific reasons for encouraging countertrade. Two main reasons are preserving hard currency and improving the balance of trade. Based on the products they trade, countries can be grouped into three categories: agrarian, developing, and developed countries.

Agrarian Countries: An agrarian country can only (or mainly) trade its agricultural products or raw mineral materials with the rest of the world. These products, called primary products, include food, food products, raw materials, minerals, and fossil fuels recovered from the land and/or enhanced with some processing.

Developing Countries: A developing country has shifted the focus of its countertrade from pure agricultural or mineral products to those produced by light industries. These products, referred to as secondary products, include textiles, machinery, and simple electronic assemblies.

Developed Countries: It is very easy to recognize this group of countries. They are often called industrial market economy nations by the World Bank. Highly sophisticated products or services are their main stock in trade. Such products or services, called tertiary, may include products such as airplanes, motorized vehicles, and high-tech electronic equipment and/or technology for improving the means of production.

In addition to the two main reasons for encouraging countertrade, different categories of countries have different motivations for engaging in countertrade.

1. An agrarian country, countertrading with developing and developed countries, can

   a. gain access to technology and know-how.

   b. increase the utilization of its labor force.

   c. gain exposure to future technical innovations.

   d. upgrade its labor skills.

2. A developing country, countertrading with an agrarian country, can

   a. gain access to alternative sources of supply.

   b. increase its production capacity.

   c. use low-cost labor.

and by countertrading with a developed country, it can

   d. gain access to technology and know-how.

   e. improve production standards.

   f. upgrade its labor skills.

   g. upgrade its marketing skills.

   h. expand its market.

   i. increase utilization of its labor force.

3. A developed country, countertrading with an agrarian country, has the same motivations as the developing country trading with an agrarian country. Since the developing countries have some degree of purchasing power and small technological differences, countertrade with them will enable the developed country to

   a. increase export sales.

   b. gain access to the developing country's markets.

   c. increase its production capacity.

   d. reduce its production costs.

The advantages of countertrade are summarized in Table 14.1 when viewed at the macro or national levels, or in Table 14.2 if viewed from the enterprise (micro) point of view. Note that the macro and micro views have much overlap. This, in a way, points out that what is good for ''the enterprise'' may also be good for the country.

However, countertrade must be recognized as a viable proactive tool for doing business. A number of American manufacturers have recently created corporate level positions to do this. Among these are Monsanto, TRW, and Boeing Aircraft. A methodology for a proactive approach to seeking out countertrade opportunities is discussed in Reisman et al. (1989).

NOTE

This chapter is reprinted by permission of the publisher from A. Reisman, D. C. Fuh, and G. Li, ''Achieving An Advantage with Countertrade,'' *Industrial Marketing Management* 17(1): 55–63, copyright 1988 by Elsevier Science Publishing Co. Inc.

Table 14.1
Countertrade Advantages Versus Levels of Development Matrix Macro (Country) Point of View

LEVEL OF ECONOMIC DEVELOPMENT	TRADING PARTNERS COUNTRY	Agrarian	Developing	Developed	Agrarian	Developing	Developed	Agrarian	Developing	Developed
ADVANTAGES	HOME COUNTRY	Agrarian	Agrarian	Agrarian	Developing	Developing	Developing	Developed	Developed	Developed
Preserving Hard Currency		*	*	*	*	*	*			
Improving Balance of Trade		*	*	*	*	*	*			
Accessing Technology & Know-How			*	*			*			
Upgrading Labor Skills			*	*			*			
Upgrading of Market Skills			*	*			*			
Improving Production Standards			*	*			*			
Exposure to Future Technical Innovations			*	*			*			
Access to Alternative Source of Supply					*			*	*	*
Increasing Production Capacity					*	*		*	*	*
Unloading Excess Inventory		*	*	*	*	*	*	*	*	*
Working Out Trade Deal Under Constraints			*	*	*	*	*	*	*	*
Taking Advantage of Sales Opportunities					*			*	*	
Gaining Access to New Markets		*	*	*	*			*	*	
Helping to Introduce a New Product Model					*			*	*	
Reducing Risk of Over Demand Forecast					*			*	*	*
Taking Advantage of Tax & Tariff Laws		*	*	*	*	*	*	*	*	*

Table 14.2

Countertrade Advantages Versus Economic Development Level of Trading Enterprise's Home Country*

LEVEL OF ECONOMIC DEVELOPMENT / ADVANTAGES	COUNTRY OF ENTERPRISE TRADED WITH → HOME COUNTRY OF ENTERPRISE ↓	Agrarian / Agrarian	Developing / Agrarian	Developed / Agrarian	Agrarian / Developing	Developing / Developing	Developed / Developing	Agrarian / Developed	Developing / Developed	Developed / Developed
Preserving Hard Currency		*	*	*	*	*	*			
Improving Balance of Trade		*	*	*	*	*	*			
Accessing Technology & Know-How			*	*			*			
Upgrading Labor Skills			*	*			*			
Upgrading of Market Skills			*	*			*			
Improving Production Standards			*	*			*			
Exposure to Future Technical Innovations			*	*			*			
Access to Alternative Source of Supply					*			*	*	*
Increasing Production Capacity					*	*		*	*	*
Unloading Excess Inventory		*	*	*	*	*	*	*	*	*
Working Out Trade Deal Under Constraints			*	*	*	*	*	*	*	*
Taking Advantage of Sales Opportunities					*			*	*	
Gaining Access to New Markets		*	*	*	*			*	*	
Helping to Introduce a New Product Model					*			*	*	
Reducing Risk of Over Demand Forecast					*			*	*	*
Taking Advantage of Tax & Tariff Laws		*	*	*	*	*	*	*	*	*

*Based on the following assumptions:

1. An enterprise in an agrarian or developing country has abundant raw materials and labor and a potentially large consuming market but lacks hard currency, technology and know-how.
2. An enterprise in an agrarian or developing country is subject to countertrade constraints imposed by government.
3. An enterprise in a developed country has no hard currency or technology restrictions but needs raw materials and sales opportunities.

REFERENCES

Aggarwal, R. 1989. "International Business Through Barter and Countertrade." *Long Range Planning* 22(3): 75–81.

Banks, G. 1983. "The Economics and Politics of Countertrade," *The World Economy* 6(2): 159–82.

Briggs, J. A. 1984. "Back to Barter." *Forbes* 133(6): 40–42.

Bussard, W. A. 1987. "An Overview of Countertrade Practices of Corporations and Individual Nations." In *International Countertrade*, edited by C. M. Korth, 13–28. New York: Quorum Books.

Cohen, S., and J. Zysman. 1986. "Countertrade, Offsets, Barter and Buybacks." *California Management Review* 28(2): 41–56.

Cooper, R. N. 1984. "Why Countertrade?" *Across the Board* 2(3): 36–41.

Mellaart, J. 1967. *Catal Hüyük: Neolithic Town In Anatolia*. New York: McGraw-Hill.

Reisman, A., R. Aggarwal, and D. C. Fuh. 1989. "Seeking Out Profitable Countertrade Opportunities." *Industrial Marketing Management* 18(1): 65–72.

Reisman, A., D. C. Fuh, and G. Li. 1988. "Achieving an Advantage with Countertrade." *Industrial Marketing Management* 17(1): 55–63.

Chapter 15

Countertrade in the Not-for-Profit Sector

INTRODUCTION

As indicated in Chapter 14, the world of not-for-profits encompasses organizations that are varied in terms of employment levels and/or dollar levels. Moreover, the entities are functionally diverse, and may well be geographically dispersed. The not-for-profit sector is the greatest contributor to making ours a kinder and gentler society, yet, as indicated in Chapter 14, the Reagan administration, as a matter of ideology, has contributed to privatization of a number of services previously provided by government (Blumstein 1987) and this trend is not likely to be reversed in the near future.

The need to make the available resources "go further" is perceived by managers of independent sector entities ranging from the Red Cross Society to the tiniest neighborhood association. Much has been written (O'Neill and Young 1988) about this need, especially during the waning years of the Reagan administration. Moreover, prognoses exist for the post-Reagan years indicating that the need will still be there (Salamon and Abramson 1982; Skloot 1987).

This chapter addresses what the independent sector, or not-for-profit agencies, do to parlay their resources to higher levels. Clearly going "hat-in-hand" for more donative resources is standard practice. However, even *philanthropy* has been known to be expanded by countertrading.

Specifically, the chapter discusses the various formats of countertrade, from simple barter to complex joint ventures, as a means of expanding financial and other resources by nonprofit institutions. Examples of the various types of agreements practiced by the various types of institutions are provided and summarized. Lastly, the chapter calls for greater levels of institutional commitments to proactive seeking and consummating countertrade agreements.

Times are getting hard boys, money's getting scarce. If times don't get no better boys, I'm bound to leave this place.

So goes the refrain in one of the American folk ballads. The first part of the refrain is being heard these days, perhaps in somewhat different language, among the management of not-for-profit institutions. However, they have a way out. They need not succumb to the second part of the refrain. One answer lies not in cutting back the quality, quantity, or accessibility of services but in countertrade.

Countertrade practices have deep roots in the not-for-profit sector as well. In the 1730s, Benjamin Franklin (1955 printing) promoted the Free Library Company of Philadelphia, not as a philanthropy to serve the poor but as a device to facilitate book exchanges. By clubbing books in a common library, he and his literary friends each had the advantage of using other members' books—an early form of time sharing. From Franklin's book-clubbing among friends to the great interlibrary loan systems and computer bulletin boards of today, effective not-for-profit organizations have always used countertrade to expand their resources and increase their capacities. But countertrade opportunities cannot be used if they are not recognized. It is the aim of this chapter to encourage the identification of countertrade opportunities by providing a range of examples and a taxonomy of countertrade practices in the not-for-profit sector.

The examples were chosen so as to demonstrate the diversity of the practice in terms of the types of institutions involved and the media of exchange used. This diversity is summarized in Tables 15.1 and 15.2 using the parenthetical numbering of the examples in the text.

DISCUSSION

The commonness and diversity of countertrade in the contemporary not-for-profit sector becomes evident if we consider the various *types of participants*. Many bartering arrangements occur within a single organization. Often these are very large organizations. Within United Way Services of Greater Cleveland, for example, the agency relations and fund raising departments exchange staff at their differing periods of peak activity, and incidentally provide staff members with stimulating and broadening experience.(1) According to a Red Cross executive, departments within her agency frequently engage in department-to-department exchanges on a "cooperative/collaborative" basis.(2) As John Seeley and his associates showed in their classic study of the Indianapolis Community Chest, moreover, every organization that relies on volunteers offers at least some of those volunteers, knowingly or not, a tangible or intangible benefit distinct from the opportunity to work for a deeply valued religious or personal purpose (Seeley et al. 1957). One veteran of parent teachers association (PTA) and church work notes that volunteers sometimes "earn" the opportunity to have their way paid to a convention.

Countertrades also take place with considerable frequency between not-for-profit organizations that provide *similar* services. The Hillel Foundation and the Newman Club on the same university campus, for example, may exchange

Table 15.1
Types of Exchanges Versus Types of Traders

TRADING PARTNERS → HOME INSTITUTION ↓	Private / Private	Public / Private	For-Profit Manufacturing / Private	For-Profit Retailing / Private	For-Profit Service / Private	Private / Public	Public / Public	For-Profit Manufacturing / Public	For-Profit Retailing / Public	For-Profit Service / Public
Tangible Property* for Tangible Property	8,9 12**	9 26	9 23		9	9	9	9 23		9
Tangible Goods for Tangible Goods	27 33	27 33	23		25	27 33	27 33	23		
Tangible Property for Services	11,15 16,27	27	23			27	27	23		
Tangible Goods for Services	3,34, 35	34 35	23				31	23	27	27
Services for Services	1,2,3 4,5,8 9,14,18	9	9		9	9 22	9	9		9 27
Tangible Property for Intangibles	13	20 21	23	18				23	18	
Tangible Goods for Intangibles		32	17 23	17 19		32		23		
Services for Intangibles	3,28		28	28	28 29	28		28	27 28	27,28 29
Intangibles for Intangibles	8,27	27	23			24	27	27	23		

(Left margin vertical label: E X C H A N G E S)

* Tangible property exchanges include but are not limited to occasional use of.

** Numbers in Table 15.1 refer to examples interwoven in the text.

meeting rooms, personnel skills, supplies, and the like.(3) A group of children's mental health centers run regular softball games using a field belonging to one center, umpires from a second, and snacks from a third.(4) Two recreational and rehabilitative centers for the aged exchange the computer programming skills of the staff at one for a recreational-training program at the other.(5) As an associate director of the Society for Crippled Children put it in describing exchanges of professional expertise in activities such as the preparation of annual

Table 15.2
Matrix of Potential Trading Partner Types

TRADING PARTNER

HOME INSTITUTION			Private				Public				For-Profit		
			Cultural	Medical	Educational	Humanitarian*	Cultural	Medical	Educational	Humanitarian	Manufacturing	Retailing	Service
PRIVATE		Cultural	8 33 35	35	33 35	35	33		20 33		17 28	17 28	28
		Medical	11 35	2,4 22,34 35	13 35	12 35	16	32 34		15	28	28	24,28 29
		Educational	30 35	13 35	7 23 35	35			7,23	26	23 28	28	25,28 29
		Humanitarian		35	35	1,3 5,6 10,35				27	18 27 28	18 27 28	27 28
PUBLIC		Cultural	33		33		31 33		33		28	28	28
		Medical		22 34	14			32 34			28	28	28,29
		Educational	20		23				23		23 28	28	28 29
		Humanitarian				27					18 27 28	18 27 28	27 28

* Humanitarian institutions in this context include the various social and/or religious services.

** Numbers in Table 15.2 refer to examples interwoven in the text.

+ Examples of library reciprocities described by 20 can be found for each of the Table 15.2 cells.

reports, the creation of mailing lists, and procedures for strategic planning, "why use valuable dollars for consultants when we share the same goals?"(6)

Barter between similar not-for-profit organizations can, indeed, become so routine that it becomes institutionalized under the aegis of an association. Museums and opera companies increasingly join together to mount projects too large for any single institution or community; the annual meetings of their professional associations provide opportunities for at least the preliminary discussions. As described later, science and technology museums share large-scale traveling exhibits under the auspices of the Association of Science and Technology Centers.(7) The Cleveland Ballet/San Jose Ballet is not the only example of a performing arts company that is supported by not-for-profit associations in two widely separated cities.(8) Interlibrary loan programs have become wonderfully diverse and pervasive in the United States, operating among the great variety of private, public, and corporate libraries in most metropolitan areas.(9) Blood banks, sperm banks, and organ banks provide another example; still another application of the idea is being encouraged by the Robert Wood Johnson Foundation with its Service Credit Banking Program for the Elderly, through which healthy older people provide personal services to the disabled in return for ''service credits'' on which they may draw in their turn.(10) In still another field, cooperative welfare-service information services are at least as old as the Charity Organization Society's *Charities Directory* that appeared in Boston, New York, Philadelphia, and other cities in the 1880s.

Countertrade also takes place between not-for-profit organizations that provide *different* services; for example, between a community hospital and a neighboring cultural institution. Such was the case when the Cleveland Orchestra performed for the dedication of a new outpatient facility at the Cleveland Clinic in exchange for use of a clinic hall for the orchestra's annual ball.(11) As another example the Cleveland Clinic swapped some land to develop more convenient parking with some neighboring churches in exchange for repaving church parking lots.(12) The Cleveland Health Education Museum allows Cleveland Clinic patients free access to its exhibits in exchange for occasional use of clinic meeting rooms.(13)

Similarly, a mental health program for youth trains students from a music school in techniques of music therapy, receiving in return music lessons for its clients.(14) In an exchange between two organizations from other parts of the not-for-profit field, one northeastern Ohio county Planned Parenthood Association provides certain tests and other services to patients in a maternal health clinic in exchange for the use of space in a community development agency's premises.(15) The American Red Cross of Greater Cleveland has provided storage space for a vehicle owned by a not-for-profit organization in another field, in return for regular use of the vehicle.(16) The Jewish Vocational Service of Cleveland has bartered printing services for staff training. It seems likely that barter between different kinds of not-for-profit organizations is becoming more and more common, and that some community welfare federations or United Ways are already trying to formalize exchanges of staff training, expertise, and perhaps of vehicles and space.

Moreover, for-profit companies have been known to countertrade goods or services for space and/or services with cultural, medical or educational institutions. The Cleveland Playhouse provided advertisement space in one of its program brochures to the Sherwin Williams Co. in exchange for some dated paint stock.(17)

Profit-making organizations often provide services or goods in exchange for advertising or other promotional benefits; examples range from the provision of a truck, emblazoned with corporate advertising, to a group of hunger centers (18), to the provision of an $80,000 marketing campaign to a national campaign in return for the prestige and exposure provided by a small statement on campaign materials used in the 164 largest metropolitan markets in the United States.(19)

Swaps have also taken place between private not-for-profits and public institutions. Cleveland State University, for example, donated some stage equipment to the Cleveland Playhouse in exchange for training one of its students.(20) Red Cross chapters on occasion provide vehicles for community use in return for official or semi-official acceptance of Red Cross activities or support of Red Cross fund raising campaigns.(21) In an interesting and complex variation on the not-for-profit/government exchange, mental health centers have taken over responsibility for patients, thus reducing the patient census at a government agency, in return for staff assistance needed for those patients.(22)

Still more complex arrangements can involve organizations from all three sectors. Public and private museums have traditionally exchanged exhibits within highly organized networks such as memberships in the Association of Science and Technology Centers mentioned earlier. Some of these exhibits have originated in swaps with capital equipment manufacturers in the fields of communications, nuclear power, medical imaging, transportation, and the like, as well as producers of pharmaceuticals, foods, and other consumables. Such swaps have included exchanges of artifacts for a subtle form of brand-name advertising and/or public awareness. Some have involved artifacts for use of, or free access to, the exhibits.(23)

The following describes a good example of innovative marketing by a medical institution collaborating with a for-profit service company.

Some 50,000 American Express card members in Greater Cleveland were invited to tour the Cleveland Clinic campus and attend a health-care seminar on one of eight dates in October or November. The direct mail invitations were the result of an innovative and unique cooperative marketing program between American Express and the Clinic. The pilot program sought to inform American Express card members about services at the Clinic, and to encourage them to use their American Express card to pay for health-care services there.

The small-group tours, which were led by employees, gave cardholders a behind-the-scenes look at the Clinic. The complimentary seminars, conducted by members of the professional staff, covered topics ranging from sports medicine to aesthetic medicine. The program was organized by the departments of Marketing and of Consumer Affairs. (*Innerpulse Update* 1987).(24)

Other examples of subtle marketing trades include the following. The Cleveland Institute of Music is swapping air-time on WCLV, a commercial radio station specializing in classical music, for a page promoting WCLV on its brochure.(25) The Cleveland Institute of Art is using gallery space in the Ohio State Office building.(26) Both institutes are independent not-for-profit institutions.

Similarly, it is not uncommon to find in-service, in-kind, and other reciprocities between public and/or private social service agencies with each other and with the for-profit sector.(27) Such a case is currently being negotiated between the Cuyahoga County (Ohio) Mental Health Board and several community development corporations. The objective is to find permanent housing in the community for the mentally ill. In the proposal, the board would provide 40 percent of the total cost of building redevelopment for an allocation of 25 percent of the units to board clients over a forty-year contractual period. The board contracts with private businesses via a private non-profit organization called Panta Rhei, Inc., to provide office cleaning, furniture stripping, and a variety of manufacturing processes performed by mentally ill clients referred from various mental health centers in the community. Panta Rhei, Inc., performs office cleaning services for the Free Clinic in exchange for blood monitoring services performed on Panta Rhei clients and supervisors working in the furniture stripping operations.

The entire field of volunteerism in the not-for-profit sector is based on reciprocity. Services are provided in return for self-satisfaction on the part of the volunteers at one extreme.(28) At the other extreme fairly tangible returns from the networking accrue to the participants. Such is the case when lawyers and accountants serve on committees or boards along with corporate executives and/or business entrepreneurs. Medical and dental schools use dental practitioners in the clinical education of neophytes in exchange for professorial titles, a prestige factor to the practitioner in attracting and keeping (clients) patients.(29)

In most metropolitan areas, different kinds of libraries (e.g., public, county, and/or city) have exchange privileges in the form of interlibrary loans, searches, and even pickup and delivery systems with private sector counterparts. The latter may be in not-for-profit institutions or in the corporate world, for example, industry and/or services such as law firms.(30)

Lastly, exchanges often take place across national boundaries. Some of these are arranged for on a government-to-government basis. Other exchanges are arranged for by an institution dealing with a government of another country. Such was the case between the Ontario Science Center and the People's Republic of China trading exhibit making services for a "7000 Years of Science in China"(31) exhibit. Some trades are arranged directly between institutions, as was the case between the Cleveland Clinic and the London Independent Hospital.(32) The purpose of that program is to facilitate collaboration in neuroscience research and education aimed at improving clinical care for epilepsy patients in the United States and Great Britain (Affiliate Agreement 1987).

The structure of Table 15.1 provides a generic summary of the kinds of exchanges that are possible in relation to the types of trading partners and the structure of Table 15.2 further breaks down the potential trading partner types. The numbers within each of these tables refer to the examples cited in the text and are so referenced.

Although both of these tables implicitly assume two-way exchanges, this is not always true. As in the for-profit sector one can find three-way and four-way exchanges, for example, institution *A* provides goods or services to institution *B*, *B* provides goods or services to institution *C*, and *C* repays in kind to *A*, and so on. More specifically, theater sets, costumes, and other ancillaries are often traded between two or more private and/or public institutions with the same interest.(33) The Panta Rhei, Inc., operations often involve multiple entities.

In the not-for-profit sector, it is also useful to classify the goods and services involved in countertrade in accordance with distinctions that are particularly relevant to organizations in that sector. The following taxonomy draws a line between property, goods, and services used in the ordinary course of business and those specially related to the special missions (religious, educational, medical, therapeutic, patriotic, aesthetic) for not-for-profit organizations. The taxonomy also draws a line between the different kinds of "intangibles" that come into play in the not-for-profit sector, namely the intangibles that can serve immediate practical purposes (opportunities for making contacts, building networks and alliances, gaining visibility and prestige) and the intangibles represented by opportunities to serve ultimate religious or personal values.

Tangible Property	indoor space, outdoor space, vehicles, indoor, outdoor, or print media advertising space, and the like, used in ordinary conduct of business.
Tangible Goods	capital goods, consumer goods, office supplies, medical supplies, mailing lists, and the like, used in ordinary conduct of business.
Special Goods	books, works of art, museum displays, theatrical sets and props, blood, and the like, necessary to the mission of a not-for-profit organization.
Staff Services	leadership training and techniques, professional, managerial, financial, education and training, and other services utilized by staff members in their effort to carry on the activities of their organization.
Professional Client Services	medical, psychological, counselling and case work, therapeutic, educational, and other services utilized by the clients of not-for-profit organizations.
Personal Client Services	cooking, cleaning, errand running, grooming, and other personal services provided to the clients of not-for-profit organizations.
Performances and Exhibits	musical, theatrical, art, historical, and the like.
Intangibles: Networks and the like	networking opportunities, visibility, contacts, prestige, and the like.
Intangibles: Ultimate Values	opportunities to serve basic religious or personal values.

The purpose of this chapter is to identify some of the key characteristics of countertrade or barter in the not-for-profit sector, not to measure the extent of such trade. Yet a preliminary analysis of the thirty-odd cases assembled here suggests several observations about patterns of exchange among different elements. Future research will indicate whether these hypothesized patterns are in fact commonly found. If they are, we will know where the managers of not-for-profit organizations ought to look first in their search for resource-enhancing countertrades. The preliminary observations are

1. Not-for-profit organizations rather frequently engage in the trade of tangible goods and tangible property used in ordinary business. Perhaps this is due to the relative ease in which equivalent values can be agreed on in this case. Many such trades involve advertising of one sort or another; this fact may reflect in part the prevalence of barter in the advertising business.

2. Exchanges of "special" goods among not-for-profit organizations are often highly organized (through interlibrary loan and blood bank systems, for example). This is consistent with the fact that it is the mission of many not-for-profit organizations to increase access to scarce, highly valued objects.

3. The staffs of not-for-profit organizations often exchange specialized staff services with one another (trading accounting expertise for strategic planning advice, for example). This would seem to reflect the demand for and the scarcity of specialized management skills in not-for-profit organizations.

4. Board members and other nonstaff friends of not-for-profits often provide staff services in return for a variety of intangibles.

5. Professional client services rarely figure in trades. Perhaps this is because not-for-profit social agencies are set up to raise the money needed to pay professionals to provide services that potential clients cannot afford—or for which they would not choose to pay. Perhaps, also, the canons of ethics in some professional fields forbid the provision of services without money payment. (Professional courtesy among medical doctors is a special case that does not constitute an exception to the generalization that professional services for the *clients* of not-for-profit organizations are rarely subject to barter.)

6. Personal services to clients are quite frequently involved in trades between not-for-profit organizations.

7. Artistic performances, museum exhibits, and educational work figure in trades fairly often, and seem not to be restrained by customs like those that control professional services.

8. Intangibles are rarely traded for intangibles. Perhaps this reflects the fact that not-for-profit organizations usually have intangibles to offer and are sadly short of tangible resources.

Table 15.3 provides yet another way (e.g., based on types and exchanges) of classifying countertrade transactions in the nonprofits.

Countertrades, moreover, are not limited to one-time transactions, albeit these are the most prevalent. They may well be long-term contractual obligations as is the case in *joint ventures*, for example, a number of independent not-for-profits forming a new organization to provide a commonly needed service but with the benefits of "economies of scale." Indeed, joint ventures are probably

Table 15.3
Matrix of Potential Countertrade Combinations

	Tangible Property	Tangible Goods	Special Goods	Special Services	Professional Client Services	Personal Client Services	Performances and Exhibits	Intangibles: Networks etc.	Intangibles: Ultimate Values
Tangible Property									
Tangible Goods									
Special Goods									
Staff Services									
Professional Client Services									
Personal Client Services									
Performances and Exhibits									
Intangibles: Networks etc.									
Intangibles: Ultimate Values									

the most well established mode of countertrade in the not-for-profit sector, albeit they are rarely called that. Group buying by hospitals dates back to 1917 (34), according to Van Tassel and Grabowski (1987; see the Center for Health, Greater Cleveland Hospital Association). Joint or united fund raising predates group buying by at least fifteen years. The Cleveland Federation of Jewish Charities, a precursor to the still existing Jewish Community Federation dates back to 1903 (Van Tassel and Grabowski 1987). In 1957, a number of independent Cleveland cultural, educational, and medical institutions, located in a park-like setting, banded together to form University Circle Inc. (UCI 1987). This organization is still operational. It provides security, transportation, parking, planning, and land management services to thirty-nine independent member institutions and twenty-six associate member organizations.(35)

Table 15.4 lists various joint venture formats called linkages by its author. For each of the linkages, the table indicates the respective resource requirements, incentives, time duration, and extent of impact on accessibility, continuity, and efficiency. Note that in the above, even though some of these ''linkages'' show up as being of ''short'' time duration, few with perhaps the exception of a

Table 15.4
Linkages: Their Impact and Resources as Well as Incentives and Time Needed to Develop Them

Linkages	Requirements Resources/Incentives	Time	Impact on Accessibility Continuity and Efficiency
Joint budgeting	Formal authority control over fund access: support staff	Long	High
Joint funding including in-kind	Cash; persuasion	Moderate	Medium high
Purchase of service	Cash	Short	High
Consolidated personnel administration (excl. training)	Formal authority; control over fund access	Long	High[b]
Training	Persuasion; cash; expertise	Short	Medium high
Joint use of staff	Formal authority; persuasion shared objectives; control over fund access[a]	Moderate	Medium
Staff transfer	Shared objectives; formal authority[a]: control over fund access[a]	Long	Medium
Colocation	Formal authority; facility; control over fund access[a]	Short-Moderate	High
Staff outstationing	Shared objectives; client bridge or buffer; formal authority	Short-Moderate	High
Joint planning	Formal authority; control over fund access; support staff	Long	High
Joint development of operating policies	Formal authority; control over fund access; persuasion	Short	High
Information sharing	Persuasion	Short	Medium
Joint programming	Support staff; access to funds; persuasion formal authority; control over fund access	Short-Moderate	Medium-high
Joint evaluation	Formal authority; control over fund access; support staff	Moderate-Long	High
Record keeping	Formal authority[a]; control over fund access; common facility	Moderate-Long	Medium

Table 15.4 (continued)

Linkages	Requirements Resources/Incentives	Time	Impact on Accessibility Continuity and Efficiency
Grants management	Control over fund access; limited number of grants	Short-Moderate	Medium
Central support	Support staff	Short	High
Outreach	Staff; formal authority; control over fund access; common facility	Short	High
Intake	Staff; formal authority; control over fund access; common facility	Moderate-Long	High
Diagnosis	Staff; formal authority; control over fund access[a]; common facility	Short-Moderate	High
Referral	Staff; formal authority; control over fund access[a]; common facility	Short	High
Follow-up	Staff; formal authority; control over fund access[a]; common facility	Short	High
Modes of case coordination	Common facility; persuasion	Short-Moderate	High

[a] Hypothesis not directly indicated by fieldwork.

[b] Impact probably confined to efficiency.

From [UNKNOWN SOURCE]

"purchase of service" are in the nature of a single transaction such as swapping goods for a one-time advertisement in a theater program.

Academic communities in the Western world have shied away from any serious consideration of the various formats of what is known as countertrade. In fact, such material does not appear in the curricula of business management nor in those curricula catering to teaching administration for the various not-for-profit sectors. Moreover, research studies of countertrade appear to be a virgin area in the management sciences, administrative sciences, as well as in economics, finance, and marketing. The literature on the subject is at most descriptive and/or anecdotal.

SUMMARY

Some of the specific reasons for engaging in countertrade discussed in Reisman et al. (1989) and in Reisman (1991) are summarized below:

To serve as an alternative to
- Additional fund raising
- Raising fees for services
- Cutting back on
  * Quality of services offered
  * Quantity of services offered
  * Mix of services offered
  * Accessibility to services offered
    —Physical (geographic locations)
    —Temporal (extended hours)
    —Economic (reduction of fees based on ability to pay)

To help ease the burden of acquiring needed but costly
- Plant/Facilities
- Land
- Technology
- Equipment
- Professional Knowhow/Skills
- Materials
  * Consumables
  * Disposables
  * Reusables

To boost cash imcome

To expand usage of excess capacity
- Plant/Facilities
- Equipment
- Personnel

To off-load excess
- Plant
- Equipment

- Materials
  - * Consumables
  - * Disposables
  - * Reusables
To upgrade
- Personnel Skills
  - * provider personnel
  - * service personnel
  - * marketing personnel
  - * fund raising personnel
  - * public relations personnel
To access alternative sources of supply
To reduce risk of lowered future demand
To open new "markets"/catchment areas for
- clients
- volunteers
- donors
- donations
- exposure

CONCLUDING REMARKS

It was indicated earlier that countertrading in its various formats has been practiced in the non-profit sector for generations. In some branches of this sector, such as the museums, it is highly institutionalized at least in terms of exhibit trading. In most other branches, such as social or community services, it is at best an ad hoc practice. This chapter suggests that each institution should consider adapting this mode of expanding and extending its resources and should do so in a systematic proactive manner.

In an earlier chapter directed to the for-profit sector we suggest a proactive approach to seeking out profitable countertrade opportunities. It can be shown that the approach is transferable to the various not-for-profit type institutions discussed in this chapter (Reisman 1991). However, in order to take full advantage of the myriad of potential opportunities, institutions must follow the lead of corporate giants, such as TRW, Monsanto, and the like, who have recently established corprorate-level positions with the responsibility of identifying and structuring countertrade deals. The "Enterprises" section of the Ontario Science Museum is one example of this type of thinking in the world of non-profits.

NOTE

This chapter is based on "Countertrade: A Means of Expanding Financial Resources in the Not-for-Profit Sector," by A. Reisman and D. Hammack, Technical Memorandum #640, Department of Operations Research, Case Western Reserve University, Cleveland,

Ohio. This work was partially supported by a grant from the Mandel Center for Nonprofit Organizations, CWRO, Cleveland, Ohio.

REFERENCES

Affiliate Agreement. 1987. The Cleveland Clinic Foundation. Cleveland, OH.

Blumstein, A. 1987. "The Current Missionary Role of OR/MS." *Operations Research* 35(6): 926–29.

Cooper, R. N. 1984. "Why Countertrade?" *Across the Board* 2(3): 36–41.

Franklin, Benjamin. 1955 printing. *Autobiography.* New York: Washington Square Press.

Fuh, D. C., A. Reisman, and G. Li. 1987. "Ranges for Negotiating Countertrade Transactions Under the Comparative Advantage Theory." Technical Memorandum #616, Department of Operations Research, Case Western Reserve University, Cleveland, Ohio.

Innerpulse Update. 1987. The Cleveland Clinic Foundation, vol. 2, no. 38, September 21.

O'Neill, M., and D. Young. 1988. *Educating Managers of Non-Profit Organizations.* New York: Praeger Publishers.

Reisman, A. 1991. "Enhancing Philanthropy via Countertrade (Barter)." *Nonprofit Management and Leadership* 1(3): 253–65.

Reisman, A., R. Aggarwal, and D. C. Fuh. 1989. "Seeking Out Profitable Countertrade Opportunities." *Industrial Marketing Management* 18(1): 65–72.

Reisman, A., D. C. Fuh, and G. Li. 1988. "Achieving an Advantage with Countertrade." *Industrial Marketing Mangement* 17(1): 55–63.

Salamon, L. M., and A. Abramson. 1982. *Federal Budget and the Non-Profit Sector.* Washington, D.C.: Urban Institute Press.

Seeley, John et al. 1957. *Community Chest.* Glencoe, Ill.: The Free Press.

Skloot, E. 1987. "Enterprise and Commerce in Non-Profit Organizations." In *Non-Profit Sector: A Research Handbook*, edited by W. W. Powell, 380–93. New Haven, Conn.: Yale University Press.

UCI (University Circle Inc.). 1987. Annual Report, Cleveland, Ohio.

Van Tassel, D. D., and J. J. Grabowski, eds. 1987. *Encyclopedia of Cleveland History.* Bloomington and Indianapolis, Ind.: Indiana University Press.

Section 4

Management Science Methodology

The preceding six chapters discussed taxonomies intended for a fairly comprehensive description of several significant fields of knowledge. All of these fields are ripe for some form of management science type structuring.

The next two chapters address two highly explored management science areas. Both discounted cash flow analysis (DCFA) and mathematical programming (MP) have been part of the management scientist's "tool bag" for a number of decades. Both subjects have been, and are still being, taught by starting with the most simple of cases and then introducing, in incremental steps, greater levels of generality.

As discussed in Chapter 1, such has also been the approach of engineering schools in introducing fluid mechanics even though the field possessed generalized formulations in the form of the Navier-Stokes equations.

Following up on the challenge of Chapter 1, we next introduce general formulations for DCFA and for MP in order to illustrate the most general case of the taxonomy of taxonomies presented in Chapter 3.

Chapter 16 presents a mathematical model describing a very general case in discounted cash flow analysis. A systematic study of all other cases, in the order of decreasing complexity, follows. The general model reduces to their present worth all disbursements and receipts involved in the possession and operation of a succession of equipment having varying initial costs, life spans, salvage values, and income and cost functions. All possible special cases of the general model are presented in a systematic fashion. Finally, previous models and working decision rules are fit into the framework of this model as special cases.

Chapter 17 attempts to unify a broad, although not exhaustive, arena of mathematical programming (MP). The approach involves development of a general MP formulation, which is shown to reduce, in a deductive manner, to each of the major MP subfields. A taxonomy for classifying these subfields is provided and the premiere algorithms for solving each of the cases are duly indicated and referenced.

Discounted Cash Flow Analysis: A Generalized Formulation and Classification

INTRODUCTION

The general model of DCFA as initially published (Reisman and Buffa 1962) reduces, to their present worth, all disbursements and receipts involved in the possession and operation of a succession of equipment having varying initial costs, life spans, salvage values, and income and cost functions.

Mathematical relationships for all of the less complicated cases in equipment investment policy may be obtained by merely dropping or simplifying certain terms in the general model expression. Thus, it is possible to cover the entire field in a systematic manner. The section that follows defines all of the cases that may arise in equipment investment policy decisions. Subsequent sections treat some of these cases individually.

Let C symbolize the fact that the equipment in question will be replaced at some intervals of time. The intervals in this "chain," in general, are not periodic. In addition,

E symbolizes the operating expenses or disbursements for each individual piece of equipment

R symbolizes the revenues of receipts that are due to the possession and/or operation of a piece of equipment

B symbolizes the purchase price of the equipment

S symbolizes the salvage value

Thus, the case involving C, E, R, B, and S (*CERBS*) is the worst possible, or most general, situation. It considers a chain or succession of equipment. Each item in this chain has its own individual purchase price, salvage value, operating income, and expense functions, as well as its economic life span. The great majority of management decisions, however, are based on the comparison of cases less complicated than *CERBS*, but from it they can all be derived. For

Figure 16.1
Structure of Special Cases of the General Model *CERBS*

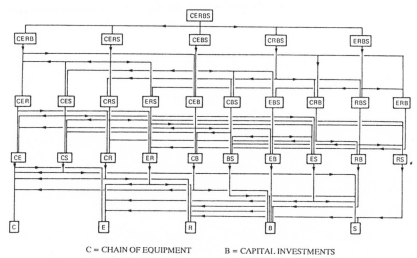

C = CHAIN OF EQUIPMENT   B = CAPITAL INVESTMENTS
E = OPERATING DISBURSEMENT   S = SALVAGE VALUE   R = OPERATING RECEIPTS

example, should management be faced with a decision among several alternative items of equipment, which are not to be succeeded, a comparison of *ERBS* is required. Furthermore, should the piece of equipment in question not have any assignable income or revenue function, only *EBS* need be considered. Following this type of thinking, all possible cases may be formulated. Figure 16.1 presents graphically all major subgroupings.

DERIVATION OF THE GENERAL MODEL

Purchase Price

The price of each unit in a chain or succession of equipment may, in general, have its own characteristic value. Hence, the first item can be bought for B_0, but its first replacement will cost B_1 and the second replacement can be had for B_2. In general, the jth replacement will cost B_j. The worth of the first item at the time management has decided, or will decide, to follow through on the investment program at T_0 or time $= 0$, is B_0. However, the present worth of the purchase price of the first replacement at time $= 0$ is less than B_1. The sum B_1 will not be needed until replacement time, which is at the end of the economic life period T_1 of the initial item of equipment purchased for B_0. Hence, to raise a sum of money equal to B_1 during the interval between time 0 and T_1, management can invest at time zero the sum $B_1 e^{-rT_1}$ and let it earn interest at the rate r so that at time $= T_1$, B_1 will be available. The term $B_1 e^{-rT_1}$ is therefore the "present worth" at time zero of the value B_1.

The worth at time zero of the money required to purchase the second replacement is $B_2e^{-r(T_1+T_2)}$, where T_2 represents the economic life of the first replacement. Note that the second replacement will take place $(T_1 + T_2)$ units of time from time zero. Similarly, the jth replacement will take place

$$(T_1 + T_2 + T_3 + \cdots + T_j) = \sum_{i=0}^{j} (T_i) \qquad (16.1)$$

units of time from time zero. Hence, the present worth at time zero of the money required to buy the jth replacement, which will take place at the time described by equation (16.1), is

$$B_je^{-r\sum_{i=0}^{j}(T_i)}$$

Consequently, the worth at time zero of the investments to be made for purchasing n items of equipment, each item replacing the one before it, is

$$
\begin{aligned}
B &= B_0 + B_1e^{-rT_1} + B_2e^{-r(T_1+T_2)} + \cdots + B_je^{-r(T_1+T_2+\cdots+T_j)} \\
&\quad + \cdots + B_ne^{-r(T_1+T_2+\cdots+T_j+\cdots+T_n)} \qquad (16.2) \\
&= B_je^{-r_i\sum_{i=0}^{j}(T_i)}
\end{aligned}
$$

Salvage Value

The value of a piece of equipment, when it is retired from service, may, in general, vary from one to the next succeeding item in a chain. This value may be positive, negative, or zero. However, unless it is zero, it must be considered. It can only be realized at the end of its life period T. Hence, the worth at time zero of the salvage value S of the first piece of equipment in a chain is

$$S_0(T_0) = S_0(T_1)e^{-rT_1}$$

The salvage value of the first replacement discounted to time zero is

$$S_1(T_0) = S_1(T_2)e^{-r(T_1+T_2)}$$

and the discounted salvage value of the jth replacement is

$$S_j(T_0) = S_j(T_{j+1})e^{-r(T_1+T_2+\cdots+T_j+T_{j+1})} = S_j(T_{j+1})e^{-r\sum_{i=0}^{j}(T_{i+1})}$$

The total salvage value of the chain at time zero therefore is

$$S = \sum_{j=0}^{n} S_j(T_{j+1})e^{-r\sum_{i=0}^{j}(T_{i+1})} \qquad (16.3)$$

Expense Function

Expenses attributable to the operation, possession, and/or ownership of a piece of equipment are incurred by the enterprise throughout the life of the equipment

This being opposed to the lump payment or receipt at the beginning or end of the item's economic life as in the cases previously considered (i.e., purchase price and salvage value). Hence, it is necessary to consider all expenses as they incur and discount them first to the beginning of the item's life and second to time zero. For the first item in the chain, the beginning of life is often time zero. Hence, the expenses E incurred throughout its life are

$$E(T) = \int_0^{T_1} E(t)\,dt$$

where $E(t)$ is some function of time describing the expected rate of expense accumulation.

In line with a previous statement regarding expenses being incurred continuously, they have to be capitalized or discounted in the same fashion, hence the present worth at time zero of $E(t)$ is

$$E = \int_0^{T_1} E(t)e^{-rt}\,dt \tag{16.4}$$

Now, if the beginning of the economic life does not coincide with time zero, then it is necessary to further discount equation (16.4). Thus, the present worth at time zero of all expenses incurred by the jth item in a chain is

$$\begin{aligned}
E_j &= \int_0^{T_{i+1}} E_j(t)e^{-rt}\,dt\ e^{-r(T_1+T_2+\cdots+T_j)} \\
&= \int_0^{T_{i+1}} E_j(t)e^{-rt}\,dt\ e^{-r\sum_{i=0}^{j} T_i}
\end{aligned} \tag{16.5}$$

Consequently, the worth at time zero of all expenses incurred by all items in a chain of equipment is

$$E = \sum_{j=0}^{n}\left[e^{-r\sum_{i=0}^{j} T_i} \int_0^{T_{i+1}} E_j(t)e^{-rt}\,dt \right] \tag{16.6}$$

Revenue Functions

The meaning and derivation of the revenue function R parallels exactly that of the expense function. Hence, only the final result will be stated:

$$R = \sum_{j=0}^{n}\left[e^{-r\sum_{i=0}^{j} T_i} \int_0^{T_{i+1}} R_j(t)e^{-rt}\,dt \right] \tag{16.7}$$

General Model

The worth P at time zero of all receipts and disbursements attributable to the ownership and/or possession, as well as operation, of a succession of equipment is

Figure 16.2
Structure of Variables in the Special Cases of *CERBS*

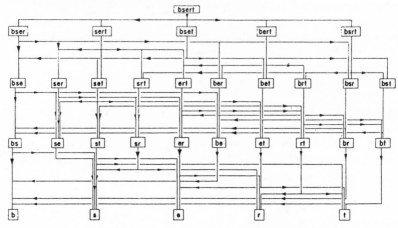

b = VARIABLE PURCHASE PRICE   r = VARIABLE REVENUE FUNCTION

s = VARIABLE SALVAGE VALUE   t = VARIABLE LIFE PERIOD   e = VARIABLE EXPENSE FUNCTION

$$P = B - S + E - R$$

or

$$P = \sum_{j=0}^{n}\left[B_j e^{-r\sum_{i=0}^{j} T_i} \right] - \sum_{j=0}^{n}\left[S_j(T_{j+1})e^{-r\sum_{i=0}^{j}(T_{i+1})} \right]$$

$$+ \sum_{j=0}^{n}\left[e^{-r\sum_{i=0}^{j} T_i} \int_0^{T_{i+1}} E_j(t)e^{-rt}\, dt \right] \qquad (16.8)$$

$$- \sum_{j=0}^{n}\left[e^{-r\sum_{i=0}^{j} T_i} \int_0^{T_{i+1}} R_j(t)e^{-rt}\, dt \right]$$

Each item in a succession of equipment may, in the general case, have its own characteristic purchase price, salvage value, revenue and expense function, and economic life. Thus, the particular case symbolized by *CERBS* has no less than thirty-one subgroups. Figure 16.1 presents the thirty-one subgroups of CERBS. Note that in each of these subgroups, all of the items *E, R, B, S,* and *T* appear whether they are variable or not. Hence, a tabulation similar to Figure 16.1 can be developed for each of the subgroups of *CERBS* to indicate which of the terms *C, E, R, B, S,* and *T* appear as variable in the *CERBS* case. This is done in Figure 16.2 by using lower case letters. It can be shown that the most popular models used in investment analysis are special cases of the general model symbolized by *CERBS*.

THE UNIFICATION

It should be recognized that many, if not all, of the questions to which traditional engineering economy approaches have addressed themselves are, in fact, special cases of equation (16.8) and can be thus handled. We next discuss most of these methodologies, formulate them, and deduce their mathematical models from that equation. We also delineate for each methodology its specific case designation based on the *CERBS/bsert* classification scheme.

It will become quite evident that when the various standard methodologies of managerial or engineering economy are deduced from the general model, equation (16.8), the term

$$\sum_{j=0}^{n} e^{-r \sum_{i=0}^{j} T_i} = \sum_{j=0}^{n} e^{-rj} \tag{16.9}$$

keeps recurring. This is so because standard approaches are based on equal time increments, that is $T_1 = T_2 = T_3 = \cdots = T_j$. Moreover, the T_js are usually unity (equal to 1).

SINKING FUND

A question often raised in economy studies is what uniform series of end-of-period payments $\bar{R}$ must be made for n periods at compound interest r (nominal) in order to assure a future amount S? Using equation (16.8), we may formulate the problem as follows: The present worth of a series of deposits on payments spanning over a period of n years must be equal to the present worth of a fixed sum S at the end of this period. Thus, if we consider the sum S as a form of "salvage value," then equation (16.8) can be seen to reduce to

$$P = 0 = \sum_{j=0}^{n} Re^{-\sum_{i=0}^{j} rT_i} - S(n)e^{-\sum_{i=0}^{n} rT_i} \tag{16.10}$$

However, since our series of payments must begin at the end of each period, as opposed to its beginning, and there must be n such payments, and not $n + 1$, we must make a modification to the first term on the right-hand side of equation (16.10). This modification merely subtracts out the contribution that would otherwise be made by a payment occurring at time zero, that is, the term $\bar{R}e^{-0r}$, which is, of course, $\bar{R} \times 1$. Figure 16.3 graphically depicts the cash flow and discounting procedures for this case. Inasmuch as $\bar{R}$ in this case is a constant, we can take it outside the summation sign. Furthermore, the T_is in this case are all equal, generally one year, we can therefore drop to T_i notation here. Combining above modifications, the first term results in

Figure 16.3
Sinking Fund: The Discounting of a Series of Payments and of the Accumulated Sum to Their Present Values

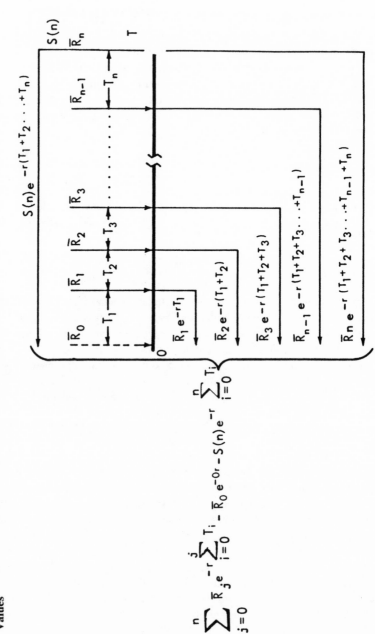

$$\bar{R} \left(\sum_{j=0}^{n} e^{-rj} - 1 \right) \tag{16.11}$$

Moreover, the multiplicand of the second term is seen to be

$$e^{-\sum\limits_{i;0}^{n} rT_i} = e - rn \tag{16.12}$$

Thus, solving explicitly for $\bar{R}$, the resulting sinking fund equation is

$$\bar{R} = S(n) \frac{e^{-rn}}{\left(\sum\limits_{j=0}^{n} e^{-rj} - 1 \right)} \tag{16.13}$$

Under the above formulation this is seen to be the *RS* subcase of *CERBS* and the 0 (zero) subcase of *bsert*.

UNIFORM-SERIES COMPOUND AMOUNT

Given a uniform series of n end-of-the-period payments $\bar{R}$, what will this series accumulate to at compound interest (nominal) r? This question is not at all unlike the one asked in the immediately preceding section. As a matter of fact, it is identical except for the fact that here we are given $\bar{R}$ and are seeking the value of $S(n)$. Thus, the formulation and delineation of the *CERBS* classification here is identical to the one already performed, but the resulting equation is, of course, a rearrangement of equation (16.13):

$$S(n) = \bar{R} \frac{\left(\sum\limits_{j=0}^{n} e^{-rj} - 1 \right)}{e^{-rn}} \tag{16.14}$$

ANNUITY

What is the present worth of an annuity or a series of equal payments for n periods (say years) if the going rate of interest is r? This is, of course, the zero subcase of *bsert*, that is, all the factors of *CERBS* that are effective in a nonvarying fashion. That is, the revenue function R is a constant $\bar{R}$ throughout. The periods T_i are, in fact, each equal to one year. Now, since only R is effective here, this is the R or, at best, the *CR* subcase of *CERBS*, depending on the position taken regarding the annual payments.

We note this to be a special case of the sinking fund. Inasmuch as we are merely interested here in the present worth of the series of payments, we are not accumulating any given sum at the end of the period as we did in the preceding two sections. The cash flow diagram for this case is therefore seen in Figure 16.4 to be a simpler version of that of Figure 16.3.

Figure 16.4
Annuity: The Discounting of a Series of Payments to Their Present Worth

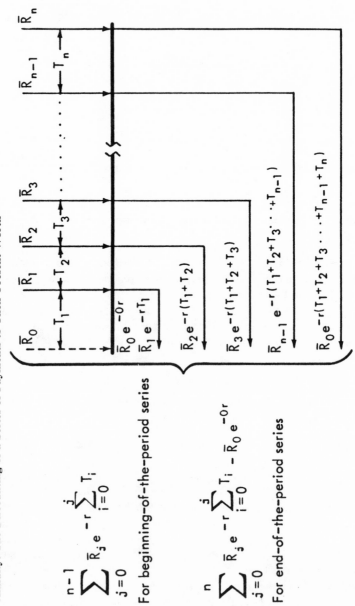

$$\sum_{j=0}^{n-1} \bar{R}_j e^{-r \sum_{i=0}^{j} T_i}$$

For beginning-of-the-period series

$$\sum_{j=0}^{n} \bar{R}_j e^{-r \sum_{i=0}^{j} T_i} - \bar{R}_0 e^{-0r}$$

For end-of-the-period series

Just as in the previous two sections, we must be careful here in our understanding as to whether the payments are made at the beginning or the end of the time interval. Thus, if payments are to be made over a period of n years, and they are to be paid at the beginning of each year starting at time zero, then the present worth equation is seen to be

$$P = \sum_{j=0}^{n-1} \bar{R}_j \, e^{-r \sum_{i=0}^{j} T_i} \tag{16.15}$$

The limits of our summation span from 0 to $n - 1$. As can be seen from the diagram, this is required because otherwise, that is, if our upper limit were taken as n, the number of payments that would be involved would be $n + 1$. One can verify this by drawing a diagram similar to Figure 16.5 and picking a given value for n. Another way of justifying above is to recognize that the end of the period that began with the $(n - 1)$th payment is, in fact, the end of the nth period.

Now, if our series of payments is to be made at the end of each year or calendar period, then we must, of course, keep within our series the nth payment $\bar{R}_n$, that is, the one at the end of the nth year but, we must remove the 0th payment $\bar{R}_0$. The present worth equation for the end-of-the-period payment series therefore is

$$P = \sum_{j=0}^{n} \bar{R}_j \, e^{-r \sum_{i=0}^{j} T_i} - R_0 \, e^{-0r} \tag{16.16}$$

Inasmuch as the time periods are equal,

$$T_1 = T_2 = T_3 = \cdots = T_i$$

one year in general practice and the payments are equal,

$$R_1 = R_2 = R_3 = \cdots = R_n$$

both equations (16.15) and (16.16) can be rewritten as follows:

Beginning-of-the-period annuity

$$P = \bar{R} \sum_{j=0}^{n-1} e^{-r \sum_{i=0}^{j} T_i} = \bar{R} \sum_{j=0}^{n-1} e^{-rj} \tag{16.17}$$

End-of-the-period annuity

$$P = \bar{R} \left(\sum_{j=0}^{n} e^{-r \sum_{i=0}^{j} T_i} - 1 \right) = \bar{R} \left(\sum_{j=0}^{n} e^{-rj} - 1 \right) \tag{16.18}$$

Note that the (-1) term in the parentheses represents e^{-r0} being subtracted from a series that includes it and that is so tabulated in Reisman (1968).

Alternatively, the question may be raised, what is the rate of return on in-

Figure 16.5
Deferred Annuity

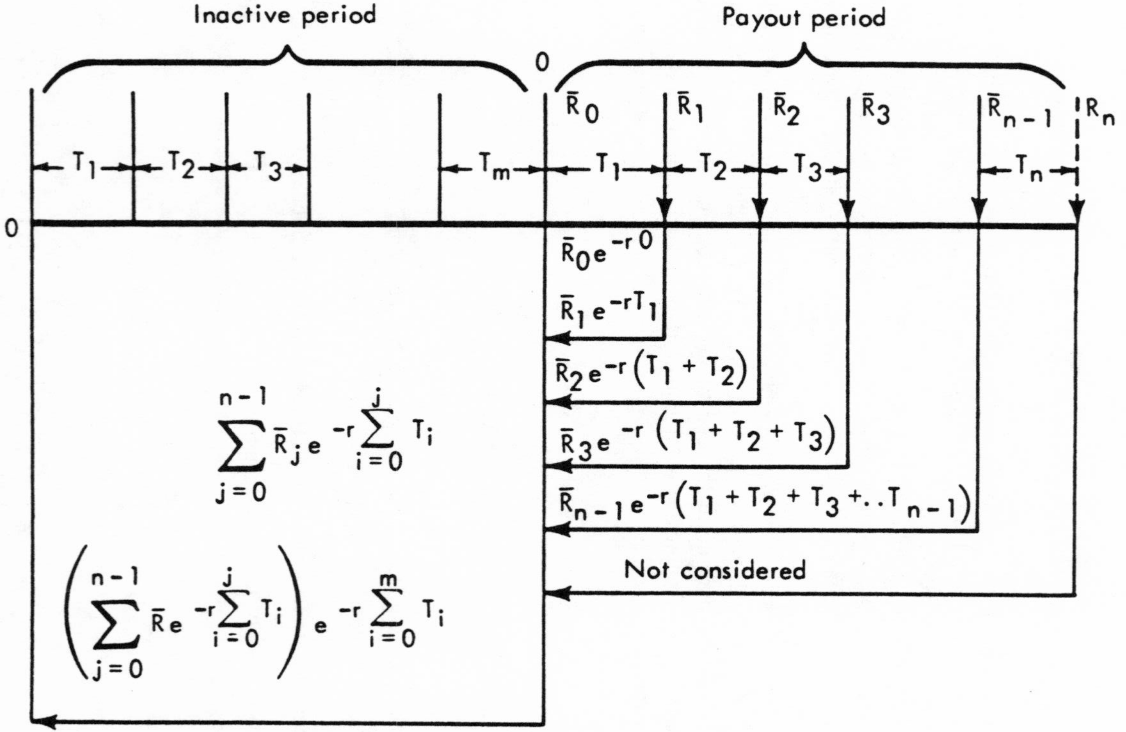

$$\sum_{j=0}^{n-1} \bar{R}_j e^{-r\sum_{i=0}^{j} T_i}$$

$$\left(\sum_{j=0}^{n-1} \bar{R} e^{-r\sum_{i=0}^{j} T_i}\right) e^{-r\sum_{i=0}^{m} T_i}$$

vestment of P dollars if R dollars are to be withdrawn at the beginning of each and every year for a period of n years. It should be recognized, of course, that in the usual case of this type of problem, the solution requires some trial-and-error algorithm. Fisher (1966) developed the first computer software for doing this. Currently such capability is widely available even for hand-held computers.

DEFERRED ANNUITY

We now raise the question of what the present value of an annuity lasting n years is if it is to begin paying out m years from now, and if money can be invested at r percent nominal interest. Under one formulation this can be shown to be the r subcase of $bsert$, inasmuch as R changes from zero to $\bar{R}$ at the end of m periods, and the ERB subcase of $CERBS$. The R is included in ERB inasmuch as the purchaser will derive a revenue in terms of the $\bar{R}$ payments for a period of n years. The B is included inasmuch as the annuity was bought for some fixed price. The E is included due to the fact that the purchaser of the annuity has foregone the interest on his or her B_0 dollars for a period of m years, that is, the "inactive" period of the annuity's life. Equation (16.8) therefore, for this group or family of cases, reduces to

$$P = 0 = B_0 + B_0(e^{rm} - 1) - \sum_{j=0}^{n-1} \bar{R}e^{-\sum_{i=0}^{j} rT_i}$$

$$= B_0[1 + (e^{rm} - 1)] - \bar{R}\sum_{j=0}^{n-1} e^{-rj} \qquad (16.19)$$

Here we see that the last term corresponds to a simple annuity for n years at r percent; the second term corresponds to the interest foregone for m years on B_0 dollars; and the B_0 is, in fact, the purchase price of the annuity. The present worth of this cash flow stream P is, of course, 0.

An alternative and more straightforward formulation for this problem is to take the n annual payments, discount them to the beginning of the payment period, and then further discount this sum to the present or time zero as seen in Figure 16.6. Thus,

$$P = (e^{-rm}) \sum_{j=0}^{n-1} \bar{R}e^{-\sum_{i=0}^{j} rT_i} = (e^{-rm}) \sum_{j=0}^{n-1} \bar{R}e^{-rj} \qquad (16.20)$$

where the term in parentheses discounts the present worth at the beginning of the payout period of the periodic payments to the present worth at time zero. Under this formulation, this problem, or course, is represented by the R subcase of $CERBS$ and the zero subcase of $bsert$.

Another alternative formulation of the annuity paying $\bar{R}$ dollars per year for n years and having payments beginning m years from time zero is to consider an annuity beginning at time zero and running for $m + n - 1$ years. If, from

Figure 16.6
A Deferred Annuity Having Eleven Payments Starting at End of Six Calendar Periods

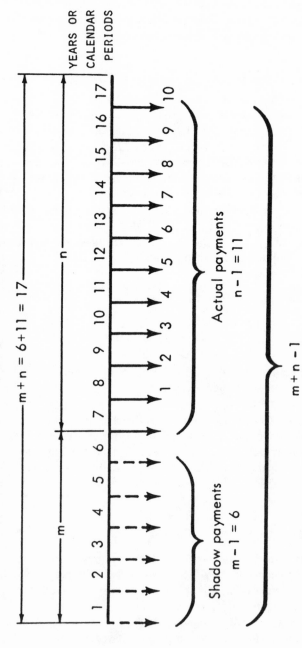

this flow stream, an annuity beginning at time zero and running for $m - 1$ years is subtracted, the result is identical to those above. Hence,

$$P = \sum_{j=0}^{m+n-1} \overline{R}e^{-r\sum_{i=0}^{j}\tau_i}$$

$$- \sum_{j=0}^{m-1} \overline{R}e^{-r\sum_{i=0}^{j}\tau_i} = \overline{R}\left(\sum_{j=0}^{m+n-1} e^{-rj} - \sum_{j=0}^{m-1} e^{-rj} \right) \quad (16.21)$$

The reason for subtracting a sum of $m - 1$ terms as opposed to a sum of m terms is that the problem, as stated, assumes payment at the end of the mth year. Now the end of the mth year is, of course, the beginning of the $m + 1$ year, and since our summation assumes beginning-of-the-period payments, we must be consistent. Let us look at this problem graphically for a specific case where $m = 6$ and $n = 11$. Starting at the end of the mth year, we see in Figure 16.6 the beginning of a series of actual payments of which there are $n - 1$ inasmuch as we are consistently considering the initial or first payment to be R_0 and not R_1.

If our series were to begin at time zero, there would be an additional $m - 1$ payments as seen from the diagram. These, in fact, are the shadow payments the present worth of which must be subtracted from the present worth of the total $m + 1 - 1$ series.

It should be noted from the three formulations of the deferred annuity that there is more than one way of reducing equation (16.8) to the case describing any specific problem. Applications of alternative formulations for a given problem, such as those shown, provide a means of checking one's work.

It should be quite clear that questions regarding the size of the payments in a deferred annuity given its present worth; rate of interest; the number of years in, and the year of onset of, the payout period can be handled in a manner similar to that of a simple annuity. Thus, using the second formulation or equation (16.20), $\overline{R}$ can be solved for through

$$R = \frac{P}{e^{-rm} \sum_{j=0}^{n-1} e^{-rj}} \quad (16.22)$$

The alternative question regarding the rate of return on a deferred annuity given all the other variables, of course, requires a trial and error solution.

CAPITAL RECOVERY

This method addresses itself to the question: What is the uniform end of the calendar-period payment $\overline{R}$ that can be secured for n years from a present investment of P dollars? The capital recovery factor is the factor by which the present capital investment P is multiplied to find the future series $\bar{R}$ that will exactly recover P with the interest r. This can be seen to be a special case of an annuity: the annuity that will start at the end of the first period and pay itself off in n such periods. Thus, it is again the zero subcase of *bsert* and the R subcase of *CERBS*.

In our formulation of this case we may go to the deferred annuity to deduce the required model, our deferment being for one period only, that is, $m = 1$ in this case. Therefore,

$$P = e^{-r1} \sum_{j=0}^{n-1} \bar{R}e^{-rj} \qquad (16.23)$$

We thus see that the capital recovery factor of the literature is in our terms either

$$\frac{1}{e^{-r} \sum_{j=0}^{n-1} e^{-rj}} \qquad (16.24a)$$

or

$$\frac{1}{\sum_{j=0}^{n-1} e^{-rj} - 1} \qquad (16.24b)$$

if we choose to use the end-of-the-period formulation for an annuity.

The e^{-r} term outside of the summation of the first formulation above could, of course, be brought inside the summation sign. However, doing this would defeat our purposes as the tables cited can handle the two factors separately very nicely; whereas, if the two were combined, a new table would be necessary and then we would have no advantage over the traditional presentations of this material.

In the last few sections we have shown that all of the classical equations of DCFA can be deduced from the general model equation (16.8). In the following sections we show that each of the more general formulations of DCFA appearing in the literature also can be classified on the basis of *CERBS/bsert* and hence, are special cases of equation (16.8).

THE DREYFUS (1960) MODEL

This model is in principle comparable to the *bsert* subcase of *CERBS*, although its formulation follows the dynamic programming methodology. It can be used to evaluate the optimum replacement policy for a chain or succession of machines having varying purchase prices, salvage values, economic life periods, expense function, and revenue functions.

THE SMITH (1957) MODEL

This is the *er* subcase of *bsert* in *CERBS* as it provides for varying revenue and expense functions while maintaining purchase prices, salvage values, and life periods constant.

THE BOWMAN AND FETTER (1957) MODEL

The most general case presented in Bowman and Fetter (1957) can be shown to be the zero subcase *bsert* in *CERBS*. It involves a chain of machines with nonvarying revenue functions, expense functions, purchase prices, salvage values, and life periods. This model is essentially the same as the one developed by Alchian (1952).

THE TERBORGH (1958) MODEL

If Terborgh's "operating inferiority" is considered to be the expense function, then his model reduces to the *EB* subcase of *CERBS*. Terborgh's "adverse minimum" is found by forcing to zero the first derivative with respect to *T* of the product of the present worth of *EB* and of the capital recovery factor.

THE DEAN (1951) MODEL

This is the *ERBS* subcase of *CERBS*.

THE RIFAS (1957) MODEL

This model may be classified as the *e* subcase of *CEB* since it considers a chain of machines with only the expense function varying.

THE ORENSTEIN (1956) MODEL

This is a special case, that is, it involves a linear expense function of the *EBS* subcase of *CERBS*.

THE CLAPHAM (1957) MODEL

This model is a special case of the *EBS* subcase of *CERBS*, since no discounting is considered.

PRESENT WORTH AND ANNUAL COST METHODS

Inasmuch as *CERBS* reduces all disbursements and receipts to their present worths, direct comparison is possible. Actually, however, applications of these methods in the past have been limited to cases involving nonvarying parameters, in other words, the zero subcase of *bsert* in Figure 16.2. Annual cost methods are entirely comparable to present worth methods.

SHORT PAYOFF METHODS

If it is assumed that the short payoff method means the time at which all costs have been recovered, then the period T is obtained by forcing P (the present worth of all of the receipts and disbursements at a given interest rate) to zero in any of the *CERBS* subcases. Once again, it can be said that in past applications of the short payoff method, all of the cases considered involved nonvarying parameters, that is, the zero subcase of *bsert*.

GLOSSARY OF TERMS

C	A symbol signifying that the model includes a provision for a chain or succession of investments.
E	A symbol signifying the provision for expenses.
R	A symbol signifying the provision for revenues.
B	A symbol signifying the provision for purchase prices.
S	A symbol signifying the provision for salvage values.
P	Present worth.
$R(t)$	Revenue time function.
$E(t)$	Expense time function.
$\bar{R}$	A uniform discrete payment.
T	Time interval.
e	Base of natural logarithms.
i	General time subscript.
j	General time subscript.
r	Continuous rate of interest, opportunity cost or cost of capital.
n	Final time period.
m	Specific time period.

NOTE

This chapter is based on A. Reisman and E. S. Buffa, "A General Model for Investment Policy," in *Management Science*, 8(3): 304–10, April 1962. It is also based on A. Reisman, "Unification of Engineering Economy: The Need and a Suggested Approach," which appeared in *Managerial and Engineering Economy* by the same author, published by Allyn and Bacon Publishers, Boston, 1971.

REFERENCES

Alchian, A. 1952. "Economic Replacement Policy." Report R–224, Rand Corporation, Santa Monica, Calif.

Bowman, E. H., and R. Fetter. 1957. *Analysis for Production Management*. Homewood, Ill.: Richard D. Irwin, Inc.

Clapham, J. C. R. 1957. "Economic Life of Equipment." *Operations Research Quarterly* 8(4): 181–90.

Dean, J. 1951. "Replacement Investments." In *Capital Budgeting*, Chapter VI, 89–120. New York: Columbia University Press.

Dreyfus, S. E. 1960. "A Generalized Equipment Replacement Study." *Journal of the Society of Industrial and Applied Mathematics* 8(3): 425–35.

Fisher, L. 1966. "An Algorithm for Finding Exact Rates of Return." *Journal of Business* 34(January): 111–18.

Grant, E. L. 1950. *Principles of Engineering Economy*. New York: Ronald Press Co.

Orenstein, R. D. 1956. "Topics on the MAPI Formula." *Journal of Industrial Engineering* 7(6): 283–94.

Reisman, A. 1968. "Engineering Economics: A Unified Approach." Series of articles appearing in *Heating, Piping and Air Conditioning*, January 1969. Reprinted as *Engineering Economics: A Unified Approach*, 1–104. Chicago, Ill.: Reinhold Publishing.

Reisman, A., and E. S. Buffa. 1962. "A General Model for Investment Policy." *Management Science* 8(3): 304–10.

Rifas, B. E. 1957. "Replacement Models." In *Introduction to Operations Research*, edited by C. W. Churchman, R. L. Ackoff, and E. L. Arnoff, 481–516. New York: John Wiley and Sons.

Smith, V. L. 1957. "Economic Equipment Policies: An Evaluation." *Management Science* 4(1): 20–37.

Summaries of most of the models listed in this bibliography are also available in R. L. Ackoff, ed. *Progress in Operations Research*. Vol. 1. New York: John Wiley and Sons, Inc., 1961.

Terborgh, J. 1958. *Business Investment Policy*. Washington, D.C.: Machinery and Allied Products Institute.

Unification of Single Objective Mathematical Programming Problems

INTRODUCTION

Optimization methods using mathematical programming (MP) techniques are taught at various levels of mathematical sophistication ranging from high school treatments of linear programming (LP) to doctoral level courses in integer programming (IP), nonlinear programming (NLP), and so on. Typically such courses are limited to one of the basic approaches. Unfortunately all too often students leave such treatments not having been exposed to the other branches of the broad field of MP. The relationship shown between the various problem formulations and/or solution types is rarely indicated even in survey courses.

Following the approach called for in Chapter 1, suggested in Chapter 3, and delineated in Chapter 16 (Reisman and Buffa 1962), Sloane and Reisman (1968), and more recently in Brockett and Golden (1987), this chapter formulates a general optimization problem involving a single objective. The chapter then proceeds to show how this formulation can be reduced to each of the typical mathematical programming formulations, such as NLP, IP, LP, and so forth. Also, similarly to Reisman (1968), the chapter suggests a taxonomic scheme based on the classification of the objective function, and constraint set structure; the types of variables; and the number of constraints involved. Lastly, the chapter suggests the premiere algorithms for solving each of the special cases of the general formulation. Clearly the special cases are quite broad in their own right, for example LP, IP, FLP, GP, NLP, and so forth.

DISCUSSION

The Classification

The unification of this class of single objective mathematical programming problems will be initiated by introducing the $O/C/S/\#$ classification scheme where

O delineates the type of objective function involved

C delineates the type of constraint sets involved

S delineates the type of variables involved

$\#$ delineates the number of constraints

In specifying the values of O, let

L^k = Linear function of the single variable x_j, for some j, raised to the kth power[1]

N_i = Strictly nonlinear function of i variables

$\sum \cdot$ = Sum of $\cdot$

$\prod \cdot$ = Product of $\cdot$

$\cdot \div \cdot$ = $\cdot$ Divided by $\cdot$

G = General objective function

$\tilde{}$ = Coefficients of $\cdot$ are random variables

In specifying the values of C, let

L^k = Linear function of the single variable x_j, for some j, raised to the kth power[1]

N_i = Strictly nonlinear function of i variables

$\sum \cdot$ = Sum of $\cdot$

$\prod \cdot$ = Product of $\cdot$

G = General constraints

$\tilde{}$ = Coefficients of $\cdot$ are random variables or the right-hand side of the constraints is or has a random variable

In specifying the values of S, let

R = Real-valued variables

I = Integer-valued variables

Z = 0–1 variables

$\cdot + \cdot$ = Set of $\cdot$ union $\cdot$

G = General variables (real, integer, etc.)

Lastly, in specifying the values of $\#$, let

O = Unconstrained problem

1 = Single constraint problem

m = m-constraint problem

G = General problem (constrained or unconstrained)

Thus, $\Sigma L/\Sigma L/R/3$ represents an LP problem with three constraints. Additional examples demonstrating the robustness of this scheme for classifying single objective MP problems follows the development of the general problem formulation.

Formulation of the General Problem

The next step in the unification involves the development of the objective function and constraint set encompassing most, if not all, of the problem formulations typically treated in the broad field of single objective MP. The most obvious subject matter that is not included involves multiobjective optimization, goal programming, and so on.

The usual way of stating a general optimization problem is to indicate that there are n variables $(n = 1, 2, \ldots)$ and m constraints $(m = 0, 1, 2, \ldots)$ and an objective function $v(x)$ for which one should

$$\left.\begin{array}{l} \text{Min } v(x) \\ \text{s.t. } w_k(x) \le b_k \qquad k = 1, 2, \ldots, m \\ \qquad x \in) S \end{array}\right\} \qquad (17.1)$$

where $x = (x_1, x_2, \ldots, x_n) \in \mathbb{R}^n$; $v(x)$ and $w_k(x)$ are real-valued functions such that $v:\mathbb{R}^n \to \mathbb{R}$ and $w_k:\mathbb{R}^n \to \mathbb{R}$ for all $k = 1, 2, \ldots, m$; $b_k \to \mathbb{R}$ for all $k = 1, 2, \ldots, m$; and $S \in \mathbb{R}^n$ (for example, $S = \{(x_1, x_2, \ldots, x_n)|x_i \ge 0, i = 1, 2, \ldots, n\}$.

Clearly, equation (17.1) is the most succinct representation of a general mathematical programming problem. However, the statement is not robust enough to show *explicitly* how one can deduce from it statements for each of the various classes of mathematical programming problems such as LP, IP, and the like. These are literally *hidden* in such a simple formulation. It requires a person to have extensive prior knowledge of the various classes of programming problems in order to properly identify a given problem. It is for this reason that we shall develop a general statement of a mathematical programming problem that can be simplified into any of the major classes of programming problems by merely dropping and/or simplifying some of its terms in a deductive manner. Another advantage of such a formulation is the ability to vividly show the similarities and differences between the various classes of mathematical programming problems.

Let $f_{jl}(z_l)$, $h_{jl}(z_l)$, and $g_{jlk}(z_{lk})$ be what we call "strictly nonlinear functions" of z_μ, for all j, l, and k, where $z_\mu \subseteq \{x_1, x_2, \ldots, n_n\}$ and $z_{lk} \subseteq \{x_1, x_2, \ldots, x_n\}$, for all μ and k. By strictly nonlinear functions we mean all functions that cannot be represented in a, what we shall call, pseudo-linear form $\sum_{j} \prod_{i=1}^{n} x_i^{\Gamma_{ij}}$, where Γ_{ij} is real valued for all i and j; that is, functions such as

$$(x_1 + x_2)^{1/2} \quad \text{or} \quad e^{x_1 x_2}$$

are termed strictly nonlinear functions where as

$$x_1^3 \quad \text{or} \quad x_1 x_2 + x_1 x_3^3$$

are not. Clearly by multiplying each of the strictly nonlinear terms by a term of the form $\sum_j \prod_{i=1}^{n} x_i^{\Gamma_{ij}}$ the resulting function will be a general representation of any nonlinear function.

Finally, referring to (17.1), $v(x)$ may be the quotient of two functions (either linear or nonlinear); that is,

$$\left. v(x) = \frac{u(x) + \lambda}{w(x) + \beta} \right\} \tag{17.2}$$

where $u(x)$ and $w(x)$ are real-valued functions of the vector x and $\lambda, \beta \in \mathbb{R}$.

Therefore, applying these results to equation (17.1), we can obtain the following general formulation of a mathematical programming problem.

GENERAL MODEL

$$\min \frac{\sum_{j=1}^{N_o} \left\{ C_j \prod_{i=1}^{n} x_i^{r_{ij}} + \gamma_j \prod_{i=1}^{n} x_i^{\rho_{ij}} \prod_{l=1}^{\pi_o} f_{jl}(z_l) \right\} + \lambda}{\sum_{j=1}^{M_o} \left\{ d_j \prod_{i=1}^{n} x_i^{s_{ij}} + \delta_j \prod_{i=1}^{n} x_i^{\sigma_{ij}} \prod_{l=1}^{\mu_o} h_{jl}(z_l) \right\} + \beta}$$

$$\text{s.t.} \sum_{j=1}^{N_k} \left\{ a_{kj} \prod_{i=1}^{n} x^{t_{ijk}} + \alpha_{kj} \prod_{i=1}^{n} x_i^{\tau_{ijk}} \prod_{l=1}^{\pi_k} g_{jlk}(z_{lk}) \right\}$$
$$\leq b_k \quad k = 1, 2, \ldots, m \quad x \in S \tag{17.3}$$

where $z_\mu \subseteq \{x_1, x_2, \ldots, x_n\}$ for all μ, and $z_{\mu k} \subseteq \{x_1, x_2, \ldots, x_n\}$ for all μ and k.

We next show that each of the common optimization problem statements is a special case of the general model (17.3). For each of these problem statements we shall discuss all of the terms in the numerator of the objective function, for example, the pseudolinear term

$$\sum_{j=1}^{N_o} C_j \prod_{i=1}^{n} x_i^{r_{ij}}$$

the strictly nonlinear term

$$\sum_{j=1}^{N_o} \gamma_j \prod_{i=1}^{n} x_i^{\rho_{ij}} \prod_{l=1}^{\pi_o} f_{jl}(z_l)$$

and the constant term λ.

More specifically, for each of the above terms we shall discuss all the parameters such as N_o, r_{ij}, and C_j's; the variables x_i in the pseudolinear term; the parameters γ_j, ρ_{ij}, and π_o; the function $f_{jl}(\cdot)$, the variables z_μ for the strictly nonlinear term; and lastly the constant λ.[2]

We shall then to the same for the denominator of the objective function. More specifically, we shall discuss the parameters M_o, d_j, s_{ij}, as well as the variables x_i in the pseudolinear term,

$$\sum_{j=1}^{M_o} d_j \prod_{i=1}^{n} x_i^{s_{ij}}$$

the parameters δ_j, σ_{ij}, and μ_o; the function $h_{jl}(\cdot)$; and the variables z_l in the strictly nonlinear term,

$$\sum_{j=1}^{N_o} \delta_j \prod_{i=1}^{n} x_i^{\sigma_{ij}} \prod_{l=1}^{\mu_o} h_{jl}(z_l)$$

and lastly the constant β.

In the constraint set we shall discuss the parameters N_k, a_{kj}, and t_{ijk} and the variables x_i in the pseudolinear term,

$$\sum_{j=1}^{N_k} a_{kj} \prod_{i=1}^{n} x_i^{t_{ijk}}$$

the parameters α_{kj}, τ_{ijk}, π_k; the function $g_{ilk}(\cdot)$, and the variables x_i and z_{lk} in the strictly nonlinear term,

$$\sum_{j=1}^{N_k} \alpha_{kj} \prod_{i=1}^{n} x_i^{\tau_{ijk}} \prod_{l=1}^{\pi_k} g_{jlk}(z_{lk})$$

Lastly, we shall discuss the nature of the right-hand side of the inequality, that is, b_k.

The discussion will then include a standard formulation for each class of such problems, an example, and reference the major algorithms for its solution. Lastly, the problem will be classified using the $O/C/S/\#$ taxonomic scheme presented earlier in the chapter. Hybrids such as mixed integer programming ($\Sigma L/\Sigma L/R + I/m$), fractional integer programming ($\Sigma L \div \Sigma L/\Sigma L/I/m$), and the like will not be considered because the list would be endless.

LINEAR PROGRAMMING

I. OBJECTIVE FUNCTION—numerator

A. Pseudolinear term

$N_o \leq n$

C_j real valued (if $r_{ij} = 0$, for all i, then $C_j = 0$)

r_{ij} 1 if $i = j$ and $C_j \neq 0$, for at least one j

    0 otherwise

B. Strictly nonlinear term[3]

γ_j 0 for all $j = 1, 2, \ldots, n$

C. Constant term

λ real valued

II. OBJECTIVE FUNCTION—denominator

A. Pseudolinear term

d_j 0 for all $j = 1, 2, \ldots, n$

B. Strictly nonlinear term

δ_j 0 for all $j = 1, 2, \ldots, n$

C. Constant term

$\beta + 1$

III. CONSTRAINT

A. Pseudolinear term

$N_k \leq n$

a_{kj} real valued (if $t_{ijk} = 0$, for all i, then $a_{kj} = 0$)

t_{ijk} 1 if $i = j$ and $a_{kj} \neq 0$ for at least one k,

    0 otherwise

B. Strictly nonlinear term

α_{kj} 0 for all $k = 1, 2, \ldots, m$ and $j = 1, 2, \ldots, n$

S each x_j is defined over some continuous interval; that is, $a_j \leq x_j \leq b_j$, where a_j and b_j are any real numbers or $\pm$ infinity

IV. Right-Hand Side

b_k real valued

STANDARD PROBLEM FORM

$$\min \sum_{j=1}^{n} C_j x_j + \lambda$$

$$\text{s.t.} \sum_{j=1}^{n} a_{kj} x_j \leq b_k \qquad k = 1, 2, \ldots, m$$

$$x_j \in \mathbb{R} \qquad j = 1, 2, \ldots, n$$

EXAMPLE

$$\min 2X_1 + 5X_2 + X_3$$
$$\text{s.t. } 5X_1 + 7X_2 + 7X_3 \leq 8$$
$$X_1 + X_3 \geq 5$$
$$2X_1 + 6X_2 + 3X_3 = 4$$
$$X_1, X_2, X_3 \geq 0$$

MAJOR ALGORITHMS FOR SOLUTION

Simplex Method (Hadley 1962; Solow 1984)

CLASSIFICATION

$\Sigma L/\Sigma L/\mathbb{R}/m$

INTEGER PROGRAMMING

I. OBJECTIVE FUNCTION—numerator

A. Pseudolinear term

N_o $\leq n$
C_j real valued (if $r_{ij} = 0$, for all i, then $C_j = 0$)
r_{ij} 1 if $i = j$ and $C_j \neq 0$, for at least one j
   0   otherwise

B. Strictly nonlinear term

γ_j 0 for all $j = 1, 2, \ldots, n$

C. Constant term

λ real valued

II. OBJECTIVE FUNCTION—denominator

A. Pseudolinear term

d_j 0 for all $j = 1, 2, \ldots, n$

B. Strictly nonlinear term

δ_j 0 for all $j = 1, 2, \ldots, n$

C. Constant term

β $+1$

III. CONSTRAINT

A. Pseudolinear term

N_k $\leq n$
a_{kj} real valued (if $t_{ijk} = 0$, for all i, then $a_{kj} = 0$)
t_{ijk} 1 if $i = j$ and $a_{kj} \neq 0$ for at least one k
   0   otherwise

B. Strictly nonlinear term

α_{kj} 0 for all $k = 1, 2, \ldots, m$ and $j = 1, 2, \ldots, n$
S each x_j is integer valued

IV. RIGHT-HAND SIDE

b_k real valued

STANDARD PROBLEM FORM

$$\min \sum_{j=1}^{n} C_j x_j + \lambda$$

$$\text{s.t.} \sum_{j=1}^{n} a_{kj} x_j \le b_k \qquad k = 1, 2, \ldots, m$$

$$x_j \in \mathbb{R} \qquad j = 1, 2, \ldots, n$$

$$x_j \text{ integer} \qquad j = 1, 2, \ldots, n$$

EXAMPLE

$$\min 2X_1 + 5X_2 + X_3$$
$$\text{s.t. } 5X_1 + 7X_2 + 7X_3 \le 8$$
$$X_1 + X_3 \ge 5$$
$$2X_1 + 6X_2 + 3X_3 = 4$$
$$X_1, X_2, X_3 \ge 0 \text{ and integer}$$

MAJOR ALGORITHMS FOR SOLUTION

Gomory's Cussing Plane Algorithm (Saaty 1970; Salkin 1975)
Branch and Bound Enumeration Techniques (Saaty 1970; Salkin 1975)

CLASSIFICATION

$\Sigma L / \Sigma L / \mathbb{R} / m$

FRACTIONAL PROGRAMMING

I. OBJECTIVE FUNCTION—numerator

A. Pseudolinear term

$N_o \quad \le n$
C_j real valued (if $r_{ij} = 0$, for all i, then $C_j = 0$)
$r_{ij} \qquad 1$ if $i = j$ and $C_j \ne 0$, for at least one j
$\qquad\quad 0 \qquad$ otherwise

B. Strictly nonlinear term

$\gamma_j \qquad 0$ for all $j = 1, 2, \ldots, n$

C. Constant term

$\lambda \qquad$ real valued

II. OBJECTIVE FUNCTION—denominator

A. Pseudolinear term

M_0 $\leq n$

d_j real valued (if $s_{ij} = 0$, for all i, then $d_j = 0$)

s_{ij} 1 if $i = j$ and $d_j \neq 0$, for at least one j

   0   otherwise

B. Strictly nonlinear term

δ_j 0 for all $j = 1, 2, \ldots, n$

C. Constant term

β real valued

III. CONSTRAINT

A. Pseudolinear term

N_k $\leq n$

a_{kj} real valued (if $t_{ijk} = 0$, for all i, then $a_{kj} = 0$)

t_{ijk} 1 if $i = j$ and $a_{kj} \neq 0$ for at least one k

   0 otherwise

B. Strictly nonlinear term

α_{kj} 0 for all $k = 1, 2, \ldots, m$ and $j = 1, 2, \ldots, n$

S each x_j is defined over some continuous interval; that is, $a_j \leq x_j$
    $\leq b_j$, where a_j and b_j are any real numbers or $\pm$ infinity

IV. RIGHT-HAND SIDE

b_k real valued

STANDARD PROBLEM FORM

$$\min \frac{\sum_{j=1}^{n} C_j x_j + \lambda}{\sum_{j=1}^{n} d_j x_j + \beta}$$

$$\text{s.t.} \sum_{j=1}^{n} a_{kj} x_j \leq b_k \qquad k = 1, 2, \ldots, m$$

$$x_j \in \mathbb{R} \qquad j = 1, 2, \ldots, n$$

EXAMPLE

$$\min \frac{5X_1 + 7X_2 + 4X_3 + 5}{9X_1 + 6X_2 + 7X_3 + 3}$$

$$\text{s.t.} \quad X_1 + X_2 \leq 10$$
$$5X_1 + X_3 \geq 3$$
$$X_1, X_2, X_3 \geq 0$$

MAJOR ALGORITHMS FOR SOLUTION

Charnes and Cooper (1962)
Gilmore and Gomory (1963)

CLASSIFICATION

$\Sigma L \div \Sigma L / \Sigma L / \mathbb{R} / m$

QUADRATIC PROGRAMMING

I. OBJECTIVE FUNCTION—numerator

  A. Pseudolinear term

  N_o $\leq (n^2 + 3n)/2$
  C_j real valued (if $r_{ij} = 0$, for all i, then $C_j = 0$)
  r_{ij} For each j with $C_j \neq 0$, and for any two i's, say and i_2 such that
  $i_1 \neq i_2$ and $i_2 \neq j$, exactly one of the following must be true:
  1. $r_{i_1 j} = 2$ if $i = j$ and $r_{ij} = 0$ for all $i \neq i_1$
  2. $r_{i_1 j} = r_{i_2 j} = 1$ and $r_{ij} = 0$ for all $i_1 \neq i_2$
  3. $r_{i_1 j} = 1$ and $r_{i_2 j} = 0$ for all $i \neq i_1$
  4. $r_{ij} = 0$ for all i
  Also condition 1 must be true for at least one j and condition 2 must
  be true for at least one j.

  B. Strictly nonlinear term

  γ_j 0 for all $j = 1, 2, \ldots, n$

  C. Constant term

  λ real valued

II. OBJECTIVE FUNCTION—denominator

  A. Pseudolinear term

  d_j 0 for all $j = 1, 2, \ldots, n$

  B. Strictly nonlinear term

  δ_j 0 for all $j = 1, 2, \ldots, n$

  C. Constant term

  β $+1$

III. CONSTRAINT

  A. Pseudolinear term

  N_k $\leq n$
  a_{kj} real valued (if $t_{ijk} = 0$, for all i, then $a_{kj} = 0$)
  t_{ijk} 1 if $i = j$ and $a_{kj} \neq 0$ for at least one k
       0   otherwise

B. Strictly nonlinear term

α_{kj} 0 for all $k = 1, 2, \ldots, m$ and $j = 1, 2, \ldots, n$

S each x_j is defined over some continuous interval; that is, $a_j \leq x_j$
b_k $\leq b_j$, where a_j and b_j are any real numbers or $\pm$ infinity

IV. RIGHT-HAND SIDE

    b_k real valued

STANDARD PROBLEM FORM

$$\min \sum_{j=1}^{N_o} C_j \prod_{i=1}^{n} x_i^{r_{ij}} + \lambda$$

$$\text{s.t.} \sum_{j=1}^{n} a_{kj} x_j \leq b_k \qquad k = 1, 2, \ldots, m$$

$$x_j \in \mathbb{R} \qquad j = 1, 2, \ldots, n$$

EXAMPLE

$$\min 3X_1 + 4X_2 + X_1^2 + X_2^2 + X_1 X_2$$
$$\text{s.t.} \quad X_1 + X_2 \leq 5$$
$$X_1 + 3X_2 \geq 10$$
$$X_1, X_2 \geq 0$$

MAJOR ALGORITHMS FOR SOLUTION

Quadratic programming (Bazarra and Shetty 1979)

CLASSIFICATION

$\Sigma L^2 / \Sigma L / \mathbb{R} / m$

STOCHASTIC PROGRAMMING

I. OBJECTIVE FUNCTION—numerator

A. Pseudolinear term

N_o $\leq n$

C_j random variable (denoted $\tilde{C}_j$) or real-valued constant (C_j must be a random variable for at least one j if both a_{kj} and b_k are real-valued constants for all k and j)

r_{ij} 1 if $i = j$ and $C_j \neq 0$
      0   otherwise

B. Strictly nonlinear term

γ_j 0 for all $j = 1, 2, \ldots, n$

C. Constant term

λ real valued

II. OBJECTIVE FUNCTION—denominator

    A. Pseudolinear term

        d_j 0 for all $j = 1, 2, \ldots, n$

    B. Strictly nonlinear term

        δ_j 0 for all $j = 1, 2, \ldots, n$

    C. Constant term

        β $+1$

III. CONSTRAINT

    A. Pseudolinear term

        N_k $\leq n$

        a_{kj} random variable (denoted $\bar{a}_{kj}$) or real-valued constant (a_{kj} must be a random variable for at least one j if both C_j and b_k are real-valued constants for all k and j).

        t_{ijk} 1 if $i = j$ and $a_{kj} \neq 0$ for at least one k
              0   otherwise

    B. Strictly nonlinear term

        α_{kj} 0 for all $k = 1, 2, \ldots, m$ and $j = 1, 2, \ldots, n$

        S each x_j is defined over some continuous interval; that is, $a_j \leq x_j$
b_k $\leq b_j$, where a_j and b_j are any real numbers or $\pm$ infinity

IV. RIGHT-HAND SIDE

        b_k random variable (denoted $\bar{b}_k$ or real-valued constant (b_k must be a random variable for at least one j if both C_j and a_{kj} are real-valued constants for all k and j)

STANDARD PROBLEM FORM

$$\min \sum_{j=1}^{n} \bar{c}_j x_j + \lambda$$

$$\text{s.t.} \sum_{j=1}^{n} \bar{a}_{kj} x_j \leq \bar{b}_k \qquad k = 1, 2, \ldots, m$$

$$x_j \in \mathbb{R} \qquad j = 1, 2, \ldots, n$$

MAJOR ALGORITHMS FOR SOLUTION

Stochastic Programming (Sengupta 1984)

CLASSIFICATION

$\Sigma \bar{L} / \Sigma \bar{L} / \mathbb{R} / m$

SEPARABLE PROGRAMMING

I. OBJECTIVE FUNCTION—numerator

A. Pseudolinear term

$N_o \leq n$

C_j real valued (if $r_{ij} = 0$, for all i, then $C_j = 0$)

r_{ij} real valued if $i = j$ and $C_j \neq 0$

  0 otherwise

B. Strictly nonlinear term

γ_j real valued and nonzero for at least one j

ρ_{ij} real valued if $i = j$

  0 otherwise

π_1 any positive integer

f_{jl} any strictly nonlinear function of the single variable x_j or 1 if $i = j$ with at least one $f_{jl} \neq 1$ for some μ

  otherwise $f_{jl} = 1$

z_l x_1

C. Constant term

λ real valued

II. OBJECTIVE FUNCTION—denominator

A. kPseudolinear term

d_j 0 for all $j = 1, 2, \ldots, n$

B. fStrictly nonlinear term

δ_j 0 for all $j = 1, 2, \ldots, n$

C. Constant term

β $+1$

III. CONSTRAINT

A. kPseudolinear term

N_k any positive integer

Af_{kj} real valued (if $t_{ijk} = 0$, for all i, then $a_{kj} = 0$)

t_{ijk} real valued if $i = j$ and $C_j \neq 0$

  0 otherwise

B. Strictly nonlinear term

αk_{kj} real valued and nonzero for at least one j and k

τ_{ijk} real valued if $i = j$

  0 otherwise

π_k any positive integer

g_{jlk} any strictly nonlinear function of the single variable x_j or 1 if $i = j$ with at least one $g_{jlk} \neq 1$ for some k and l otherwise $g_{jlk} = 1$

z_{lk} x_l

S   each x_j is defined over some continuous interval; that is, $a_j \leq x_j \leq b_j$, where a_j and b_j are any real numbers or $\pm$ infinity

IV. Right-Hand Side

b_k real valued

STANDARD PROBLEM FORM

$$\min \sum_{j=1}^{N_o} \left\{ C_j \prod_{i=1}^{n} x_i^{r_{ij}} + \gamma_j \prod_{i=1}^{n} x_i^{p_{ij}} \prod_{l=1}^{\pi_o} f_{jl}(x_j) \right\} + \lambda$$

$$\text{s.t.} \sum_{j=1}^{N_o} \left\{ a_{kj} \prod_{i=1}^{n} x^{t_{ijk}} + \alpha_{kj} \prod_{i=1}^{n} x_i^{\tau_{ijk}} \prod_{l=1}^{\pi_k} g_{jlk}(x_j) \right\}$$

$$\leq b_k \quad k = 1, 2, \ldots, m \quad x \in \mathbb{R}$$

EXAMPLE

$$\min X_1^3 - 6X_1 + X_2^2 - 8X_2 - X_3$$
$$\text{s.t.} \ X_1 + X_2 + X_3 \leq 5$$
$$X_1^2 - X_2 \leq 3$$
$$X_1, X_2, X_3 \geq 0$$

MAJOR ALGORITHMS FOR SOLUTION

Separable Programming (Bazaraa and Shetty 1979; Lasdon 1970)

CLASSIFICATION

$\Sigma N/\Sigma N/\mathbb{R}/m$

GEOMETRIC PROGRAMMING

I. OBJECTIVE FUNCTION—numerator

A. Pseudolinear term

N_o any positive integer
C_j real valued (if $r_{ij} = 0$, for all i, then $C_j = 0$)
r_{ij} real valued for all i and j and for at least one j and some of the i's, say i_1 and i_2, if $t_{ijk} = 0$ or 1 for all i, j, and k, then r_{i_1j} and r_{i_2j} do not equal 0 or 1.

B. Strictly nonlinear term

γ_j 0 for all $j = 1, 2, \ldots, n$

C. Constant term

λ real valued

II. OBJECTIVE FUNCTION—denominator

  A. Pseudolinear term

    d_j 0 for all $j = 1, 2, \ldots, n$

  B. Strictly nonlinear term

    δ_j 0 for all $j = 1, 2, \ldots, n$

  C. Constant term

    β $+1$

III. CONSTRAINT

  A. Pseudolinear term

    N_k any positive integer
    a_{jk} real valued (if $t_{ijk} = 0$, for all i, then $a_{kj} = 0$)
    t_{ijk} real valued for all i, j, and k

  B. Strictly nonlinear term

    α_{kj} 0 for all $k = 1, 2, \ldots, m$ and $j = 1, 2, \ldots, n$
    S each x_j is defined over some continuous interval; that is, $a_j \leq x_j \leq b_j$, where a_j and b_j are any real numbers or $\pm$ infinity

IV. RIGHT-HAND SIDE

    b_k real valued

STANDARD PROBLEM FORM

$$\min \sum_{j=1}^{N_o} C_j \prod_{i=1}^{n} x_i^{r_{ij}} + \lambda$$

$$\text{s.t.} \sum_{j=1}^{N_o} a_{kj} \prod_{i=1}^{n} x^{t_{ijk}} \leq b_k \qquad k = 1, 2, \ldots, m$$

$$x_j \in \mathbb{R} \qquad j = 1, 2, \ldots, n$$

EXAMPLE

$$\min X_1^2 X_2^3 + X_1 X_2 X_3$$
$$\text{s.t.} \ X_1 X_2 + X_2 X_3 + X_1^2 X_3 = 1$$
$$X_1, X_2, X_3 \geq 0$$

MAJOR ALGORITHMS FOR SOLUTION

Geometric Programming (Duffin and Peterson 1967; Beightler and Phillips 1976)

CLASSIFICATION

$\Sigma \Pi L^k / \Sigma \Pi L^k / \ \mathbb{R}/m$

NONLINEAR PROGRAMMING

I. OBJECTIVE FUNCTION—numerator

A. Pseudolinear term

N_o any positive integer
C_j real valued (if $r_{ij} = 0$, for all i, then $C_j = 0$)
r_{ij} real valued for all i and j with $C_j \neq 0$
O   otherwise

B. Strictly nonlinear term

γ_j real valued and nonzero for at least one j
ρ_{ij} nonzero if $i = j$
     0 otherwise
π_0 any positive integer
f_{jl} any strictly nonlinear function of the variables in the set z_μ or 1 if $i = j$ with at least one $f_{jl} \neq 1$ for some l otherwise $f_{jl} = 1$ if $g_{ilk} = 1$ for all i, l, and k.
z_l any subset of the set $\{x_1, x_2, \ldots, x_n\}$; that is, f_{jl} is a function of some of the variable $x_1, x_2, \ldots, x_n$ for all l and furthermore f_{jl} is a function of at least two variables for l if $g_{ilk} = 1$ or is a function of a single variable for all l.

C. Constant term

λ real valued

II. OBJECTIVE FUNCTION—denominator

A. Pseudolinear term

d_j 0 for all $j = 1, 2, \ldots, n$

B. Strictly nonlinear term

δ_j 0 for all $j = 1, 2, \ldots, n$

C. Constant term

β $+1$

III. CONSTRAINT

A. Pseudolinear term

N_k any positive integer
a_{kj} real valued (if $t_{ijk} = 0$, for all i, then $a_{kj} = 0$)
t_{ijk} real valued for all i, j, and k if $a_{kj} \neq 0$
     0 otherwise

B. Strictly nonlinear term

α_{kj} real valued and nonzero for at least one j and k
τ_{ijk} nonzero if $i = j$
O   otherwise

π_k any positive integer

g_{jlk} any strictly nonlinear function of the variables in the set z_μ or 1 for
all i, l, and k with at least one $g_{i\mu k} \neq 1$ for some k and l if $f_{jl} = 1$
or is a function of a single variable for all l

z_{lk} any subset of the set $\{x_1, x_2, \ldots, x_n\}$ for all l and k

S each x_j is defined over some continuous interval; that is, $a_j \leq x_j \leq b_j$, where a_j and b_j are any real numbers or $\pm$ infinity

IV. RIGHT-HAND SIDE

b_k real valued

STANDARD PROBLEM FORM

$$\min \sum_{j=1}^{N_o} \left\{ C_j \prod_{i=1}^{n} x_i^{r_{ij}} + \gamma_j \prod_{i=1}^{n} x_i^{\rho_{ij}} \prod_{l=1}^{\pi_o} f_{jl}(z_l) \right\} + \lambda$$

$$\text{s.t.} \sum_{j=1}^{N_o} \left\{ a_{kj} \prod_{i=1}^{n} x_i^{t_{ijk}} + \alpha_{kj} \prod_{i=1}^{n} x_i^{\tau_{ijk}} \prod_{l=1}^{\pi_k} g_{jlk}(z_{lk}) \right\}$$
$$\leq b_k \qquad k = 1, 2, \ldots, m \qquad x \in \mathbb{R}$$

where

$z_\mu \subseteq \{x_1, x_2, \ldots, x_n\}$ for all μ

$z_{\mu k} \subseteq \{x_1, x_2, \ldots, x_n\}$ for all μ and k

EXAMPLE

$$\min \exp(x_1 x_2)$$
$$\text{s.t. } x_1 + x_2 \leq 5$$

MAJOR ALGORITHMS FOR SOLUTION

Penalty and Barrier function algorithm (Luenberger 1973, 1974)

Method of feasible directions (Bazaraa and Shetty 1979)

CLASSIFICATION

$\Sigma \Pi N_k / \Sigma \Pi N_k / \mathbb{R}/m$

CONCLUDING REMARKS

This chapter has attempted to unify the class of optimization problems involving a single objective. In designing our classification, we have erred on the side of parsimony much like what was done in the commonly used $A/B/C$ classification of queueing problems (Kendall 1953). Hence, we can not distinguish subclasses of problems (e.g., all network problems such as transportation, assignment, shortest path, and max-flow problems are classified as linear programming problems, i.e., $\Sigma L/\Sigma L/R/m$). To have included such a fine "sieve" would have been at the cost of a rather complex and cumbersome taxonomy.

Furthermore, the reader may have noticed that the strictly nonlinear term in the denominator of the objective function does not appear in any of the major classes of single objective optimization problems considered; that is, classes such as fractional nonlinear programming $(\Sigma \Pi N_k \div \Sigma \Pi N_k / \Sigma \Pi N_k / \mathbb{R} / m)$ are not mentioned. At the current state of the art, such problems are nearly impossible to solve; hence, they are not part of the currently main-line literature. The term was included in the general formulation for completeness and as a challenge to future algorithm developers.

NOTES

This chapter is based on the paper G. Pollock and A. Reisman, "Unification of the Single Objective Mathematical Programming Problems," Technical Memorandum #641, Department of Operations Research, Case Western Reserve University, Cleveland, Ohio.

1. It is assumed throughout the chapter that all functions are in their "most expanded" form; that is, functions such as $(a_1 x_1^2 + a_2 x_2)^2 = a_1^2 x_1^4 + 2a_1 a_2 x_1^2 x_2 + a_2^2 x_2^2$, where a_1 and a_2 are constants.

2. It should be noted that in the discussion of the specific MP problem statements only those parameters and variables that are applicable will be discussed, for example, omission implies that the parameter in question is not part of the particular formulation.

3. The reader is again reminded that discussed in these sections are only those parameters that apply to the specific case at hand.

REFERENCES

Bazaraa, M. S., and C. S. Shetty. 1979. *Nonlinear Programming Theory and Algorithms*. New York: John Wiley and Sons, Inc.

Beightler, C. S., and D. T. Phillips. 1976. *Applied Geometric Programming*. New York: John Wiley and Sons, Inc.

Brockett, P. L., and L. L. Golden. 1987. "A Class of Utility Functions Containing All the Common Utility Functions." *Management Science* 33(8): 955–63.

Charnes, A., and W. Cooper. 1962. "Programming with Linear Fractional Functionals." *Naval Research Logistics Quartery* 9(3, 4): 181–86.

Duffin, R. J., E. L. Peterson, and C. Zener. 1967. *Geometric Programming*. New York: John Wiley and Sons, Inc.

Gilmore, P., and R. Gomory. 1963. "A Linear Programming Approach to the Cutting Stock Problem, Part II." *Operations Research* 11(6): 863–88.

Hadley, G. 1962. *Linear Programming*. Reading, Mass.: Addison-Wesley.

Kendall, D. G. 1953. "Stochastic Processes Occurring in the Theory of Queues and Their Analysis by the Method of Imbedded Markov Chains." *Annals of Mathematical Statistics* 24:338–54.

Lasdon, L. 1970. *Optimization Theory for Large Systems*. New York: Macmillan.

Luenberger, D. 1973. *Introduction to Linear and Nonlinear Programming*. Reading, Mass.: Addison-Wesley.

Luenberger, D. 1974. "A Combined Penalty Function and Gradient Projection Method for Nonlinear Programming." In *Journal of Optimization Theory and Applications* 14(5): 477–95.

Reisman, A. 1968. "Unification of Engineering Economy: The Need and a Suggested Approach." *The Engineering Economist* 14(1): 1–24.

Reisman, A., and E. S. Buffa. 1962. "A General Model for Investment Policy." *Management Science* 8(April): 304–10.

Saaty, T. L. 1970. *Optimization in Integers and Related Extremal Problems.* New York: McGraw-Hill Book Co.

Salkin, H. 1975. *Integer Programming.* Reading, Mass.: Addison-Wesley.

Sengupta, J. K. 1984. *Stochastic Programming: Methods and Applications.* New York: North-Holland.

Sloane, W. R., and A. Reisman. 1968. "Stock Evaluation Theory: Classification, Reconciliation and General Model." *The Journal of Financial and Quantitative Analysis* 3(June): 171–204.

Solow, D. 1984. *Linear Programming: An Introduction to Finite Improvement Algorithms.* New York: North-Holland.

Epilogue

The overriding message of this book emphasizes the great need for meta-research in the management sciences. There are several objectives of such meta-research. These are:

1. *Consolidation.* Making the knowledge base more unified within each subdiscipline as well as across the many OR/MS subdisciplines
2. *User-friendliness.* Making OR/MS knowledge more amenable for use by the researcher, the practitioner, the educator, and the student
3. *Expansion.* Providing a vehicle for major strides forward in expanding the knowledge base both in theory and in practice

The above objectives can be served, as summarized in Figure E1, by one or more of the following approaches.

1. *Meta-research*, or research on research. This is a more systematic, less anecdotal, more rigorous version of the traditional literature review.
2. *Taxonomies.* This is both a means to several ends and an end in itself. Taxonomies create a structure and/or a vehicle for doing meta-research. They provide a vehicle for classifying the existing literature in a way that is efficient yet robust. Also, taxonomies can serve as a means for identifying literature voids.
3. *Generalization.* Many subdisciplines of OR/MS can be unified while, at the same time, they are expanded through work that generalizes on existing models and thereby subsumes each and all of them into its structure as special cases.
4. *Expert Systems.* With the advent of this technology it is possible, based on the characteristics specified by the inputer, to have a computer select and suggest the most appropriate model, algorithm, and/or heuristic from the entire universe of potential approaches.

Figure E1
The Objectives and the Means for Meta-Research in OR/MS

		THE MEANS			
		Research on Research	Taxonomies	Generalization	Expert Systems
	Consolidation	X	X	X	X
T H E O B J E C T I V E S	User Friendliness Researcher Practitioner Student/Teacher	X X	X X X	X X X	X X
	Expansion of Theory	X	X	X	
	Expansion of Practice	X	X	X	X

Figure E1 indicates that neither the *objectives*, the rows of the incidence matrix, nor the *means*, the columns of the matrix, are mutually exclusive. In fact, they are all complimentary and supplementary to the overall objective of meta-research.

Figure E2 classifies the chapters of this book using the matrix of Figure E1.

It may be worthwhile to note that the cells in the *expert systems* column of Figure E1 are not empty except for the one addressing *expansion of theory*. Yet, Figure E2 does not reference any chapters in this column. This may be due to the fact that the author has not published in this area and has not done the homework necessary to write on the subject or reference the relevant literature. It may also be due to the relative newness of expert systems and a time lag in bridging that technology with the various subdisciplines of OR/MS.

If the latter case is true, then the transfer of expert systems technology to OR/MS represents an area of great potential for productive research. Such research, in addition to opening up new vistas for publishing articles, and creating new journals, may even do some good in making the existing models, algorithms, heuristics, and the like more user-friendly for the researcher but more importantly for the practitioner, the student, and the teacher. If it is successful in this regard, it may even contribute to the expansion of practice by improving the quality of

Figure E2
Chapters in this Book Addressing Meta-Research in OR/MS

		THE MEANS			
		Research on Research	Taxonomies	Generalization	Expert Systems
T H E O B J E C T I V E S	Consolidation	12	3,10,11,13, 14,15	2,16,17	
	User Friendliness				
	Researcher	5,12	3,5,10,11,13,14,15	2,4,16,17	
	Practitioner		3,5,10,11,13,14,15		
	Student/Teacher	5,12	3,5,10,11,13,14,15	2,4,16,17	
	Expansion of Theory	5,12	3,5,13,14,15	2,4,16	
	Expansion of Practice	5,11,12	3,5,14,15	16,17	

solutions to problems currently within the purview of OR/MS practitioners. It may also allow the "missionary work" called for by Blumstein to proceed with greater confidence into economic sectors currently untouched by the OR/MS professionals.

Glossary of Terms

TAXONOMY -

1. The science, laws or principles of classification,
2. BIOL., The theory, principles and process of classifying organisms in categories.

}NRUD[1]

---

1. Science or technique of classification,
2. Science dealing with the identification, naming and classification or organisms.

}RHD[2]

Classification: esp. classification of animals & plants according to their natural relationships; also, the laws and principles of such classification.

}WNID[3]

CLASSIFICATION -

1. The act or result of classifying,
2. BIOL. The systematic grouping of organisms into categories based on shared characteristics or traits: TAXONOMY

}NRUD

---

1. The act of classifying,
2. One of the groups or classes into which things may be or have been classified.

}RHD

---

1. Act of distributing into groups, as classes, families, etc; act of assigning to a proper class,
2. Result of classifying; a system of classes or groups;
3. BIOL. Systematic arrangement of animals and plants in groups or categories according to some definite plan or sequence; taxonomy.

}WNID

UNIFICATION -

1. To make into a unit: CONSOLIDATE

}NRUD

---

1. The process of unifying or uniting; union.

}RHD

---

1. Act, process, or result of unifying,
2. To make one.

}WNID

GENERALIZATION -

1. An act or instance of generalizing,
2. A general principle, statement or idea.

}NRUD

1. *New Riverside University Dictionary*, 1984, New York: Houghton Mifflin Co.
2. *Random House Dictionary*, 2nd ed. 1987. S.B Flexner, Editor-in-Chief New York: Random House Publishing Co.
3. *Webster's New International Dictionary*, 2nd ed., 1956, W.A. Neilson, Editor-in-Chief, Springfield, Mass: Merriam Co.

| | 1. | The act or process of generalizing, | ⎫ |
| | 2. | A result of this process; a general statement, idea or principle. | ⎬ RHD |

	1.	To make general,	⎫
	2.	To reduce to general laws, to give a general form to,	⎬ WNID
	3.	To derive or induce from particulars.	⎭

SYNTHESIS -

| | 1. | Fusion of separate elements or substances to form a coherent whole., | ⎫ |
| | 2. | CHEM. Formation of a compound from its constituents. | ⎬ NRUD |

	1.	The combining of the constituent elements of separate material or abstract entities into a single or unified entity,	⎫
	2.	A complex whole formed by combining,	⎬ RHD
	3.	A process of reasoning in which the conclusion is reached directly from given propositions and established or assumed principles.	⎭

| | | Composition or combination of parts, elements, etc. so as to form a whole; of immaterial things, the combining of factors, forces, ideas or the like into one complex. | ⎬ WNID |

ANATOMY -

	1a.	The structure of a plant or animal or of any of its elements, b. The constituent structure of something,	⎫
	2.	The science of the form and structure of organisms and their elements,	
	3.	A treatise on anatomical science,	
	4.	The dissection of a plant or animal to disclose the various elements and their positions, structure, and interrelation,	⎬ NRUD
	5.	A skeleton,	
	6.	A detailed analysis or examination,	
	7.	The human body.	⎭

	1.	The science dealing with the structure of animals and plants,	⎫
	2.	The dissection of all or part of an animal or plant in order to study its structure,	⎬ RHD
	3.	An analysis or minute examination.	⎭

| | 1. | The art of dissecting or artificially separating the different parts of any animal or plant to ascertain their position, relations, structure and function, | ⎫ |
| | 2. | The science or branch of morphology which treats the structure of animals. | ⎬ WNID |

MORPHOLOGY -

1. Study of the structure and form of living organisms,
2. An organism's structure and form, excluding its functions,
3. GEOL. Geomorphology,
4. Study of word formation in a language, including inflection, derivation, and the formation of compounds.

}NRUD

1. The branch of biology dealing with the form and structure of plants and animals,
2. The patterns of word formation in a particular language, including inflection, derivation and composition.

}RHD

1. The branch of biology dealing with the form and structure of animals and plants,
2. The science of structure or form; of language, that branch of linguistic study which deals with the history & functions of inflections and derivational forms.

}WNID

GESTALT -

A physical, psychological, or symbolic configuration or pattern so unified as a whole that its properties cannot be derived from its parts.

}NRUD

1. A unified whole; a configuration, pattern, or organized field having specific properties that cannot be derived from the summation of its component parts.

}RHD

1. Literally, form; shape,
2. PSYCHOL., a structure or system of phenomena, whether physical, biological, or psychological, so integrated as to constitute a functional unit with properties not derivable from its parts.

}WNID

STRUCTURE -

1. Something made up of a number or parts held or put together in a specific way,
2. The manner in which parts are arranged or combined to form a whole,
3. Interrelation of parts in a complex entity,
4. Relatively intricate or extensive organization,
5. Something constructed, esp. a building or part.

}NRUD

	1.	Mode of building, construction, or organization; arrangement of parts, elements, or constituents,
	2.	Something built or constructed,
	3.	A complex system considered from the point of view of the whole rather than of any single part.

> RHD

INDUCTION -
1. The act or process of deriving general principles from particular instances or facts.

> NRUD

1. Act or process of reasoning from a part to a whole, from particulars to generals.

> WNID

1. Any form of reasoning in which the conclusion, though supported by the premises, does not follow from them necessarily.
2. The process of estimating the validity of observations of part of a class of facts as evidence for a proposition about the whole class.

> RHD

DEDUCTION -
1. The drawing of a conclusion by reasoning;
2. The process of reasoning in which a conclusion follows necessarily from the stated premise: inference by reasoning from the general to the specific.

> NRUD

1. Act, process or result of deducing; inference in which the conclusion follows necessarily from the premises,
2. A deriving of a conclusion by reasoning; inference from evidence, whether facts or principles; as, to reach an opinion through deduction.

> WNID

1. A process of reasoning in which a conclusion follows necessarily from the premises presented, so that the conclusion cannot be false if the premises are true.

> RHD

1. Act of building; construction,
2. Manner of building, form,
3. The interrelation of parts as dominated by the general character of the whole.

> WNID

INDUCTIVE -
1. Of, pertaining to, or utilizing induction (the inductive process),
2. ELEC. - Of or resulting from inductance (inductive reactance),
3. Causing or influencing: INDUCING,
4. Introductory.

> NRUD

	1.	Of, pertaining to, or involving electrical or magnetic induction,
	2.	Of, pertaining to, or employing logical induction: inductive reasoning.

RHD

	1.	Leading or drawing; persuasive; tempting,
	2.	Tending to induce or cause,
	3.	Of or pertaining to logical induction, as inductive method or inductive reasoning.

WNID

	1.	The act or process of deriving general principles from particular instances or facts.

NRUD

	1.	Act or process of reasoning from a part to a whole, from particulars to generals.

RHD

	1.	Any form of reasoning in which the conclusion, though supported by the premises, does not follow from them necessarily,
	2.	The process of estimating the validity of observations of part of a class of facts as evidence for a proposition about the whole class.

WNID

DEDUCTIVE -	1.	Of or based on deduction,
	2.	Involving deduction in reasoning.

NRUD

	1.	Based on deduction from accepted premises: deductive argument, deductive reasoning.

RHD

	1.	Of or pertaining to deduction; employing deduction in reasoning; inferential.

WNID

Index

About the Author

ARNOLD REISMAN is a Professor of Operations at Case Western Reserve University. He has authored 12 books on management, including the book, *Managerial and Engineering Economics*, which won the Lanchester Prize in 1971. As Chairman of the Global Countertrading Group, he teaches, consults, and structures businesses within the Soviet Union. As consultant to the UN, he has traveled widely in the Americas, India, and the Caribbean.